Women's Edge
HEALTH ENHANCEMENT GUIDE™

Fight Fat

Secrets to Successful Weight Loss

By Alisa Bauman
and the Editors of

PREVENTION
Health Books™

Rodale Press, Inc.
Emmaus, Pennsylvania

Printed in Italy by Rotolito Lombarda S.p.A

"What Are Your Appetite Triggers?" on page 40 is excerpted from "The Development and Validation of an Eating Self-Efficacy Scale" by Shirley M. Glynn and Audrey J. Ruderman, which originally appeared in *Cognitive Therapy and Research*, volume 10, number 4. Copyright © 1986. Reprinted by permission of Plenum Publishing Corporation.

Bauman, Alisa.
    Fight fat : secrets to successful weight loss / by Alisa Bauman
and the editors of Prevention Health Books.
        p.   cm. — (Women's edge health enhancement guide)
    Includes index.
    ISBN 1–57954–157–7 hardcover
    1. Weight loss—Popular works.   I. Prevention Health Books.
II. Title.   III. Series.

2 4 6 8 10 9 7 5 3   hardcover

OUR PURPOSE

*"We inspire and enable people to improve
their lives and the world around them."*

Fight Fat Editorial Staff

MANAGING EDITOR: Sharon Faelten
STAFF WRITER: Alisa Bauman
CONTRIBUTING WRITERS: Jennifer Barefoot, Denyse Corelli, Jennifer L. Kaas, Nanci Kulig, Sandra Salera Lloyd, Linda Mooney, Kristine Napier, Margo Trott
ASSISTANT RESEARCH MANAGER: Anita C. Small
LEAD RESEARCHER: Sandra Salera Lloyd
EDITORIAL RESEARCHERS: Susan E. Burdick, Lori Davis, Christine Dreisbach, Carol J. Gilmore, Jennifer L. Kaas, Teresa A. Yeykal, Shea Zukowski
SENIOR COPY EDITORS: Amy K. Kovalski, Jane Sherman
ART DIRECTOR: Darlene Schneck
COVER AND BOOK DESIGNER: Lynn N. Gano
ILLUSTRATORS: Gayle Kabaker, Narda Lebo, Tom Ward
LAYOUT DESIGNERS: Karen Lomax, Donna G. Rossi
MANUFACTURING COORDINATOR: Patrick T. Smith
OFFICE MANAGER: Roberta Mulliner
OFFICE STAFF: Julie Kehs, Suzanne Lynch, Mary Lou Stephen

Rodale Health and Fitness Books

VICE-PRESIDENT AND EDITORIAL DIRECTOR: Debora T. Yost
EXECUTIVE EDITOR: Neil Wertheimer
DESIGN AND PRODUCTION DIRECTOR: Michael Ward
RESEARCH MANAGER: Ann Gossy Yermish
COPY MANAGER: Lisa D. Andruscavage
BOOK MANUFACTURING DIRECTOR: Nigel Osborne, Christa Gronbech

Contents

PART THREE
Stoke Your Fat-Burning System

PART FOUR
Think Yourself Thin

For the best interactive guide to weight loss, fitness, nutrition, and living a more fulfilling life, visit our Web site at http://www.healthyideas.com.

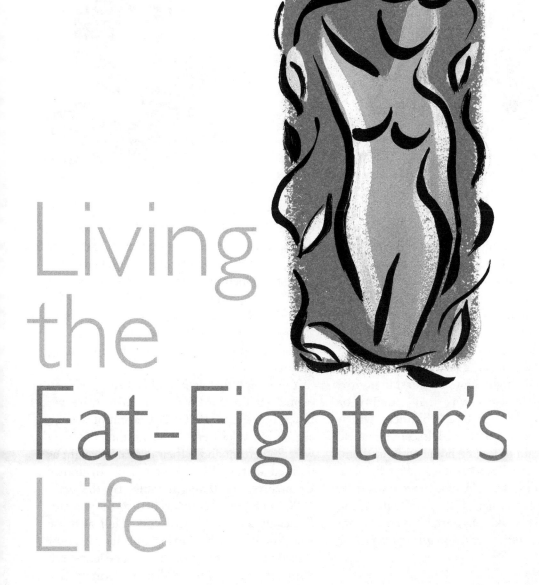

PART ONE

Living the Fat-Fighter's Life

Goodbye, Diet!

The Best Diet Is No Diet at All

Women wear diet blinders. Screening out much of the taste, smell and enjoyment of food, the blinders leave us focused on how much body fat particular foods will create. So we look at cake and see fat hips. We look at fried chicken and see fat thighs. We look at cheesecake and see a fat behind.

When wearing such blinders, we tend to tabulate and calculate. A slice of cake now plus some aerobics tonight minus breakfast tomorrow equals an "I-can-live-with-that" tummy or thighs. We're so used to the blinders, which most of us have worn since adolescence, that we wouldn't dream of leaving home without them. Yet, if we want to become successful fat-fighters, we must discard them. "Although we think diets are making us thinner, all they really do in the long run is make us fatter," says Debra Waterhouse, author of *Outsmarting the Female Fat Cell*.

Yes, Diets Are Fattening

The average woman who diets starts a new one about three times a year. She may try eliminating "bad" foods – things like chocolate, cake, peanut butter, beer and steak. She may try eating particular foods almost exclusively – going on grapefruit diets, cabbage soup diets and olive-and-egg diets. She may skip meals. Or slash calories. At any rate, it all comes down to the same thing: She deprives herself until the pounds drop off. And then she begins eating normally again.

You'd think that with all this dieting, women would get thinner. We don't. In fact, we get fatter. In the mid-1970s, 26 percent of women age 20 and older were obese, meaning that they were 20 percent above their desirable weight as defined in the Metropolitan Life Insurance Company height/weight table. By the early 1990s, the percentage swelled to 35 percent. Basically, dieting doesn't work. Half of those who lose weight by cutting calories regain or exceed their weight within a year. The long-term numbers are even more dismal. "Ninety-five percent of women who lose weight regain it all within five years," says Sue Cummings, R.D., a clinical dietitian who specialises in weight loss

Why do diets fail? Researchers have come up

with a number of reasons.

1. *Diets make your fat cells fatter.* Every woman has about 30 billion fat cells. Such cells can grow in size and number – up to 100 billion or so. Diets only speed this fattening process. "Trying to starve a fat cell only improves its ability to retain fat," says Waterhouse. "Diets act essentially as fitness programmes for fat cells: They boost the ability of fat cells to store fat, to take in new fat and in some cases to increase their numbers" Why? Evolution. Fat cells evolved to keep us alive during times of famine, and they react to a low-calorie diet as just that – famine. Fat cells respond to famine, or calorie restriction, by holding on to the fat they already have and by becoming more aggressive at taking in new fat once the diet is over.

2. *Diets mess with your enzymes.* Our cells manufacture enzymes, tiny protein molecules that either en-courage the body to burn fat or store fat, depending on the type. Dieting can double the number of fat-storing enzymes and halve the amount of fat-burning enzymes.

3. *Diets put the brakes on your metabolism.* When you diet, you risk starving your body of some vital nutrients because nutrient intake is tied to calorie intake. Very low calorie diets can trigger a complex chain of reactions that will eventually tell your metabolism to stop burning so many calories. You may lose weight initially after cutting calories. Eventually, how-ever, the weight becomes harder to

WOMAN TO WOMAN

She Stopped Dieting and Lost Wight

Cindy Guyette, a travel agent in Birmingham, jumped off the diet roller coaster two years ago, hit the ground running with a new exercise plan, and took off 5 stone. Here's her story.

Strike the word *diet* from the dictionary – diets don't work!

I've fought the battle of the bulge since the second form. You name it; I've tried it – weight-loss centres, packaged meals, diet drinks, fasting. Each diet brought a glimmer of hope – a promise of quick, easy weight loss. They all worked for a while, but soon I slipped back into my old ways and the weight bounced back, bringing with them even more unwelcome inches.

Shortly after graduating from college, I hit rock bottom. I weighed more than ever before – I could barely get into a size 18. I couldn't stand to look in the mirror. I hated myself. I was desperate. I knew I had to do something to turn my life around. I ended an unhappy relationship, started a new job and decided to do something about my weight for good. Since dieting had failed me so often, I sought a new strategy: I joined a gym.

Believe me, at my weight, going to a gym wasn't easy. At first I couldn't do much, but I persevered and gradually it got better. The weight started to melt away. Now I go to the gym five days a week. I'm addicted.

When I got serious about exercising, the pieces of my life fell into place. I started eating better, having less fat and more vegetables. Now if I eat a fast-food hamburger, I feel really sick. I eat vegetables galore. I've found that small changes add up, like cutting out cheese and mayonnaise on sandwiches and eating two slices of pizza instead of five.

Weight loss, like life, is all about choices. If I choose to have a biscuit as a snack, then I decide to eat a little lighter that evening. If I opt not to go to the gym, then I resolve to eat a little lighter that day. If I do have a heavy eating day, I tell myself, "Relax, that's only 1 out of 365 days in the year."

Five stone lighter, I have tons more energy and I feel great. I will never diet again. Shake off all those inhibiting diet ideas – empower yourself and stop dieting.

drop. Then, when you start eating normally, it takes your metabolic rate a while to get back up to speed – and you gain weight.

4. *Diets make you rebellious.* The more you focus on what foods you are allowed to eat and what foods you are not allowed to eat, the more deprived you feel, says Susan Olson, author of *Keeping It Off: Winning at Weight Loss.* Then you rebel. Instead of just eating a small amount of the "bad" food, you binge, eating well beyond fullness. "If you say you are going on a diet tomorrow, then you probably are going to stuff yourself tonight," says Dr. Olson. Such binge eating can actually make you wolf down more food than you normally would without the diet. Binge eating also makes you store more fat than you normally would had you spread the same number of calories throughout the day. "If you eat more calories than your body can burn in a few hours, the remainder will be stored as fat," says Waterhouse.

5. *Diets don't last.* You need to change your eating and exercise habits for a lifetime to lose weight and keep it off. By definition, however, diets mean temporary deprivation. So while you may lose a little weight, once you return to your normal eating habits, the weight returns. "If it doesn't work in the long term – and that's what matters – it's not effective," says Frances Berg, author of *Health Risks of Weight Loss.*

Diets do more than hamper your weight-loss efforts. They can hamper your health. Restraining your appetite causes stress and anxiety. You end up so preoccupied with dieting that you lose some of your mental sharpness, needing more time to balance your cheque book, forgetting to

REAL-LIFE SCENARIO
She Can Escape the Starver-Stuffer Syndrome

Anita is a career dieter. Her current strategy is to eat lean during the week so that she can splurge on the weekends. A typical weekday menu consists of dry toast and coffee for breakfast, a big salad for lunch, and chicken or fish with veggies and rice for supper. Friday, Saturday, and Sunday nights she eats in restaurants, enjoying everything from soup to dessert. Not only is Anita not losing, her weight is gradually creeping up. What is she doing wrong?

Anita is more than a career dieter; she's a *classic* dieter. Restricting calories and fat during the week and splurging on weekends is the typical scenario for classic dieters. And it's one of the many reasons that diets don't work.

Since Anita undereats all week long, it's no wonder that she goes overboard on weekends. Her skimpy breakfast, for example, is too low in calories, is virtually all carbohydrates, and is metabolised in about three hours. As a result, she's starving by lunchtime, and while her lunch salad may be filling because it has fibre, it is still very low in calories. Even her "healthy" supper can't make up for the day's deprivation. By the time the weekend rolls around, Anita is craving what she really desired all week – more calories and fat – and she indulges in everything from

get milk when you're at the shops and not hitting the brakes as fast as usual when other cars stop suddenly. Even the most modest calorie restriction can lead to low vitamin levels, causing fatigue. Rapid weight loss can even make you moody.

The No-Diet Fat-Fighting Plan

Now don't get discouraged. Yes, dieting doesn't work. Once you give up dieting, however, you'll

cocktails to fettuccine Alfredo to Mississippi mud pie. Consequently, she gets little benefit from being "good" all week – and it doesn't help that her weekend is three days long. If she were to count up the calories that she consumes all week, she would be sure to find that she's taking in more than she's expending. And that's why she's gaining rather than losing.

The fact that Anita always splurges in restaurants is another problem, since she exerts much less control over what she's eating there. And like all classic dieters, she views dining out as more of a celebration than just another meal, so she eats foods that she would never think of eating at home.

What Anita needs to do is eat sensibly during the week so that she's more in control and can order sensibly in restaurants. But she'll need to cut back there, too. Soup to dessert isn't going to do it if she wants to lose weight. If she includes low-fat – not nonfat – foods in her diet and doesn't restrict her calories so severely during the week, she will minimise weekend cravings and have the willpower to pass on the desserts and heavy sauces, or at least eat considerably less of them. It would also help if she'd think of her weekend as two days instead of three. This way the weight will begin to melt – not as fast as a scoop of vanilla ice cream with pie, but they'll melt.

Expert consulted
Franca Alphin, R.D.

be ready to embark on a better, easier, more effective way to fight fat forever. Instead of a transitory quick-fix diet, the *Fight Fat* plan gives you the ammunition you need to outsmart the craftiest of your fat cells and turn down your appetite. You'll also learn how to use food, exercise and even your brain to make your body burn more fat and calories in three ways.

1. *At rest.* The rate at which your body burns calories to complete general day-to-day activities such as breathing, swallowing and pumping blood is called your basal metabolic rate (BMR). Your BMR slows as you age. But the *Fight Fat* plan will give you numerous ways to keep this important fat-fighting furnace running strong.

2. *During movement.* Every time you use a muscle, whether you're picking up clothes from the floor, slamming on your brakes or climbing a flight of stairs, you burn calories over and above your BMR. To help you burn even more calories, the *Fight Fat* plan gives you doable exercises that will easily fit into your hectic schedule.

3. *During digestion.* Yes, you burn calories just to digest the food you eat. And some foods make you burn more calories than others. The *Fight Fat* plan lets you in on some of the best-kept secrets about fat-burning foods.

You'll also learn tons of mental strategies designed to help you stick with the *Fight Fat* plan for a lifetime, so you can lose the fat and keep it off. Based on the latest research, the plan focuses on six basic fat-fighting principles. You'll find them mentioned throughout this book.

Let food happen. Women should affix bumper stickers to their cars that read, "Food happens," says Dr. Olson. Women tend to focus excessively on "good" and "bad" foods, which actually hampers attempts at weight loss, she says. The good-food/bad-food focus makes us crave the "bad" food even more. That's why in the *Fight Fat* plan, there are no bad foods. Sure, you'll be cutting back on dietary fat, but you don't have to give up your favourite foods. To fight fat, you'll actually work your treasured fatty dishes into your meal plan and instead cut back on other fatty foods that you couldn't care less about.

Eat early and often. Unlike most diets, this plan has you eating more, not less. "Frequent eating works with your metabolism, which speeds up a little each time you eat," says Patricia Giblin Wolman, professor of human nutrition. "Also, if you eat regular meals, starting with breakfast, you're less likely to feel ravenously hungry and overeat at any one meal." In the *Fight Fat* programme, you'll eat breakfast, lunch, supper and snacks. There's even room for dessert.

Take the work out of working out. Our bodies were designed for movement. But if you overexercise, you can get fat. Excessive exercise can deplete the body of chromium, which helps regulate blood sugar. The body may respond by increasing the production of insulin, which will make you ravenous. Also, since excessive exercise makes you miserable, you may do it for a while, but as with dieting, you'll eventually quit. And you don't burn extra calories by sitting on your behind. With the *Fight Fat* plan, you'll create your own exercise programme, one so comfortable that it eliminates excuses. Your programme may be as simple as getting up from your desk for a 10-minute walk break three or four times a day.

Lift your weight. Of all the calories burned in your body, 50 to 90 percent are burned by your muscles. Weight training can boost your metabolism by building calorie-hungry muscles. Don't worry, though, you're not going to spend hours in a gym with a bunch of sweaty 30-year-old men. The *Fight Fat* plan shows you a weight-lifting routine that can be done at home with dumbbells. And it doesn't take more than an hour a week.

Don't "should" on yourself. Women know only too well how they *should* eat and how they *should* exercise, even how they *should* think. The thing is, no one likes to be "should" on. And you really can't "should" yourself into doing anything for a long period of time.

"Women 'should' themselves to death," says Dr. Olson. "I would bet that 99 percent of the women who come to me say, 'Sue, I know what I *should* do. Why don't I do it?' Of course, they don't realise that they already have the answer. The more you 'should' yourself, the more you meet resistance."

What really helps is to create your own fat-fighting programme, based on the advice and suggestions you read in *Fight Fat*. Slowly incorporate doable advice into your life. Don't try to force yourself to switch to habits that you really are unwilling to stick with.

Practice mind mastery. Different emotions and thoughts can hamper your ability to stick with the *Fight Fat* plan. Women tend to eat when they feel stressed or depressed, for instance. "One woman I know said, 'If you name a feeling, I can eat for it,'" says Dr. Olson. The *Fight Fat* plan will teach you ways to manage your emotions and stressful feelings so they don't drive you to the refrigerator.

The Rest of Your Life

There you have it. No more forbidden foods. No more deprivation. No more guilt. No more impossible exercise routines. Today you have taken the first step towards what will become a lifetime of thin habits. As you read this book, you'll learn more and more ways to live the fat-fighter's life. *Fight Fat* will finally give you a practical plan that actually works.

The Fat Facts

How Women Are Different from Men

True or false? When your body burns fat during exercise, the fat melts and comes out your pores as sweat.

True or false? When you eat a slice of rich cake, the calories head straight for your hips (or other fatty zone), where they sidle up to fat and make themselves comfy.

Both statements, of course, are false. But if you had even the smallest doubt about the answers, chances are that there's a whole lot more you need to know about how your body makes and uses fat. And knowing the manoeuvers this marauding menace uses to sneak up on you is your first defence in winning the fat wars. So let's get armed.

The Making of a Fat Cell

So where do all those calories go when you eat that scrumptious, rich cake?

Once it's been savoured by your taste buds, the cake slides down your throat and goes into your stomach, where digestive juices work on it. Then it moves into your small intestine. Here's

where fat and nutrients are absorbed part and parcel through the intestinal wall and shipped off through your bloodstream to various cells in your body.

Once in your bloodstream, the fat that you eat is easily converted into body fat. Since a gramme of fat carries more calories than a gramme of carbohydrate or protein, your body stores fat about twice as easily as it does carbohydrate and protein.

Unfortunately, our bodies' ability to store fat is nearly limitless. And when space in our fat cells gets a little tight, they even have the ability to grow.

Fat cells can also multiply. We're all born with a genetically determined number of these cells, but as we grow, our bodies continue to manufacture them until adulthood, when new fat cell production usually stops. By this time, we've accumulated about 30 billion of them, give or take a few million.

Only two things can trigger more fat cell production in adulthood: One is the purely female prerogative of pregnancy. The other is weight gain. Yes, as nasty as it sounds, gaining weight only makes fat cells feistier. But they do give us a bit of a break: They only begin to replicate when you start pushing the scales at more than 160 percent of your ideal weight. So if your normal weight is 10 stone, you wouldn't start greeting new fat cells unless you tipped the scales at 14 stone. Once you make a new fat cell, though, you have it for life.

Fat cells are intended as reservoirs for energy, with each pound of captive fat holding 3,500 calories of energy. When the body can't find enough carbohydrates and protein to burn for energy, a fat cell will release a glob of fat from captivity into the bloodstream, where an enzyme called lipoprotein lipase will be waiting to break it down and direct it towards needy cells.

Why Women Wear Fat Genes

When it comes to producing fat cells, women have it all over men, thanks to a heritage that dates back to prehistoric days. During those times, women's primary job was to keep the population growing through breeding. The men's job was to keep the population growing through feeding.

We could argue that women were a lot better at their calling than their men. It was a feast-or-famine existence. Many times, while men were gone for days on end hunting for food, women were often left behind with little sustenance other than their own fat stores to protect them and their unborn children from starvation. Women needed extra fat to sustain themselves through pregnancy and nursing, so the female

WOMEN ASK WHY

Why does fat stick to my thighs like Krazy Glue, while my husband can diet away his gut in a couple of weeks?

Women have been plagued by this injustice since day one. Although there are some men who have thunder thighs, the accumulation of stubborn fat in the buttocks and thighs has always been a peculiarly female phenomenon. And you could argue that men are to blame.

During the Stone Age, women's bodies developed the ability to store fat in order to nurture growing fetuses during the long wait for men to bring home food from the hunt. Don't suppose for a minute that skinny ones like Wilma Flintstone actually survived in the days before supermarkets. Women back then were built to breed future generations.

Despite progress, many women still carry around this excess weight. Since we're genetically programmed to store fat efficiently, we're naturally going to have a hard time dieting it away. In fact, the type of fat stored in the lower part of the body is much more difficult to burn than abdominal

body, because of the times, was conditioned to store it.

"The male fat cell developed so that it could protect one person – its male owner – from starvation during a famine. The female fat cell evolved so that it could protect two – its female owner and her developing fetus," says Debra Waterhouse, R.D., author of *Outsmarting the Female Fat Cell*. "The better a woman's fat-storing ability, the greater the chances that she, and the entire species, will survive. In fact, if the female fat cell hadn't evolved to be so stubborn, we might not be here today."

Today, however, we don't have to go days or months without food, so we probably don't need

and upper-body fat because upper-body fat breaks down more easily than other types. Abdominal fat is "easy come, easy go" because it accumulates quickly when there is a calorie surplus but is broken down just as quickly when there is a calorie deficit.

Since men tend to store most of their fat in the gut, they are naturally going to have better luck at losing it. That's why your husband's gut seems to be so easy to get rid of.

There is some good news tucked amid those fat folds, however. Since women once stored fat out of necessity, our bodies store it not only more efficiently but also more safely than men's bodies do. Research has discovered that there is a correlation between fat that settles above the waist and the typical health problems associated with obesity, such as diabetes, high blood pressure, high cholesterol and heart disease.

If that's not enough of a comfort, remember that exercise has a toning effect, and it may improve the shape of your thighs and reduce the wobble. And if having a scapegoat helps, blame it on those cavemen who missed their targets.

Expert consulted
Ellen Parham, R.D., Ph.D.

quite as much fat. Yet our bodies have not adapted. Women still carry around a lot more fat than men – about 8 percent more. That's 120,000 extra calories stored as fat to see us through any situation. And compared to men, women face some fat-fighting obstacles.

❧ We gain weight during pregnancy to adequately nourish the growing fetus. Part of the weight we gain during and after pregnancy has to do with a heavier uterus (which can expand from 2 to 24 ounces in weight), extra breast tissue and up to 4 pounds of extra blood. But we also gain between 8 and 11 pounds of fat (most of it in the form of new fat cells) and fluid.

"Women store fat very efficiently during pregnancy because they are designed to support the life of this newborn for six months to a year after birth," says Joanne Curran-Celentano, R.D.

❧ Women have less muscle than men. Since a pound of muscle burns about 30 to 50 more calories than a pound of fat, men burn fat more easily simply because their metabolisms are higher.

❧ The female hormone oestrogen makes a woman's fat cells, especially in the hips, thighs and buttocks, nearly diet-proof. Some theories suggest that oestrogen lives in fat, where it activates and multiplies fat-storing enzymes. According to Waterhouse, "oestrogen is a fat cell's best friend, keeping a woman's body pear-shaped and fertile." Science has proven oestrogen's fat-loving role: In studies, when men were given oestrogen, they gained weight in their lower bodies almost instantly and had a hard time losing it.

Fat Shapes a Woman

Because the lower body is a convenient place to store fat for pregnancy, that's where most women carry their fat – on their thighs, hips, and buttocks. Such fat gives many women a pear shape, with narrow shoulders and wider hips.

Some women and most men, on the other hand, tend to have most of their fat in the abdomen, making them apple-shaped. As opposed to the fat on the thighs and buttocks, abdominal fat, also called visceral fat, is a "harder" kind of fat that doesn't feel soft and flabby. "Visceral fat is the type of fat associated with diseases like blood sugar problems, adult diabetes, high blood pressure, high blood

(continued on page 12)

GAINING AND AGING – WHAT TO EXPECT

Like grey hair and wrinkles, gaining weight seems to be a natural consequence of aging. The typical woman gains weight every decade of her life after age 20 until she reaches her midsixties. Then she starts losing somewhat naturally. Between ages 24 and 34, for instance, most women can expect to gain about eight pounds; between 34 and 44, they add about six pounds, and between 44 and 54, about two. For the next 10 years, their weight should remain relatively stable. Then weight loss very slowly begins.

To understand why, we went to Maria A. Fiatarone Singh, M.D. Here's a breakdown of when we gain weight and why.

Ages 24 to 34. Weight gain usually begins during our midtwenties with the onset of adult responsibilities. Once we start working and raising families, we have less time for the activity-filled life that we led when we were younger. We no longer get summers off, and our jobs

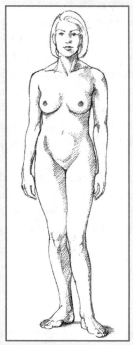

Ages 34 to 44

confine us to sitting most of the day. This gives us the biggest fat gains, primarily along our hips and thighs.

We also tend to get pregnant in our midtwenties and thirties, and pregnancy pads our hips and thighs with even more fat. This is one of the few times in life that a woman's body can manufacture new fat cells – cells that never die. That's one reason why we have a tough time losing weight that we gained during pregnancy.

Ages 34 to 44. We continue to gain weight, although not as quickly, as we enter our midforties because our metabolisms are idling at a

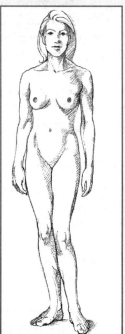

Ages 24 to 34

slower rate. The lack of activity during the past 15 years has allowed our muscles to shrivel up. As a result of this, we burn fewer calories because muscle is one of the body's primary calorie-burners.

Ages 44 to 54. Now we're nearing menopause. A drop in levels of the hormones oestrogen and progesterone slows our metabolisms even further, making us gain fat in our abdomens.

Ages 54 to 64. Weight gain continues to slow during this decade. As we age, we may lose some of our appetite, so we eat less without even trying.

If you find that you are on the plump side during your midsixties, however, you shouldn't worry too much about losing that weight. "Some studies suggest that older

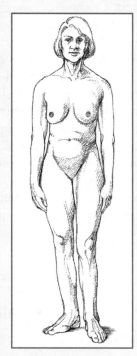

Ages 54 to 64

women who are a bit plumper live longer than those women who are not," says Dr. Fiatarone Singh. Of course, as is often the case with such studies, others have found that not to be the case.

None of this, obviously, is written in stone. How closely you follow the pattern depends a great deal on your personal level of physical activity, your eating habits, and your genes. In fact, you can help keep the lid on weight gain and even reverse it by following the advice given in this book.

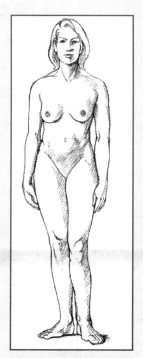

Ages 44 to 54

cholesterol and heart disease," says Dr. Curran-Celentano.

Although apple-shaped women are at more risk for disease, they do have one thing over the more common, pear-shaped women: They have an easier time losing weight. Abdominal fat is more metabolically active than the fat on the hips and thighs. "It accumulates faster, but it also breaks down faster than fat on the thighs or butt," says Jill Kanaley, Ph.D. Usually, when you lose weight, your body takes fat from your breasts, then your abdomen and finally from your hips, thighs and buttocks.

Corralling the Female Fat Cell

So there you have it. Female fat is pretty darn durable. But that doesn't mean that it's undefeatable. This book is filled with savvy ways to get rid of fat forever. And a good place to start is with some strategies aimed directly at the female fat cell.

Don't starve. According to Waterhouse, "Trying to starve a fat cell only improves its ability to retain fat." Women feed their fat cells by embarking on an average of 10 diets in their lifetime. "Diets teach fat cells to defend themselves, for reasons that cut to the heart of why we have fat in the first place," says Waterhouse. In a word: survival.

"Fat cells evolved to keep us alive during times of famine, and they interpret a low-calorie diet as just that – famine," says Waterhouse. "Fat cells respond to famine, or calorie restriction, by holding on to the fat they already

---

FAT: THE REAL WAR BETWEEN THE SEXES

When it comes to fat, men and women were not created equal. Men have less. They carry it in different places on their bodies. Not only that, they tend to lose it more quickly. This is definitely a war that's hard to win. Below you'll find our strategic locations.

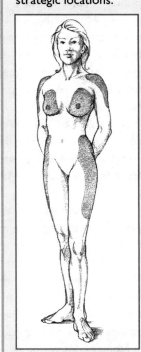

➤ Before menopause, women tend to gain fat here to accommodate childbearing. Because of its composition, fat in this area is the toughest to burn. When you burn fat in these areas, it usually means that the entire body is getting thinner.

---

have and by becoming more aggressive at taking in new fat once the diet is over. The result is a system of fat protection that can be very difficult to crack, especially if the system becomes stronger each time we diet."

Slow down. To lose weight and keep it off, aim for slow losses, not fast ones. A reasonable rate is $\frac{1}{2}$ to 1 pound a week. Slow losses will prevent your fat cells from mounting a defence.

Go 10 weeks at a time. It takes time to break old patterns and establish new ones. If you've been having three pats of butter on your

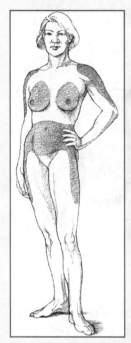

→ After menopause, women tend to gain fat here as levels of the female sex hormones oestrogen and progesterone drop.

→ During pregnancy and lactation, the breasts temporarily become larger and fatter.

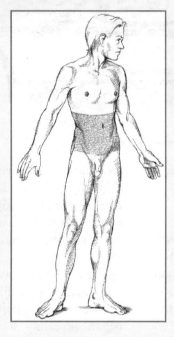

→ Men tend to gain fat here. Such fat puts men at a higher risk for heart disease, but it's also easier to lose than the type of fat found on women's thighs and buttocks.

more calories than fatty tissue. In fact, women who exercise for an hour a day use up about 8 percent more calories than the average couch potato, even while they rest. And finally, exercise conditions your fat-burning enzymes to break down fat faster, so even when you are not exercising, your body continues to burn fat.

Take advantage of breast-feeding. If you are of childbearing age and you are thinking about having a baby, plan to breastfeed instead of bottle-feed. Your body will burn tons of calories just in the act of producing the milk for your baby.

"Not only does it take calories to make the milk, but when the milk is secreted, lots of calories go with it," says Dr. Curran-Celentano. Pregnancy and lactation mark one of the only times in a woman's life when her body will preferentially burn lower-body fat. So take advantage of your breast-feeding routine as well as getting some exercise and getting back to your regular eating habits.

toast every morning and you switch to using a teaspoon of all-fruit jam, for example, it will take weeks before you're used to the new routine. You should pledge your body to 10 weeks of effort, experts advise. If you're still eating low-fat after 10 weeks, you've probably established the healthy new behaviour.

Move. Overeating is not the largest problem in obesity – underexercise is. Exercise helps weight loss in three ways. First, it burns calories over and above what we would usually burn in one day. Second, it builds muscle, which burns

Whose Fault Is It, Anyway?

Check Out Your Genes to Size Up Your Size

Some people are born to fatness. Others have to get there.

—Les Murray, Australian poet

Fat isn't fair. It seems as if some women, for instance, can eat *all the time*, sit on their behinds all day long, snack while they watch TV at night and indulge in decadent desserts. Yet they never appear to gain an ounce, and they can wear their skinniest jeans even right after Christmas.

On the other hand, it seems that some women can eat hardly anything. They watch each crumb they eat. They walk whenever they can and never eat a thing when watching TV. Yet for them, gaining weight comes as easy as growing hair.

If you fall into the I-eat-hardly-anything-but-still-can't-seem-to-slim-down department, don't blame yourself. It's not necessarily your fault. Blame it on your genes.

The Gene Trap

Yes, a lot of women who struggle with their weight have their ancestors to thank. But don't feel that this gives you license to wave the red flag and reach for a bag of biscuits. Your genes may be working against you, but you can fight fat. It's just that you might have to work harder at it than other women, says Barbara Hansen, Ph.D.

Historically, an overweight or obese woman was thought to eat like a glutton. Then studies conducted during the late 1980s and early 1990s began revealing a much different picture, showing that many overweight women did not necessarily eat more than their thinner counterparts. Instead, such women had more complicated, biologically seated factors working against them. Here's the evidence.

❧ Six days a week for 100 days, researchers fed identical twins 1,000 calories more than usual. Even though everyone was overeating, some eaters gained more weight than others. For each set of twins, however, the amounts gained were similar.

❧ When another study looked at identical twins who were raised apart, researchers found that both twins gained similar amounts of weight regardless of their eating and exercise habits.

* Native Americans, Pacific Islanders, Hispanics and African-Americans seem to store fat more easily than other ethnic groups. Researchers speculate that members of these groups may possess a "frugal gene" that encourages efficient energy storage during times of plenty to tide them over in times of famine.

* In a laboratory, researchers isolated a gene in mice (called the ob gene) that caused increased appetite and slower metabolism. Later, a similar fat gene was found in humans; right now, however, the evidence suggests that it rarely causes obesity in humans.

Although research is just beginning to unravel how our genes may make us fat, scientists speculate that a few different fat genes may have survived from past generations of people who struggled against starvation during times of food scarcity. Such genes allowed them to eat and store calories when food was plentiful. Then, when food was scarce, the genes helped the people burn fewer calories so that they could live off their fat as long as needed, thus helping them to survive, researchers theorise.

"Most likely, it's a complex interaction of many genes – kind of like a symphony – that works together to predispose a woman towards obesity," says Dr. Hansen.

Who inherited the fat genes? To narrow it down, just take a look at photos of your

WOMAN TO WOMAN
She Dodged Her Genetic Inheritance

A graduate student in her midtwenties, Robyn Bright of Brighton, welcomed a number of family hand-me-downs – her mum's extra set of tableware, her grandma's handmade quilt – but there was one legacy that she hoped would skip her branch on the family tree: big thighs. And it has. Here's how she outwitted Mother Gene.

I've never struggled with weight, but I knew early on that I would have to battle with heavy thighs. I used to look at my relatives and wonder, "Am I going to look like that one day?"

I became certain that it was a genetic shortcoming that would plague me like a curse. I remember convincing my mother to join a gym with me, which she did whole-heartedly. She even shed weight quickly – everywhere but her thighs. I realised that my best hope was preventing the weight from getting there in the first place. So I stayed active.

In school, I ran track and cross-country, followed by crew in college. But inevitably, my attention returned to my thighs. I began to notice that years of aggressive running and rowing, while great for my body overall, had transformed my legs into muscular trunks. Then one summer I found my answer in a pool of water – as a lifeguard.

The ongoing summer training involved lap swimming for 45 minutes every morning. It didn't take long to see that I had found my remedy. By summer's end, the fat-burning workouts had slimmed down my thighs.

Now that I'm working towards my master's and my schedule is tighter, I can't always go to the gym or head for a pool, but I still stay active. I walk almost everywhere, and when I do drive, I make it a habit to park far away and to use the stairs instead of escalators or lifts. Incorporating little habits like these into my everyday life gives me a leg up in battling my birthright.

ancestors, says Dr. Hansen.

If you inherited fat genes, you'll gain weight more easily than women who didn't, she says. You also probably inherited your appetite, your cravings and your metabolism. Yet fatness is not inevitable. You can reduce the effects of your fat genes. Here's what you need to know to slim them down.

Why You're Never Late for Supper

You would think that you'd feel full when your stomach has food in it and hungry when it doesn't. But appetite isn't that simple. Instead, a complex set of chemicals communicate with one another through telephone line–like nerves that run from your stomach and gastrointestinal tract to your brain and then back again.

On the gastrointestinal side, the levels of acids, blood sugar and insulin, which rise and fall during digestion, are communicated through the receiver ends of the nerves, which transmit those messages to a part of the brain called the hypothalamus. The hypothalamus then interprets the message. Depending on what it hears, the hypothalamus orders up a group of different brain chemicals called neurotransmitters. It's the levels of various neurotransmitters in your brain that result in messages such as, "I can't possibly eat another bite," "Well, just a few more," and "Give me some chocolate chip biscuit dough right now!"

One neurotransmitter, called neuropeptide Y, for instance, might increase your hunger, especially for sweets and starches such as chocolate bars and potatoes. Another neurotransmitter, serotonin, is believed to communicate the opposite. It might tell you, "Oh, I

> ### REAL-LIFE SCENARIO
> #### She Can Fight Heredity
>
> Sandi, who grew up in a fat family, is in her late twenties and thin. But lately, she's been struggling to maintain her weight. In her recollection, there was never a shortage of homemade sweets around the house. At a reunion of her mother's side of the family, she noticed that she was about the only thin person there. She also noticed a striking similarity among some of her aunts and cousins: thighs and bottoms the size of Ireland. Is she destined to look just like them?
>
> Well, maybe. As Sandi can clearly see, obesity does run in the family. She may have been lucky and not inherited those genes, but in case she did, her lifestyle can certainly affect the likelihood of her following suit. If she exercises, eats a low-fat diet, and avoids some of the goodies her cousins love, there's a chance she won't end up looking like them. But unfortunately for Sandi and many women like her, the size of her appetite is what is most likely to determine her destiny.
>
> You see, our ancestors give us genes that, to a large degree, regulate our appetite and metabolism. Genes carry a lot of weight, so to speak, in determining your desire for food. Also, if your metabolism is a bit sluggish, you may have to fight your genes to speed it up. That's why if Mum has a tendency to gain weight, it's likely that you will, too.

feel stuffed. Stop – stop right now." The problem is that some women's brains may not manufacture enough of the appetite-reducing serotonin, giving them voracious appetites and a sweet tooth that will not be denied. A serotonin imbalance can also cause depression. That's why medications that raise serotonin levels can boost your spirits as well as curb your appetite, says Leah J. Dickstein, M.D.

Just as a brain chemical imbalance can cause

The role that genes play in obesity can be traced to your ethnic background, in terms of both the genes you inherited and the environment in which you grew up. Travel through Europe and it's easy to see which ethnic groups have a genetic propensity for obesity. The good news is that fat genes aren't necessarily passed on to all offspring. If you're Swedish, for example, you have a good chance of being blonde. But not all Swedes are blonde and not all blondes are Swedes. The same applies to being overweight.

Since Sandi is struggling with her weight, chances are good that her genes are working against her. Since genetic influence expresses itself at different times in our lives, if she's noticing that it's her older aunts who are the heaviest, she may be genetically disposed to put on weight later in life. If she's looking at heavy cousins her own age and she's a lot thinner, then she's doing great. Unlike her friends with "thin" genes, she may never be able to eat to her heart's content without seeing the results on her scale, but she doesn't have to end up like her cousins, either. Controlling her appetite with a nutritious low-fat diet with plenty of fruits and vegetables to fill her up and stepping up her metabolism with an aerobic exercise programme will keep her the slimmest female in the family.

Expert consulted
Barbara Hansen, Ph.D.

hunger, so can a gastrointestinal chemical imbalance. The hormone insulin, for instance, usually does a good job of making sure that blood sugar gets to hungry cells. In some women, the insulin is ready and waiting, but it doesn't effectively remove sugar from the blood. The pancreas is then forced to produce increasingly larger amounts of insulin in order to maintain normal blood sugar levels. The high insulin levels may stimulate the appetite and lower the amount of sugar that is burned as energy, while at the same time increasing fat stores. This condition is called insulin resistance.

Natural Appetite Suppressants

Even if you are genetically predisposed to low serotonin levels or insulin resistance, you can turn down your appetite. Here's how.

Eat chocolate. If you do not have diabetes, an allergy, or any other medical condition that prevents you from eating chocolate, small amounts of dark chocolate can encourage the brain to produce serotonin and other feel-good brain chemicals, according to Dr. Dickstein. Self-medicating with small amounts of dark chocolate works especially well just before menstruation, she says. Also, research indicates that the type and proportions of fat in dark chocolate aren't as bad for your heart as other types of fat. And, as long as you use it in small amounts, it won't wreck your diet.

Don't drink. Alcohol depletes your brain of serotonin, says Dr. Dickstein. So if you don't drink, don't start. And if you do, you'll want to cut back.

Work off your hunger. Here's one more reason to exercise: It raises serotonin levels, says Dr. Dickstein. Also, exercise can make your body more sensitive to insulin.

Eat carbohydrates early. In laboratory animals, levels of brain chemicals that stimulate the appetite for carbohydrates peak early in the morning, says Sarah Leibowitz, Ph.D. So a high-carbohydrate breakfast may shut off the "eat carbohydrate" message and leave you stated. Try whole-wheat pancakes, oatmeal, or cold cereal in the morning instead of eggs and bacon, she suggests.

Take sugar in small spoonfuls. After you eat carbohydrates, your digestive system breaks them down into simple sugars that enter your bloodstream. When the sugars appear, the pancreas secretes insulin, which shuttles the sugar to hungry cells. If you eat too much sugar at one time, however, your pancreas over-produces insulin, making your blood sugar levels plummet. This reaction can leave you feeling tired and irritable and may bring on a craving, says Elizabeth Somer, R.D. You don't have to cut all the sugary foods you love out of your diet, she says; just don't eat them all at the same time.

Feast on fibre. Eating soluble fibre will depress your appetite and your body's post-meal insulin response. Normally, insulin levels rise after a meal, but soluble fibre keeps these levels lower. So stock up on barley, corn, oat products, beans, apples, citrus fruits and root vegetables.

Trick Your Taste buds

Your lifetime exposure to certain foods determines the majority of your food preferences. If you enjoy broccoli, for instance, it may be because you ate a lot of it as a child, says Dr. Hansen. Many of your food habits are learned early and are influenced by those around you, she says. But your genes do have some influence on the amount of food you crave and how strongly your preferences dictate what you actually eat, she adds. This explains why twins raised apart naturally gravitate towards the same body shape and weight.

Your preference for different foods, however, is actually one of the easier traits to change, says Deborah J. Bowen, Ph.D., who is conducting studies on food preferences in women. She has found that when women avoid high-sugar and high-fat foods, they lose their taste for them. Here is what you can do.

Give yourself a few months. Changing your eating habits takes time. To reduce the fat in your diet, you must start gradually and be patient. In fact, studies show that it takes about three months to derail any habit – and for most women, fat is a habit.

Slowly reduce your consumption of high-fat foods by fighting one fatty food at a time. If you regularly eat fried chicken three times a week, for instance, try to limit your consumption by indulging only once a week. And when you do, try oven-baked chicken. At the same time, increase your consumption of fruits, vegetables and grains. If you eat only one piece of fruit a day, for instance, add an apple at lunch.

Procrastinate. When you feel compelled to have a fatty food, wait 10 minutes. If you are not really hungry, the craving will pass, says Linda Crawford, eating-behaviour specialist.

Create a diversion. When you feel a craving coming on, distract yourself by engaging in an activity that requires concentration and prevents eating. Take a walk, ride your bike, paint your nails, or play with the kids, says Crawford.

Vacate the premises. Distance yourself from food by leaving the scene of the snack. Once out of sight, goodies are often out of mind, says Crawford.

Savour what you like. Decide what amount of the fattening food is reasonable to eat and then nibble on the favoured food slowly, savouring every bite. Scarfing ice cream from a 2 pint container isn't a good idea. Instead, dish out one conservative scoop of frozen yogurt, satisfy your craving, and then get on with your life.

Rev Your Metabolism

You may not feel as if you're burning a ton of calories every time your heart beats, your lungs take in a breath and your body temperature increases when you enter a cold room, but your metabolic rate – the rate at which you burn calories just to stay alive – accounts for 70 percent of the calories you burn in a day. (You burn the rest by moving around and digesting food.)

Not all metabolisms were created equal. Some experts think that your metabolism may speed up or slow down in an attempt to maintain a set body weight. So if you overeat, your metabolism burns more calories than usual, even while you are sleeping. If you diet, on the other hand, your body burns fewer. For some women, this means that their bodies will stay slender no matter how much they eat. For others, it means that their bodies will cling to a heavier weight no matter how little they eat. Your metabolic setpoint, however, is not set in stone. Genes cast at least 25 percent of the votes and maybe as much as 75 percent, influencing your hormones, the amount of muscle tone you have and how much and what you eat. Your environment, including which foods you choose and how much you restrain your caloric intake, contributes the rest. Here is what you can do.

Spice up your life. Eating spicy food may boost your metabolism for three hours after eating. In one study, people revved up their calorie-burning potential by 25 percent when they ate food with hot mustard and chilli sauce. You don't want to make every meal spicy, however. Eating spicy food about two to three

> ### DO YOUR GENES FIT?
>
> Scientists have not yet perfected tests that would let you give some blood, have it analysed, and find out whether or not you have fat genes. But they are at the point where they can look at various factors, such as whether or not your parents are fat, and let you know your chances of having a weight problem. Check the following list to discover your genetic lot.
>
> ❧ If both of your parents are overweight, you have an 80 percent chance of also having weight problems.
>
> ❧ If one parent is overweight, your odds are 40 percent.
>
> ❧ If neither parent is overweight, you have only a 10 percent chance of being overweight.
>
> ❧ If you're Afro-Caribbean, you're twice as likely as a Caucasian to be fat.
>
> ❧ If you're Native American, from the Pacific Islands or Hispanic, you'll have more trouble fighting fat than someone of European ancestry.
>
> ❧ If you're Asian, you have less chance of becoming fat than members of other ethnic groups, but beware, because any excess fat will tend to land on your abdomen.

times a week seems to produce the most benefits. "It seems that if you eat spices regularly, it may blunt the effect," says Jeya Henry, Ph.D.

Eat breakfast. You may plan to eat lunch, but your body doesn't know that. If you skip breakfast, all your body knows is that its food supply has been interrupted – maybe for a long, long time. So it starts burning calories more slowly to keep you from starving during an impending famine. To reassure your metabolism that there's plenty of food to be had and keep it purring along, eat something when you wake up.

Pick carbohydrates and pass up the fat. Your body burns energy while digesting all kinds of foods. But it may burn more calories in the process of digesting complex carbohydrates than it burns while digesting protein or fat. So make sure you get no more than 25 to 30 percent of those calories from fat and no more than 15 percent from protein foods such as meats, fish, poultry and cheese. Get the rest from complex carbohydrates such as fruits, vegetables, whole-wheat pasta, breads and rice.

Lift your weight. In addition to your setpoint, the speed of your resting metabolism depends on your muscle mass. The more muscle you have, the faster your metabolic rate. In fact, women who build muscle through weight lifting must eat 15 percent more just to maintain their weight, says Maria A. Fiatarone Singh, M.D.

Deflate Your Fat Cells

When your body has extra calories floating around in the bloodstream, it will either store them as glycogen in your muscles or as fat inside a fat cell. For a slimmer appearance, you would rather have the excess stored in your muscles, where it gets burned more readily to produce heat and energy. The problem is that some women's bodies prefer to store calories as fat instead of as glycogen in their muscles.

Here's why. Fat cells can expand to three times their size. And they can multiply. The more fat cells you have, the more easily you store fat. Some women are born with more fat cells and produce them more easily throughout life than other women. Once you have fat cells, you're stuck with them. They don't shrivel up and die, no matter how thin you get.

Enzymes also come into play. An enzyme called lipoprotein lipase draws fat to either fat or muscle cells. The more lipoprotein lipase there is on the surface of your fat cells, the more likely it is that you'll store fat there rather than in muscle cells. The average woman has three lipoprotein lipase molecules on fat cells to every one on muscle cells. So in the average woman, three times as many calories are stored in fat than in muscle. Other women fare much worse. They may have four or five lipoprotein lipase molecules on fat cells compared to every one on muscle cells. Thus, they store fat much more easily.

This is not as bleak as it may sound. You can outsmart your fat cells. Here's how.

Don't bully your body. When you try to bully your body into losing weight with crash dieting and grueling exercise, your fat cells mount a defence. Instead, go slowly and easily. It will take longer, but it's worth it, says Debra Waterhouse, R.D. "The mistake so many women make is trying to rush the process," says Waterhouse. "They end up strengthening the very systems they're trying to weaken."

Exercise comfortably. Research shows that exercising at a moderate pace is best. If you find that you're gasping for breath or can't carry on a conversation, then you're not exercising for weight loss, you're wearing yourself out. The faster you go, the sooner you'll want to call it quits. Conversely, the more you enjoy exercising, the more time you'll spend doing it.

Your Perfect Weight
Take a Positive Look at Yourself

A woman watches her body uneasily, as though it were an unreliable ally in the battle for love.

—Leonard Cohen, songwriter

Too often, women fall in love with the wrong weight.

You may have picked your perfect weight at some point when you were young, for instance, maybe in your early twenties before life events such as pregnancy padded your frame. Then, after pregnancy, you found yourself consistently starving yourself down to your pre-pregnancy weight. You'd gain. You'd diet. Today, as much as you want to get to that perfect number on the scale, it continues to elude you.

Maybe you didn't think about your perfect weight until the day you saw the body you'd love to have but didn't – yet. Although you were satisfied with the way you looked, you knew that if you dropped 10 pounds or so, you, too, could look like *that*. But try as you will, it's still not happening.

Or you may have arrived at your perfect weight with the best of intentions, based simply on what the chart in the doctor's office says is the best weight for you and your health. The problem is that you can't make it happen.

If your quest for your perfect weight is constantly frustrating you, it may be time to perfect reality. Picking a weight that you want to be but can never attain is self-defeating.

"When women get up in the morning and get on the scale, it can make or break their day, depending on what it says," says Susan Olson, Ph.D. We can try harder and harder to get the scale to show us the numbers we want to see but still fail. Even worse than making us feel bad about ourselves, trying to slim down to the wrong weight can actually hamper our ability to fight fat, she says.

"When women try to lose weight just to look thinner, they often go to extremes," says Kathy McManus, R.D. "They may try fad diets, exercise too hard or use diet pills. They may try to reach an unrealistic weight that cannot be maintained. They may harm their health."

WOMEN ASK WHY

Why is it that I can lose 10 pounds in 2 weeks, but I can't lose the last 2 pounds in 10 weeks?

Did you ever wonder why a wrestler jogs around in sweatshirts and pants when the temperature is in the 90s? Is it pure stupidity? Well, not entirely. He knows that sweating it out – essentially dehydrating himself – is the quickest way to drop five pounds before weigh-ins. Your rapid weight loss tells me that most of what you've lost so far has also been water, but instead of breaking a sweat, you've probably been restricting yourself to a very low calorie, low carbohydrate diet.

When you cut your calories severely, your body first draws on its carbohydrate reserves. When they're gone, your body turns to fat for fuel, a process that releases excess water through your urine. So it's no surprise that you lost a lot of weight in two weeks. But it was mostly water. And it doesn't last. Here's why.

After a couple of weeks, your body adjusts to your strict diet and starts to conserve energy by actually lowering its basal metabolic rate (BMR). Long periods of calorie restriction can cause your BMR to fall at least 20 to 30 percent below normal levels. At this point, your body actually requires fewer calories than it previously needed to stay alive and healthy. This explains the infamous weight-loss plateau.

There is something you can do, however, to burn off those last few pounds: Exercise. Exercise helps keep your BMR purring. Better yet, combine exercise with a sensible eating programme and you'll actually increase your BMR.

Since exercise increases muscle mass, the scale may not be the best indicator of how successful your diet has been. So as you gear up for your diet, avoid focusing on the numbers: Instead of wrestling with your weight, just fight fat.

Expert consulted
Bernestine B. McGee, R.D., Ph.D.

Getting Real

Ask any thin woman how much she'd like to weigh, and most likely she'll tell you that she could stand to lose 5 or 10 pounds. That's because women tend to want to be a lot thinner than they should be, says Dr. Olson. Many factors play into this unrealistic image that we have of ourselves.

Fashion models. Music videos, magazine covers, TV shows and films feature very thin women instead of those with more realistically filled-out figures. Yet attempts to make our bodies look like theirs are unnecessarily punishing, if not impossible. The industry standard is artificially high, set by images of models and celebrities who have the means to hire personal trainers, spend thousands of pounds on cosmetic surgery and have their photographs airbrushed to perfection. Holding them up as role models only means that you are setting yourself up to let yourself down.

Your former weight. Changing hormones and bone structures mean that the weight you easily maintained in your twenties may not be doable now without a considerable decrease in the number of calories you eat or a considerable increase in exercise. You may be able to stay on such a regimen for a short period of time, but not for the lifetime it would take to keep the weight off.

Competition. Sometimes we want to weigh what our role model or our best friend or our skinny mum weighs. The problem is, body weights can vary tremendously because of bone structure. If your bones are heavier than your friend's, she'll always weigh less than you, even if you both wear the same clothing size.

Inaccurate perceptions. Many of us think that we look fatter than we really are, so we try to slim down to too-thin proportions. But we can never get slim enough. "Women can lose weight and still think that their thighs are too fat," says Dr. Olson. In one study, when asked to estimate their body size, half of the women had inaccurate perceptions, believing that their bodies were bigger than they actually were. The less accurate a woman's self-perception, researchers found, the more likely she was to diet.

False information. We've heard over and over again how we should lose weight to stay healthy. Yet feeling stressed because we can't maintain the weight we picked from a chart may do more harm to our health than simply accepting a body that is 10 or 15 pounds heavier than it should be, says Joanne Curran-Celentano, R.D.

"There's a very large range of healthy weights, and you have to put that range in perspective," says Dr. Curran-Celentano. "If it's completely stressful for you to keep your weight at one number, I don't think it's worth it. I see women spend a whole lot of anxiety and a lot of energy trying to maintain a weight

Woman to Woman
Self-Acceptance Is Number One

For more than three decades, Maye Musk of Liverpool has made her living in front of cameras and audiences as a fashion model and a motivational speaker on ending emotion-driven eating. But despite the pressure of always being on display, she accepts herself, no matter what her weight.

Often, the women featured in magazines and on TV are extremely thin, but that doesn't suit my lifestyle. When I was 16 years old, I began modelling in South Africa, where I was raised. Over the years, I've modelled from size 8 to size 18. No matter what size I've been — and I have pictures of myself at 14 stone — I looked good. I always dressed nicely, walked tall and felt good about myself. Now, although I'm no longer a plus-size model, I am still a bit larger than other women in my field. I could blame it on age or having three children, but I have to take responsibility for my habits.

Of course, some people have criticised me for my weight. They were mostly men I was dating who, because I was a model, expected me to look like Cindy Crawford when I wore a bathing suit. I usually dropped them when they started suggesting that I lose weight and have plastic surgery. I make it a point not to mix with people who don't like me for who I am. It pulls down my self-esteem, especially if their criticism is based on looks.

Now I'm a size 12, which in the modelling world is still larger than the norm. When I go to jobs, the wardrobe people usually have size-10 clothes set out for me, but when they see that I'm a little bigger, they simply get larger clothes.

It's probably strange for a model and motivational speaker, but I almost never get on the scale. I don't want my mood to depend on my weight. I let the way I feel guide me instead. If I begin to feel sluggish or my clothes become too tight, I know it's time to eat smaller portions and lose some weight. Accepting who I am is not the same as letting myself get out of control.

The older I've become (I'm almost 50 now), the more content I am with myself. This, I think, is one of the keys to happiness. I even wrote a book, *Feel Fantastic*, based on my success.

that they think is in the appropriate range. They would be a lot freer if they would forget about that weight and concentrate on developing a healthy lifestyle."

In addition to causing anxiety and stress, picking a number that's too low on the scale sets you up for failure, says Dr. Olson. The weight-loss process will feel excruciating. Women can be such perfectionists that no matter what the scale tells us – even if it says we've lost weight – we still are not satisfied. We wish we had lost more, and we get discouraged. Then we overeat – and we gain weight.

Is Your Weight a Health Risk?

If you are obese – that is, if you are 20 percent over your normal weight – your primary goal in losing weight should be to improve your health. But here's the surprise: You don't have to get down to "normal" to benefit.

Overweight and obesity have been associated with high blood pressure, high cholesterol, heart disease, gall-bladder disease, diabetes and cancer. You don't have to figure out how far above normal weight you are to know if you are at risk – just look at your naked body in the mirror, says Joan Marie Conway, Ph.D. If you see that you can pinch more than an inch in a few places, you're probably overweight and at risk.

Losing just 10 percent of your body weight can make a big difference in your health risk, says Dr. Curran-Celentano. That means that all you need to do is aim to take off no more than a pound a week. For instance, if you weigh 12 stone, you need to lose only 17 pounds over a period of 17 weeks to significantly improve your health. Once you attain that goal and find that

---

PRESS LIFE'S PLAY BUTTON

Too often, women put their lives on hold until they lose weight. But most of the things that we postpone we could do right now, before we drop a single pound. Here are some of the most common things that women put off and some easy steps we can take to press life's play button, according to Joni Johnston, Psy.D., who specialises in body image and eating disorders.

What we avoid: Wearing a swimsuit.

Why: We're insecure or embarrassed.

How to overcome it: At first, put on your swimsuit when you're at home, but don't go out. Just walk around in it. Look at yourself in the mirror. Eventually, just the act of wearing one in private will make you more comfortable with wearing one in public. For your first few forays to a public swimming pool or beach, go with a large-size friend or a group of large women. Or take a water aerobics class designed for large women.

What we avoid: Going to the doctor.

Why: Fear that the doctor will make treatment contingent on weight loss and or that the doctor will blame all our health problems on weight.

How to overcome it: Keep shopping around until you find a doctor with whom you are comfortable. Know your body well enough so that you can stick up for yourself if your doctor blames an unrelated health problem on your weight. Be assertive. Tell the nurse that you prefer not to be weighed.

What we avoid: Asserting ourselves at work and in relationships.

Why: We feel that we don't deserve to have an opinion. We feel that the sort of person who speaks up must be thin and beautiful, a category in which we feel we don't belong.

How to overcome it: Know that everyone's opinion is valuable. Stop focusing on your body and focus on internal strengths, such as your intellect or your kindness. If you need a jump start, take an assertiveness class.

What we avoid: Enrolling in continuing education courses.

Why: Underneath our body worries, we wear a general fear of failure. We feel that we don't have enough time to focus on college until we are finished "fixing" our bodies. We feel that our weight is the big problem and our desire for learning the small problem in life. Also, for some people, there's the fear of not being able to fit at a desk.

How to overcome it: If you're wasting more time than necessary worrying about your appearance, put some of that time into your education. Realise that your desire to learn is the real issue, and your appearance is not. If you are worried about fitting into a desk, go to the school's office for people with disabilities. They are required by law to make sure that there are desks available for large people.

What we avoid: Dating.

Why: Low self-esteem; the fear of setting ourselves up for rejection; the thought, "Any man who would want me must have something wrong with him"; and the assumption that men won't find us attractive.

How to overcome it: Focus on aspects of yourself that are appealing rather than the flaw you usually obsess about. Mentally rehearse all the reasons that someone would find you desirable. Remember that you are more likely to worry about minor imperfections in your appearance than others are. Know that men are not as critical of women's bodies as women are of their own bodies. In the long run, mates choose one another based on personalities, values and morals. Appearance may rank high for first dates, but meaningful relationships are based on deeper factors.

you still want to lose, you can aim for another 10 percent.

"Even very modest losses – 5 to 10 pounds – can have a significant, positive impact on health," notes Susan Zelitch Yanovski, M.D. When a panel of 20 experts on body weight gathered for the American Health Foundation's Roundtable on Healthy Weight, they determined that the best healthy weight-loss goals for overweight women range from 10 pounds for a woman who is five feet tall to 14 pounds for a woman who is five feet eight inches tall. Such a modest loss, they concluded, was enough to turn the tide from a higher risk of disease to better health.

If you are not significantly overweight, however, losing 5, 10 or even 15 pounds may not make much of a difference to your health. The health improvements of weight loss come at the top of the scale, not the bottom. So if you weighed 8.5 stone for most of your life and then gained 10 pounds after menopause, you don't need to lose those 10 pounds for your health.

Reach for a "Look"

Most of us think of health as a secondary reason for wanting to lose weight. Looking good is the primary goal. This is where unrealistic expectations start, as in, "I could stand to lose one and a half stone. Two stone would be even better." Is it possible, though, that in reality, what you could really stand to lose is more like 10 pounds?

If you're going to set a weight-loss goal, make sure you pick a weight that you can reach and maintain, advises Dr. Curran-Celentano. Pick a number that takes into account not only how slim you want to look but also how slim your body will allow you to look.

To find that natural weight, follow this three-step process.

1. *Start small.* If your weight-loss goal is large, start with the 10 or so pounds you should lose to improve your health. This is the weight you *need* to lose, says Dr. Curran-Celentano.

2. *Find a familiar number.* Now find out what your body will let you lose based on your genes. Although this sounds complicated, it isn't. Think about a weight that has seemed natural for you as an adult. Perhaps you weighed 10 stone for many years, then suddenly began putting on the pounds. This is much different from your lowest weight, which is probably the number that you've been trying over and over again to achieve.

You're looking for your "easy-care" weight, a weight that seemed to maintain itself. Even if you ate a little more or a little less or engaged in a little more or a little less physical activity, you could pretty much maintain this weight. This is the weight that your body will let you attain, says Dr. Curran-Celentano.

3. *Then add a few.* Now rectify what you need to lose and what your body will let you lose with what you really want to lose. Your goal weight should be one that you can maintain comfortably for years to come – one that fits your lifestyle. Despite how much you want to look as slender as Cindy Crawford, you don't want to pick a weight that seems like torture to maintain. Otherwise, you'll end up gaining. So your goal weight may be somewhat lighter than your healthy weight and somewhat heavier than

THE BODIES OF TIME—PAST AND FUTURE

If you've frustrated yourself by trying to achieve an ideal body shape and size most of your life, you've been chasing a moving target. In the past century, the so-called ideal body shape has changed from thin to curvy and back again.

"Historically, the ideal female body weight usually drops as women gain economic or political progress, then goes up afterward in a sort of backlash," says Joni Johnston, who specialises in body image and eating disorders. Thin was in, for example, when women earned the right to vote in the 1920s and was back again in the 1960s when the Pill gave women sexual freedom. When each of the world wars ended and women gave up their male-oriented wartime jobs and returned to the home, the ideal womanly form was decidedly more feminine – rounder, softer, and fuller-figured.

Here's what was ideal during different periods in history.

After the population drop caused by the bubonic plague in the fifteenth century, the ideal female form was a pregnant look. Women packed the fronts of their dresses with pillows.

During the 1920s, the rail-thin flapper was in – no breasts, no hips, no curves.

Fifteenth Century: Maximised Hips

The 1920s: The Flapper

After World War II and through the 1950s, the voluptuous, curvy, rounded look was the ideal. Marilyn Monroe epitomised this body type. Many girls stuffed their bras with toilet paper to try to look larger-breasted.

In the 1960s, Twiggy was the woman to watch. Small breasts, rail-thin bodies, and straight figures were in.

Thanks to plastic surgery, the image of the ideal woman has become even more complex and unnatural. Features like huge breasts and full buttocks, which normally require women to maintain an above-average amount of body fat, are surgically placed on models and actresses who have very thin frames and wear size-three clothes.

As women become bigger players in the fashion and media industries, they are controlling more of the spending pounds available to businesses. As these women say "no more" to the unrealistic ideals of the end of the twentieth century, Dr. Johnston says diversity will gain favour in the fashion industry.

"Of course, there will be ebbs and flows with every trend, but hopefully there will be less extremes and fewer women obsessed with the ideal body image," she says.

your desired weight, says Dr. Curran-Celentano.

Figuring out your perfect weight means balancing your desires, your needs, your lifestyle and your body's natural tendencies. "There's no magic number," says Shiriki Kumanyika, R.D. "A woman cannot pick a goal weight off a chart. She has to factor in her own current weight and weight history, her family's health history, her personal health goals, her own eating patterns and her level of activity. Then she can pick a weight-reduction target that makes sense."

Post-WWII through the 1950s: The Curvy Era

The 1960s: Twiggy Times

The 1990s: The Surgically Altered Decade

The Numbers Game

Making Sense of Weights and Measures

Many women think of weight loss as a numbers game. You need to know your weight, your measurements, your percentage of body fat, the number of calories you put in your mouth each day, how many fat grammes you swallow, the serving sizes of foods you eat and the number of calories you burn.

When it comes to measuring your progress on a weight-loss programme, some numbers are more important than others. And plenty of them are downright unnecessary. We asked nutrition expert Maria A. Fiatarone Singh, M.D., which numbers we should pay attention to in planning a weight-loss programme. Here is her advice.

Chart Your Weight-Loss Course

The basic measurement that we use to decide if we need to lose weight is the number on the scale. We can determine what we need to lose in two ways: the traditional height/weight/body frame table that you find in your doctor's office or the newer body mass index (BMI) that's been

getting a lot of attention for the past few years.

The numbers game: Body mass index (BMI).

The theory: It's more complicated than the insurance table, but it's believed to be a more accurate gauge of what you should weigh. Your BMI is a ratio of height to weight that is an indication of your weight-related health risk. Once you do the calculations, you'll end up with a number between 19 and 32; the closer your BMI is to 19, the better.

How to measure: To find your BMI, you'll need a calculator. Divide your weight in pounds by your height in inches squared and then multiply the result by 705. Or look at "Your Body Mass Index (BMI)," in which the maths has been done for you.

A BMI between 19 and 22 is considered desirable. A BMI between 23 and 25 means that you are slightly overweight and may be at risk for weight-related disease. At a BMI of around 26, your disease risk starts increasing. Since some women in the range of 25 to 27 are perfectly healthy, however, you should take other risk factors, such as your family history, eating habits, age and level of physical activity into account before you get alarmed at your number. A BMI of 30 or above means that you are obese and at substantially increased risk for disease. For example, one study found that women with a BMI greater than 29 had a 230 percent greater risk of heart disease.

Strengths: Measuring your BMI goes a step beyond simply stepping onto the scale. It's probably the most accurate and scientific way to predict whether your weight could cause you to die prematurely from cancer, heart disease or some other weight-related illness. BMI has been used in longevity studies that showed that those under 30 years of age with a BMI of 19 to 22 have the greatest chance of living the longest.

Weaknesses: Women love to shoot for one number in particular, but the BMI scale does not allow for such specificity. The difference in health risk between BMIs of 23 and 24, for instance, is minimal in a weight range of 5 to 10 pounds. BMI exists purely as a measurement of health risk.

Recommendation: Calculate your BMI at the beginning of a weight-loss plan to find out if you fall into the at-risk category. If your BMI is 30 or higher, you'll want to lower it. Once you start your weight-loss plan, continue to calculate your BMI once a month until you get your result below 30. Once you're there, you don't need to spend a lot of time worrying about your BMI. The long and the short of it is that women who are lean throughout life or whose weight doesn't fluctuate greatly from year to year are more likely to lead long, healthy lives. Nevertheless, if you are overweight and lose extra pounds, you can still reduce your risk of osteoarthritis, high blood pressure, diabetes and other problems.

Your Body Mass Index (BMI)

Height	Weight (lb.)													
4'10"	91	96	100	105	110	115	119	124	129	134	139	143	148	153
4'11"	94	99	104	109	114	119	124	128	133	138	143	148	153	158
5'0"	97	102	107	112	118	123	128	133	138	143	148	153	158	163
5'1"	100	106	111	116	122	127	132	137	143	148	153	158	164	169
5'2"	104	109	115	120	126	131	136	142	147	153	158	164	169	174
5'3"	107	113	118	124	130	135	141	146	152	158	163	169	175	180
5'4"	110	116	122	128	134	140	145	151	157	163	169	174	180	186
5'5"	114	120	126	132	138	144	150	156	162	168	174	180	186	192
5'6"	118	124	130	136	142	148	155	161	167	173	179	186	192	198
5'7"	121	127	134	140	146	153	159	166	172	178	185	191	197	204
5'8"	125	131	138	144	151	158	164	171	177	184	190	197	203	210
5'9"	128	135	142	149	155	162	169	176	182	189	196	203	209	216
5'10"	132	139	146	153	160	167	174	181	188	195	202	207	215	222
5'11"	136	142	150	157	165	172	179	186	193	200	208	215	222	229
6'0"	140	147	154	162	169	177	184	191	199	206	213	221	228	235
BMI	19	20	21	22	23	24	25	26	27	28	29	30	31	32

A. First, measure your waist.
B. Next, measure your hips.
C. Finally, measure your bust.

Weight and Measurements

In recent years, research has found that where we wear our body fat has an impact on factors that are more crucial than beauty. Our body shape is an indicator of our propensity for certain diseases. If you need motivation to lose weight, you might want to get out the tape measure. But there are different ways to interpret what your measurements are saying. Here's the rundown.

The numbers game: Your measurements.

The theory: Strategically measuring your waist, hips and bust can give you an accurate idea of exactly how much smaller your body is getting, helping to motivate you as you fight fat.

How to measure: Use a flexible tape measure. For your waist measurement, wrap it around the narrowest part of your waist, roughly halfway between your bottom rib and your hipbone, keeping your stomach muscles relaxed. Then, for your hips, wrap the tape around your hips and buttocks at the widest point, slightly below your

actual hipbone. To measure your bust, wear a bra, stand erect and wrap the tape around your back and the fullest part of your bust.

Strengths: Measuring your body circumference is much more accurate than stepping on the scale. Why? Because muscle weighs more than fat. If you build muscle through exercise, you may not lose much weight on the scale. Thankfully, however, muscle is also more compact than fat, so your body size will still shrink as you lose fat and gain muscle. And that's where using a tape measure comes in. It lets you know exactly how much smaller you are.

Weaknesses: Women put too much emphasis on bust size. The areas you want to pay attention to are your trouble spots – thighs, hips and belly.

Recommendation: Go for it, but forget about measuring bust size. Instead concentrate on your waist size, which will shrink as your belly gets smaller, and your hip circumference, which will give you a good idea of how your rear end and thighs are shaping up.

The numbers game: Waist-to-hip ratio.

The theory: Research has shown that your body *shape* may be more important than your body *size* when it comes to assessing weight-related health risks. The fat most associated with health risks makes you look like an apple. It can be found on the upper body, in the abdomen and above, rather than in the thighs and hips. So if your waist is much wider than your hips, you have too much of the more dangerous upper-body fat.

How to measure: Use a measuring tape to measure your waist at its narrowest point. Then measure your hips at their widest point. Divide your waist measurement by your hip measurement. Anything above 0.85 means that you are more prone to heart disease, high blood pressure, stroke, diabetes and some types of cancer.

Strengths: Finding the ratio between the measurements of your waist and hips can give you an extremely accurate prediction of whether you will develop life-threatening diseases later in life. Looking at where your fat is distributed also takes genetic influences and lifestyle into account. Certain lifestyles, such as eating a high-fat diet and smoking, tend to make fat accumulate in the belly area. On the other hand, both aerobic exercise and resistance training, as well as oestrogen replacement therapy, have been shown to reduce belly fat.

Weaknesses: Although calculating your waist-to-hip ratio is the best method of assessing the health risks of your body shape, your measurements do not tell you how much fat you carry overall. And body measurements don't distinguish well between fat and muscle. So while measurements can accurately predict how your body shape affects your health, they don't reflect your level of fitness.

Recommendation: Your measurements are probably the most important number game of all. But you can forget about the common way that women measure themselves, which accounts for bust size. You only need to worry about your waist and hip measurements.

The numbers game: Percentage of body fat.

The theory: In addition to your bone structure, the shape of your body is dictated by the ratio of fat to muscle. This ratio is another indicator of your risk for developing certain diseases. Simply standing on a scale can't tell you whether you have too much fat or just a lot of muscle, but body fat tests can.

How to measure: You can arrange to have a test at a gym or doctor's office. There, a staff member will either pinch your skin with calipers, weigh you underwater or run a mild electric current through your body. Although no one knows for sure, some say that an optimal amount of body fat for women ranges from 18 to 22 percent. Above 30 percent is considered borderline obese and above 35 percent is considered obese.

Strengths: Finding out how much body fat you have tells you how fit you are. The more you exercise and lift weights, the more muscle you will build and the less fat you will have.

Weaknesses: Unless you buy special equipment and take a training course on how to use it, you can't measure your percentage of body fat at home. You'll have to go to someone who offers these services to measure your progress. Even with a trained professional and the right equipment, though, you may not get accurate results. Body fat is difficult to measure, so results are usually off by at least 3 percent. Also, unlike your waist-to-hip ratio or BMI, studies have not proven ideal body fat percentages.

Recommendation: Given the problems that are inherent in measuring body fat and the lack of an agreed-upon benchmark for what's considered desirable, experts advise women against using body fat measurements as a measure of weight loss.

WOMEN ASK WHY

Why does the scale say I've gained five pounds the day after a big night of pigging out? Can I really gain weight overnight?

While the scale may register a couple of pounds higher the morning after, pigging out for one night isn't likely to cause any of those pounds to be actual fat. One pound accounts for about 3,500 calories, so in order to gain just one pound of fat overnight, you'd have to eat 3,500 more calories than you burned that day! You can see just how difficult it would be to gain five pounds overnight.

So if it's not fat that's tipping the scale, what is? After a huge feast, you're probably toting around quite a bit of water weight. You see, when you store carbohydrates, they're stored with water, and we can carry a lot of water weight because we have many places to store excess water in the body. If your late-night binge included a lot of salty foods, such as potato crisps and nachos, your body will retain even more water, making the scales register even more extra pounds.

Unlike fat weight, water weight is transient, meaning that if you weighed yourself four more times the next day, the scale would probably say something different every time. In other words, you can turn around a night of overeating by making a few adjustments the next day. The key is not to become discouraged. Try to increase your activity. You may also want to eat some high-fibre foods to avoid constipation.

Finally, if you did eat a lot of salty foods the night before and you're retaining water, believe it or not, the thing to do is drink six to eight glasses of water. This will help you flush out the sodium, which is what was holding the water in. Just stay mentally positive, and you can counter an occasional overindulgence and still stay on track.

Expert consulted
Michele Trankina, Ph.D.

Food Maths

When we're not weighing and measuring our bodies, we turn our attention to food. Here is what's worth counting and what's not.

The numbers game: Fat grammes.

The theory: Eating fat is more fattening than eating carbohydrate or protein. For one thing, fat has nine calories per gramme, compared with four for both carbohydrate and protein. Also, fat is stored in fat cells more efficiently than carbohydrate or protein. The body burns off just 3 percent of its fat calories in the process of storing fat. While converting carbohydrate into fat to be stored, however, the body burns 23 percent of the carbohydrate calories. So limiting your fat intake can help you lose weight, regardless of how well you watch your calories.

How to count: Restrict the amount of fat you eat based on your goal weight and average calorie intake, limiting your fat calories to 25 percent of your daily calorie consumption. For example, if your total daily intake is 1,600 calories, you should be getting no more than 44 grammes of fat. To make it easier to figure out, we offer the following table.

Strengths: Counting how many grammes of fat you eat in a day is an extremely accurate way of knowing whether you are sticking with your new eating plan.

Weaknesses: Counting is difficult. To succeed, you would have to walk around with a fat-counting

Your Fat Gramme Quota		
Weight (lb.)	Probable Calorie Intake	Fat Limit (g.)
110	1,300	36
120	1,400	39
130	1,600	44
140	1,700	47
150	1,800	50
160	1,900	53
170	2,000	56
180	2,200	61

guide and a set of measuring cups and spoons. Every time you went out to eat, you'd have to find out exactly how the food was prepared and the size of the portions. And you'd have to write down everything you eat so you could tally it all up at the end of the day.

Recommendation: Don't you have better things to do? Don't go around counting all the time. Instead, concentrate on slowly cutting fat from your diet. One way to do this is to eat more low-fat whole grains, fruits and vegetables. These foods will fill you up. What's more, by substituting them for higher-fat foods, you automatically reduce calories. You'll find numerous other tips in this book to help you do just that. Every once in a while, you can tally up how much fat you are eating to ensure that you are on target. But don't miss out on more enjoyable ways of spending life by busying yourself with fat-gramme counts.

The numbers game: Counting calories.

The theory: It's pretty basic. Based on the proven scientific formula that a pound of stored body fat equals 3,500 calories, you should lose a pound for every 3,500 calories you save. So if it takes 2,000 calories a day to maintain your current weight, and you go on a 1,500-calorie-a-day diet, you should lose a pound a week.

How to count: Determine the number of calories that your body requires to maintain your current weight. You can do this by measuring and writing down everything you eat for two weeks. Use food labels or a calorie-counting guide to figure out how many calories are in the food you eat. Add it all up and divide by 14. The result is the average number of calories that you are eating each day to maintain your weight. Based on this number, determine how many calories you want to cut every day. For this method to work, you'll have to count your calories daily. Here's some simple arithmetic to help you out.

Weight Loss per Week (lb.)	Calories to Cut per Day
1	500
½	250
¼	125

Strengths: As with counting fat grammes, counting calories is an extremely accurate way of knowing whether you are sticking to your eating plan. And eventually, if you can maintain your calorie restriction, you can lose weight.

Weaknesses: If you've ever tried it, you know that no matter how much you stick with the calorie-counting programme, you're not necessarily going to drop the weight according to plan, especially if you use the scale as an indicator. As mentioned above, a lot of other factors need to be considered when stepping on the scale. Also, scientists have discovered that our calorie-burner has a way of slowing down when we start to conserve calories. For successful weight loss, you need more than calorie control: You need to exercise as well. In addition, counting calories is even more tedious than counting fat grammes, so this whole method can become discouraging and self-defeating.

Recommendation: Forget about it. You can

keep up the calorie-counting regimen for a month or two at best, but not for the lifetime it takes to keep weight off.

The numbers game: Tallying calories burned through exercise.

The theory: You can boost the number of calories you burn every day by boosting your energy consumption through exercise. The theory holds that exercise also stokes your metabolism so you burn calories more efficiently all day long. However, you have to build calorie-hungry muscle with weight lifting as well as get in a half-hour or more of heart-pumping aerobic exercise on most days to get the effect.

How to count: To be honest, it's really hard to gauge this accurately because so much depends on your level of fitness. There is a general rule of thumb, however, for how many calories you can expect to burn for any activity. One mile is equal to 100 calories, for example, no matter how long it takes you to cover the distance. Here are a couple of tables to help you along.

Strengths: Figuring out approximately how many calories you burn during exercise is not quite as difficult as figuring out how many calories you eat. That's about it.

Weaknesses: As we said, it's pretty hard to be accurate about this. Most people exercise

HOW THE SCALE LIES

"Don't worry about those few extra pounds. Your weight can fluctuate."

How many times have you heard that reassurance from a doctor or nutritionist or from a friend as you stepped on the scale before your evening workout at the gym?

Women are often given – and can give – many reasons for weight fluctuations during the day or even over a period of a couple of days. Here are a few reasons that women gave us for being surprised by the number they saw on a scale.

- "I ate a lot for lunch."
- "My clothes weigh at least five pounds."
- "I had a full bladder."
- "I ate a lot of salty food yesterday."
- "My shoes must weigh a ton."
- "I hadn't gone to the toilet yet."

What's the real impact of such "excuses" on what the scale tells us? To find out, we did a little experiment. We picked a fairly in-shape woman who weighs about 8.5 stone (120 pounds) and asked her to weigh herself on the same scale throughout the day under various circumstances: Before and after breakfast, wearing only her undergarments, and then after lunch, fully clothed with a full bladder, after

Your Calorie-Burning Goals

One-Year Weight-Loss Goal (lb.)	Calories to Burn per Day
5–6	150
10–12	300
15–18	450
20–25	600

Calories Burned through Exercise

Activity	Calories Burned per Half Hour
Mild walking	92
Slow cycling	122
Low-impact aerobic dance	137
Ballroom dancing	150
Easy rowing	150
Weight lifting	150
Swimming	270
Vigorous walking	277
Jogging	327

emptying her bladder, and wearing various layers of clothes. Her weight varied from 118.5 to 126.5.

Right after waking, wearing underwear	118.5
After breakfast, wearing underwear	121.75
After lunch, fully clothed with full bladder	126.5
After lunch, fully clothed after urinating	125
After lunch, after urinating, without shoes	124
After lunch, after urinating, without shoes and blazer	122.5
After lunch, after urinating, in underwear	121.75

The moral of the story: If your weight fluctuates within eight pounds on a particular day, don't assume that it's your fault. It could just be the time of day, your outfit or some other factor, such as excess water weight due to too much salt in your last meal.

To get the best reading from a scale, weigh yourself on the same scale at the same time of day each time, wearing the same type of clothing and even with the same amount of food in your stomach.

moderately, as they should. The truth is, though, that at a moderate pace, you really don't get much of a difference in calorie burning no matter what type of exercise you do, even though various calorie-burning charts like the one shown here indicate otherwise.

Recommendation: Exercise. But don't pick your exercise, time or intensity based on the number of calories you want to burn. Once you make exercise contingent on how many calories you have to burn, you're more likely to quit. Rather, think of exercise as something that helps you lose weight not merely by burning X number of calories per session but also by increasing your metabolic rate, increasing how fast your body burns off calories from food you consume and helping you to be more active and fit.

The numbers game: Food groups.

The theory: Some foods are healthier for women than others. And if you concentrate on making sure that you eat enough of the healthy foods each day, you'll automatically eat less of the fattening, unhealthy ones. You'll simply be too full on low-fat, fibrous food to fit in many high-calorie, fat-laden treats. The outcome? You'll lose weight naturally.

How to count: Each day, try to eat two or three servings of low-fat dairy products, three or four servings of fruit, four servings of vegetables, eight servings of whole grains and five servings of lean meats and other protein foods, says Joanne Curran-Celentano, R.D. Here's a rough idea of what counts as a serving in each of the food groups.

➧ Dairy: 250 ml of milk or yogurt or 45 g of nonfat or low-fat cheese

➧ Fruit: A medium apple, banana, or orange, 125 ml of chopped cooked or canned fruit, or 185 ml of fruit juice

➧ Vegetables: 90 g of raw, leafy vegetables, 90 g of other vegetables (cooked or chopped raw), or 185 ml of vegetable juice

➧ Grains: One-half bagel, one slice of bread, 60 g of ready-to-eat cereal, 90 g of cooked cereal, rice or pasta, or 120 g of popcorn

➧ Protein: 30 g of cooked lean meat, poultry or fish, one egg, 125 g of cooked legumes, 90 g of tofu, or two tablespoons of peanut butter

Strengths: Keeping track of the types of food you eat throughout the day is much easier and more practical than counting calories or fat grammes. When you eat a banana, for instance,

WOMAN TO WOMAN

She Scaled Down Her Weight – By Throwing Out Her Scale

Denise Rios, a Glasgow newspaper editor, used to weigh herself incessantly, fretting over every pound of fluctuation. Finally she put away the scale and her weight started to drop. Here is her story.

Growing up, I weighed myself frequently, but it wasn't until college that the numbers I saw ever bothered me. That was my first inactive year – and one of lousy eating. I ballooned. It was up and down from there: I'd meet a boyfriend and lose weight, get settled into the relationship and gain weight. All the while, I tracked the numbers.

I visited the scale almost every day, sometimes several times a day. If I gained two pounds, I might flip out and binge or go to the other extreme and not eat for days. At age 21, fasting worked fine, but in my late twenties, the pounds started to stick.

My self-esteem hit rock bottom at 11.5 stone – 40 pounds more than my five-foot-one-inch frame should carry. I was out of a long-term relationship and in love with chocolate cupcakes. Because I was depressed by my weight, it became increasingly difficult to control what I ate. I got a new job and moved back home to get my life together.

That's when I joined Weight Watchers. It was there that I learned not to weigh myself constantly, that weight fluctuates for many reasons and a scale can be misleading and discouraging. I donated my scale to an aunt.

I felt liberated at last. I soon realised that my compulsion had been self-fulfiling: The scale would tell me I was fat and ugly, and that's what I became. Free from the scale, I came to think of myself as okay – a healthy person.

Even today, living in the country's third fattest city, I am constantly tempted by fat-laden food – and sometimes I give in. But I've learned not to obsess over my weight, to eat appropriately, and to exercise regularly. I'm down from a size 16 to a 12, and while I'd like to drop one more size, I feel good about myself. I no longer own a scale and I haven't weighed myself in months. I'm free!

you know you've had one fruit serving. You don't have to weigh it and then look up its calorie or fat content in a book. Because you are dealing with smaller numbers, you can mentally add up what you eat rather than keeping a detailed food diary.

Weaknesses: This method doesn't take into account fruits, vegetables and grains that are also high in fat and calories, such as Aubergine Parmesan, pizza and fried courgettes. It also doesn't take body size into consideration.

Recommendation: Of all the counting methods, this one works the best. It's the easiest to stick to as well as the most satisfying. You can count food groups for the rest of your life and never feel deprived.

PART TWO

Food
and
You

Why Am I So Hungry?

Get a Handle on Your Appetite Triggers

Have you ever joked that just the sight of food makes you fat? Or that you can gain weight just by smelling food?

To some extent, it's true.

For many women, eating behaviour is motivated more by external influences, such as the sight and smell of food, than by hunger, says Beverly Cowart, Ph.D. "For some women, it's very difficult not to eat if they are around food that is very appealing."

So the sight of creamy cheesecake with gooey red strawberry syrup oozing down the sides can make you hungry. So can the smell of bacon, fried chicken or freshly baked chocolate chip biscuits made with real butter.

Other than what we see or smell, a host of situations inside the body can also arouse our appetites – a surge of the hormone insulin, for instance, or the release of specific appetite-sensitive chemicals in your brain, or, not surprisingly, an empty stomach.

Your brain, eyes, nose, tastebuds, intestines, nerves, internal chemicals and hormones all have a say in when, how much and even what you eat.

Sometimes they're all yelling at the same time that you should eat. At other times, you might get mixed messages. For instance, your stomach, brain chemicals known as neurotransmitters, and hormones may propose one thing, like "have a piece of fruit," while your eyes, nose and tastebuds lobby for chocolate cake. Your stomach, neurotransmitters, and hormones are more prudent, often signaling you to eat only when nutrients are low, urging you to eat when and what you really need to. When your eyes, nose and tastebuds tell you to eat, however, proceed with extreme caution.

Hunger Patrol

You can train your brain and stomach to be your hunger patrol. Here's how.

Smell your food. Studies have shown that once you start eating, smelling food can make you stop eating sooner by satisfying you faster. So eat more slowly and take the time to smell the food you are eating, says Susan Schiffman, Ph.D.

Keep a food diary. "Write down any

unplanned eating and the circumstances under which it occurred," says Ronette Kolotkin, Ph.D. Review your notes so that you can start anticipating appetite triggers and plan to deal with them.

Eat breakfast. Researchers put 52 overweight women on a 12-week diet during which some ate three meals a day, including breakfast, while others passed up their morning meal. The women who ate breakfast tended to snack less on high-fat, high-calorie goodies.

Spice it right. Food will satisfy you more quickly if it tastes good and has good mouth-feel. One way to guarantee flavour without resorting to large amounts of sugar, salt or fat is to use plenty of herbal seasonings or other flavourings that tend to be hot or sour, says Dr. Cowart. Think lemon juice, jalapeño peppers and chilli powder.

Eat bargain foods. On a calorie-for-calorie basis, some foods fill you up faster and satisfy your hunger better than others. The faster a food fills you up, the less of it you eat. The filling foods are apples, oranges, potatoes, whole-wheat pasta, fish, lean beef and popcorn.

Don't overdo fat. High-fat meals at any time of the day seem to induce cravings for yet more fat, says Sarah Leibowitz, Ph.D. She found that lab rats that ate meals that were more than 40 percent fat continued to produce high levels of a neurochemical that stimulates an appetite for fat.

WOMEN ASK WHY

Sometimes it seems as if the more often I eat, the hungrier I am. Can eating make me hungry?

Believe it or not, it can. Many women who skip breakfast, for example, say that if they eat in the morning, they're hungrier by lunchtime. Those hunger pangs are a signal that your metabolism is working as it should. So, yes, eating regularly means that you're going to feel hungry regularly, but that's a good thing!

Many dieting women ignore hunger because they're afraid that when they eat, they'll overdo it. They say, "If I don't eat, then I won't overeat". And there's some truth to that. If you can hold out for several hours without eating, you actually may not feel hungry anymore. But that only means that your body has adapted to a state of starvation, causing your metabolism to plummet. And if you're trying to fight fat, that's exactly what you don't want to happen.

In reality, it's appetite, not hunger, that makes you overeat. And there's a difference. Hunger is easy to appease; a little food will take care of it. Appetite is not. What sometimes happens, especially if you're constantly trying to deny your hunger, is that taking the first bite releases your inhibitions. Then it's easy to think, "Now that I'm eating, I might as well keep eating". Hunger is alleviated quickly, but you don't know it because your appetite takes over. You keep on eating.

The best way to deal with hunger is to give in to it. Satisfy your hunger with something small (munch on some carrots, for example) so you keep your metabolism steady. After all, no one else can ignore your growling stomach, so why should you? To avoid overeating, your best bet is to pay attention to your body's natural hunger cues. Eat when your stomach tells you to, and stop eating as soon as the pangs go away.

Expert consulted
Joanne Curran-Celentano, R.D., Ph.D.

A study by researchers at University of Leeds suggests that this also holds true for human appetite-control systems. A high-fat meal, it seems, simply isn't as satisfying as a high-carbohydrate meal.

Darken your eating environment. Bright colours like orange, red and yellow stimulate the appetite far more than dark ones like grey, black and brown, says Maria Simonson, Sc.D. So a dark tablecloth and napkins can tame your appetite tiger.

Avoid the buffet table. "The variety and presentation of good-tasting, calorie-rich foods that are often found on buffet tables can be too tempting," says Dr. Kolotkin.

Tune in to slow food/mood music. People chew faster and eat more to spirited tunes than to slow, restful ones, according to Dr. Simonson. So Enya may be a better dinner companion than Bruce Springsteen.

Watch for crowded encounters. Researchers have found that we all eat more when we dine with company. When dining in large groups, in fact, we tend to eat about 75 percent more than when dining alone.

Get more exercise. "Good, healthy exercise can decrease the appetite," says Dr. Simonson. A 20- to 60-minute workout three to five times a week should do it.

Play with your food. "When you

WHAT ARE YOUR APPETITE TRIGGERS?

When it comes to appetite, people eat for many reasons. Some are enticed by the mere sight of a cheesecake, or they're tempted when partying with friends. For others, just being in certain moods makes them want to eat.

To determine how much influence different social and emotional triggers have on your eating habits, start by rating how much influence you think they have, says Susan Head, Ph.D. To do so, take the following quiz, called an Eating Self-Efficacy Scale. It was developed by Shirley M. Glynn, Ph.D., and Audrey J. Ruderman, Ph.D. and is given to people who go to the Duke centre to lose weight.

For each of the following scenarios, answer the question "How difficult is it to control overeating?" by rating yourself on a scale of 1 to 7. A rating of 1 means that you have no difficulty controlling your eating, while a rating of 7 means that you can't control it. Ratings in between mean that sometimes you can and sometimes you can't, to varying degrees.

 1. After work or college _____
 2. At Christmas time _____
 3. When you're with friends _____
 4. When you're preparing food _____
 5. When you're at a social occasion that centres around food, such as a supper party _____
 6. When you're with family members _____
 7. When you feel like sitting back and enjoying food _____
 8. When you're faced with tempting food _____
 9. When the refrigerator is full _____
10. When you're hungry _____

Subtotal (questions 1–10): _____

11. When you feel restless _____

12. When you feel upset _____
13. When you feel tense _____
14. When you feel irritable _____
15. When you're annoyed _____
16. When you're angry at someone _____
17. When you're angry with yourself _____
18. When you're depressed _____
19. When you feel impatient _____
20. After an argument _____
21. When you feel frustrated _____
22. When you want to cheer up _____
23. When you feel overly sensitive _____
24. When you're nervous _____
25. When you're anxious or worried _____
Subtotal (questions 11–25): _____
Total score for questions 1–25: _____

A total score between 54 and 106 is average; most people fall within that range. That means that you are fairly confident that you can handle various appetite triggers. The lower your score, the less likely you are to eat in response to appetite triggers. A higher score means that many situations cause you to overeat. Now look over the quiz to isolate your worst appetite triggers.

Next look at your subtotals. Questions 1 to 10 deal with social situations, while questions 11 to 25 deal with emotional triggers. If your answers for the first 10 questions add up to less than 35, you have a good handle on how you eat in social situations. If your answers for questions 11 through 25 add up to less than 50, you are dealing effectively with your emotional triggers.

go to a restaurant, order food that will keep your hands busy and that will take longer to eat – hot soup, for example, or lobster in the shell," recommends Angie Day.

Wear something tight-fitting when you go out to eat. "Being a little uncomfortable is a nice little reminder that you're trying to lose weight, and it will keep you from overeating," says Day. "It's a trick that works for me – absolutely."

Think, Don't Shovel

To short-circuit automatic-pilot eating, go through the following four-step process at mealtime.

1. *Two minutes before the meal:* Sit in your chair quietly. Take five or six long, deep breaths. Let yourself feel relaxed.

2. *One minute before the meal:* Think about the work that was required to prepare and cook the food. Appreciate the fact that it's going into your body to nourish you.

3. *Midway through the meal:* Take another minute. Stop eating and take five deep breaths. Sit quietly for just a moment. You might even realise that you're not hungry anymore.

4. *Ten minutes after eating:* Take one minute to do another series of five deep breaths. Focus on the physical sensations that the food might be causing in your body. Hopefully, most are pleasant.

Cravings, Go Away!
How to Develop a Low-Fat Tooth

High-fat food makes a high-fat body. It's that simple. Gramme for gramme, dietary fat has more than twice the calories and is more readily converted into body fat than either protein or carbohydrate. So cutting your fat intake way back is a crucial element in the *Fight Fat* eating plan.

How much fat is optimal for a weight-loss plan? You've probably heard that 30 percent of calories from fat should be your goal, but this recommendation is based more on healthy living and disease prevention than weight loss. Some experts recommend 10 percent, but that's too strict and too hard to follow. (If you're seriously overweight, however, you ought to consider it. Talk to your doctor.) The *Fight Fat* plan says 25 percent of calories from fat is the way to go.

Fortunately, carving fat from your diet is not difficult. In fact, once you start eating less fat, you'll feel full more often. That's because low-fat food has fewer calories. You'll be able to eat more and still lose weight.

Women also report that fatty foods start to lose their appeal the longer they're on a low-fat diet. In one four-year study, for example, more than 2,000 women who limited their fat intake to around 25 percent of calories lost their taste for fat within six months or less. By the end of the study, the women said they honestly didn't like fatty foods anymore.

So how do you go from loving fatty foods to snubbing them?

Cutting Back Made Easy

At first, holding your fat intake to 25 percent of calories will seem tedious. That's because counting your daily fat grammes, at least for a little while, is the best way to learn how to eyeball your fat intake. For a couple of weeks, keep track of the food you eat, says Marsha Hudnall, R.D. Packaged foods have labels that will let you know the number of calories and fat grammes per serving. For non-packaged foods, you'll need to consult a calorie and fat gramme guide, available at most book shops and libraries.

For each day, add up the number of calories and fat grammes you eat. Remember, one gramme of fat has nine calories, so if you eat

1,600 calories, limit yourself to about 44 grammes of fat a day to stay within the guidelines, says Hudnall.

Once you get an idea of how much fat you are eating, you can take a look at the types of foods you wrote down and look for ways to siphon off fat. All animal foods have fat, so you'll want to start there. That doesn't mean you have to cut them out of your diet, but you can make quick fat savings in the animal-food department simply by choosing skimmed milk over whole, buying low-fat cheeses when available, and opting for lean meats such as chicken and turkey.

Making the switch to low-fat, however, doesn't mean that you must give up your high-fat favourites or resort to a life of bland, rubbery food. You and your family can still have the foods you love as long as you pay attention to portion sizes and learn how to cut fat without compromising taste. Here are some expert strategies.

Redesign your plate. If you put an average meal on one of those paper plates with dividers, the largest section – about half of the plate – is filled with meat. The rest contains refined starchy food and fat. The meal ends up with 34 to 36 percent of calories from fat rather than the 25 percent we want. Instead of plopping meat in the large section, move it to one of the smaller areas. When the meat fills a quarter of the plate, it generally becomes the 90 gramme serving that earns "very healthy" kudos.

Fill the largest section with vegetables and put grains in the other space, says Lori Wiersema,

WOMEN ASK WHY
Why can't I stop at one potato crisp?

Women have a love affair with fat. And salt. And things that crunch. Thanks to the invention of the potato crisp over a century ago, we can have all three in one food, and the combination makes crisps a prime candidate for food addiction.

That's why advertisers dare you to eat just one. They're betting that you can't do it – at least not at first. Science backs up their hunch. Studies have shown that if you swear off salt and fat, your cravings for foods like potato crisps will actually increase for the first three months. But if you can manage to hold out longer and keep your hand out of the crisps (and stick to a diet that's lower in fat and salt across the board) for five months, you'll barely be able to stand the stuff.

A recent trend in snack foods, however, just may be your saviour. That other crucial ingredient that makes it so hard to stop at one crisp – the crunch – is finding its way into a variety of low-fat foods. While crunch may have some appeal because it's often found in high-fat snacks like crisps, it has a stellar reputation of its own for satisfying all kinds of appetites. Crunch is associated with fun and freshness. In some cases, eating crunchy foods can also relieve stress.

One way to avoid eating too many salty, greasy crisps, then, is to substitute lighter, lower-fat crunchies, especially baked crisps and crackers that taste pretty close to the original. Of course, you don't want to get in too deep with those crispy goodies, either. It's easy to get carried away, even with low-fat, low-salt alternatives.

Expert consulted
Barbara Levine, R.D., Ph.D.

R.D. "Redesigning your plate to create the right fuel mix automatically slashes fat and calories to a healthy level," she says.

Use fat judiciously. "You can't just leave out the fat completely, because fat tastes really good. But you can compensate," says Marie Simmons, author of *Fresh and Fast*. "If a recipe calls for 60 ml of olive oil, for instance, instead use just 1 tablespoon of oil during cooking and then maybe add another ½ tablespoon at the end, so you still have that good taste."

Satisfy with less meat. Meat is one of the top fat sources in our diets. A great way to enjoy smaller portions of meat is to give it an intense flavour, says Marilyn C. Majchrzak, R.D.

At Canyon Ranch, for example, culinary experts top grilled fish with a richly flavoured sauce of freshly crushed herbs added to a teaspoon of melted butter. And don't forget eye appeal: When it's thinly sliced and artfully arranged, 90 grammes of chicken looks like no paltry poultry.

Think juicy. If you're accustomed to sautéing your veggies in a half-inch of oil, cook them in a non-stick pan over low heat in a mixture of a little oil plus water, says Simmons.

Be spicier. If you learn to cook with herbs and spices, you won't miss the taste of butter or oil on your veggies.

Be saucy. To pare fat calories from muffins, cakes and other home-baked goodies, swap the cooking fat for applesauce. This trick works best in recipes containing liquid ingredients such as skimmed milk or fruit. Merely substitute one part applesauce for one part oil, butter, or margarine. Instead of using 80 ml oil and two whole eggs when preparing lemon cake from a packet mix, for example, use 80 ml applesauce and three egg whites. You'll save almost five grammes of fat and 40 calories per slice.

Serve special spuds. You'll never miss fat-

FOODS THAT STOP CRAVINGS

Sometimes the best thing you can do when you have a craving is to follow the advice of your stomach: "Eat something."

You don't, however, have to eat something fattening to satisfy your yearning. Here are some alternatives.

Suck on a pickle. Pickles are a wonderful combination of powerful flavour and almost no calories. The upshot is that your tastebuds get a satisfying workout while your fat cells are left out to dry.

Combine peppermint and fruit. A really strong craving for sweets can often be stifled by eating a peppermint and washing it down with a glass of fruit juice or a few nibbles of fruit such as an apple or pear, says Maria Simonson, Sc.D., Ph.D.

Spike a yogurt. "Cinnamon, vanilla and nutmeg can satisfy a sweet tooth, since these spices add a sweet flavour without

---

drenched french fries if you can make delicious, nutrient-rich yam or sweet potato fries instead. Cut the unpeeled potatoes into thick slices (about 1 cm), then dredge them in a mixture of low-sodium soy sauce and a few drops of sesame oil. Grill until crisp and golden.

Retrain Your Tastebuds

Instead of seeing your entrance into the low-fat world as torture, view it as an adventure, one where you get to try new recipes and taste new foods. That simple change in your mindset can go a long way towards helping your tastebuds adjust to this new way of eating, thus reducing some of those cravings for high-fat foods. Here are some other strategies.

Take baby steps. Instead of shocking your tastebuds by avoiding all of the foods you love the most, take on a smaller battle. For instance, if you're a real meat or chicken person, don't go

the calories," says Elizabeth Somer, R.D., author of *Food and Mood* and *Nutrition for Women*. Add the flavourings to yogurt or steamed milk, she says.

Sip some soup. Due to its sheer volume, soup takes up more space in your stomach than other foods, but since it's mostly liquid, you feel fuller on fewer calories. And unless you truly enjoy scalding your mouth, hot soup also forces you to eat slowly.

Sniff a banana, green apple or peppermint. In one study, men and women sniffed from inhalers scented with banana, green apple, or peppermint whenever they felt the urge to have something to eat. On average, they lost almost five pounds a month, even though they were told not to change their usual eating patterns. The more people sniffed, the more weight they lost. Researchers speculate that the smell may have short-circuited their appetites.

cold turkey. Instead, try going from a stuffed pork chop to a centre-cut pork loin medallion, from a full-size steak to a baby filet mignon, or from a whole chicken breast to half a breast. "Also, once a week have a meatless meal, featuring pasta or grains and vegetables, or maybe a lentil-and-brown-rice pilaf. Little by little, increase the number of these dishes," urges Bernice Veckerelli, chef.

Or let's say that you decide to eat less red meat. Keep track of how much you usually eat in a week. If you find that you're eating seven meat meals a week, for example, first cut back to six by substituting a fish or vegetarian meal. Then go to five, then four, then three. And don't try to be perfect, because it just leads to guilt and frustration and quitting. Instead of zero, aim for three.

Don't get bored. "Eat a variety of foods," says Veckerelli, even if you're having weight-loss success with particular tried-and-true items. "A lot of the time, people think that dieting means nothing but grapefruit or fruit and cottage cheese, and eventually they get bored and hungry," she says. But if you make a point of experimenting at mealtime, particularly trying to increase your intake of whole grains, fruits and vegetables, which are very filling and satisfying, you'll perk up your palate and be more apt to stick to your weight-loss plan.

Allow for some fat. Remember that you are reining in your fat count to 25 percent of calories, not 15 or 10 or 5. Many women crave high-fat foods because they are over-restricting their fat intake, says Hudnall. They feel deprived. And usually, they eventually pig out on fried chicken, french fries and cheesecake. You can cut such intense fat cravings by allowing for 25 percent of calories from fat and budgeting for an occasional high-fat food, which will fight deprivation cravings best. This is a low-fat diet, not a no-fat diet.

Never say "just a taste." Women love these three words, but they can be damning to your diet and your psyche. Chances are, you'll eat more if you keep picking from the bag of crisps than you would if you ate a full meal. In other words, those little "tastes" can add up, and you can end up eating more than if you set out to eat a predefined portion. Even worse, your psyche won't be satisfied. "If you're yearning for a particular food, serve yourself a reasonable portion," says Jennifer Stack, R.D. You'll feel freed of your hunger – and your craving – after allowing yourself a snack that's sizable enough to satisfy you.

Walk away from cravings. The kind of craving that kicks in at the sight of an ice cream sandwich may dissipate after 10 or 15 minutes if you get moving, says Maria Simonson, Sc.D. So walk around the building a few times while on the way to the vending machine. By the time you get there, the ice cream may have lost its appeal.

Lift weights. Weight lifting may naturally curb your hankering for fat. In a study 30 women who did nine common strength-training exercises naturally cut back on their fat intake within six weeks – without anyone telling them to. Researchers suspect that the positive physical changes brought about by weight lifting gave the women the inspiration they needed to change their diets as well.

Take a small bite out of chocolate cravings. Chocolate cravings are harder to resist than most, says Elizabeth Somer, R.D., nutritionist and author of *Nutrition for Women* and *Food and Mood*. If you can't resist, try getting by with a very small piece of something chocolate. To make sure you have only a little, eat your treat with a meal. When you eat chocolate with a meal, you're less likely to overdo it than if you tackle a jumbo chocolate bar and nothing else. Another strategy: If you must have chocolate, choose baked goods made with low-fat cocoa powder, she says.

Get the lowdown on high-risk situations. "Different people have different vulnerabilities," says Joyce D. Nash, Ph.D. You might, for instance, do fine at an ice cream stand but lose all control at a buffet table. Someone else might handle buffets like a pro but go to pieces at the sight of Mars bars.

"Ask yourself what your high-risk situations are," says Dr. Nash. "Is it going out with friends? When you're feeling down and sorry for yourself? When you're in a bakery? Do a personal analysis. Once you know your eating triggers, you can focus your efforts and determine which strategies you can use to cope better," she says.

Limit alcohol. Although alcohol itself doesn't have fat, drinking it can make you crave fatty foods, says Cindy Wachtler, R.D. "Drink a glass of wine before dinner, and suddenly the food looks better and tastes better and your judgment of quantities diminishes," she says.

Nix the fat-free bingeing. "Remember, there are calories in fat-free foods," says Stack, "so don't think they're free." It's better to eat that one full-fat chocolate bar and satisfy your craving for the day than to load up on twice as many calories by eating foods made with fat facsimiles.

Mini-Meals
When More Means Less

Here's a tale of two dieters on a typical day.

Woman number one is a mini-meal muncher. She breakfasts each morning on some cereal and orange juice, then heads off to work. About mid-morning she takes a break and gets a plain bagel to nibble on while she works up proposals. A few hours later she stops for lunch – a sandwich and some veggies. By late afternoon she's at the vending machine getting some pretzels. After work she heads home and whips up some baked fish and a small potato for dinner. Later, when her chores are done, she sits down to watch TV and snacks on low-fat yogurt and some grapes. Then it's time for bed.

Woman number two is a calorie-watcher. She's out the door in the morning without any breakfast and ignores her hunger pangs until lunch. She picks at a small salad and then ignores her hunger all afternoon. About 5:00 P.M., she heads home, polishes off a nice dinner, watches some TV and heads for bed.

Who's going to be the winner at losing?

Woman number one, of course.

Why More Is Best

You would think that skipping meals would result in eating fewer calories, which in turn would result in less body fat. But your body doesn't work that way. It actually burns fat more effectively when you eat small amounts of food more often. In fact, scientists have discovered that eating four to six small meals a day actually helps to speed up your fat-burning system. Here's why.

❧ If you bypass breakfast and skimp on lunch, you're going to overload at dinner. "After an all-day fast, the body is ravenous and you end up doubling the quantity of food you eat," says Diane Grabowski-Nepa, R.D. Too much food at any one time is too much for your body to handle, and it encourages fat storage. On top of that, your body is more efficient at storing fat in the evening than earlier in the day, when you're more active. So if you overeat at dinner, more calories get stored as fat than, say, if you overeat at breakfast.

❧ Skipping meals can slow your metabolism by as much as 5 percent. That's because an empty stomach makes your brain think that your body is starving, so it turns down its calorie-burning thermostat in an effort to live longer off its stored fat. On the other hand, when you eat small meals all day long, your stomach never gets a chance to be empty, thus keeping your metabolism purring along.

❧ When you eat a big meal such as a huge dinner, your body produces insulin, which prevents fat cells from releasing fat into the bloodstream to be picked up by other tissues and burned. In other words, high insulin levels put a lock on your fat-releasing ability. Higher insulin levels also stimulate appetite, which makes you want to eat more. On the other hand, when you eat small meals all day long, you never experience the insulin surge that larger meals create.

❧ Spreading your daily calories over four meals or more can help you dampen your appetite by keeping food in your stomach at all times. Instead of always feeling deprived, you always feel full, so you don't binge.

❧ Your stomach expands and contracts with food load, apparently losing its tone when repeatedly pushed to the max. So once it's over-stretched, it takes more food to satisfy you, according to studies by scientists at the obesity research centre at St Luke's-Roosevelt Hospital Center in New York City. Eating small amounts of food all day doesn't stretch the stomach, so you feel full more quickly.

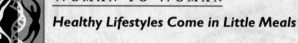

Because she was overweight and diabetic, Anita Beattie's doctor gave her a harsh ultimatum: "Enter a hospital programme to lose weight or don't come back to see me, because you are wasting my time and your money." That push was just what Anita needed to encourage her to drop the extra 2.5 stone that she was lugging around and, with her doctor's guidance, to taper off the insulin that she used to control her diabetes.

My doctor put me in the hospital for four days to teach me enough about diet and exercise so that when I left the hospital, I could carry out these lessons on my own. The hospital nutritionist put me on an exercise programme and a low-calorie diet. I started walking for 20 minutes a few times a week, and I began eating several mini-meals throughout the day instead of the all-day meal I used to eat. My husband was a great support – he measured all my food and created my menus. He helped me learn about portion sizes. I was surprised to learn, for instance, that a piece of cheese as long as the distance from the tip of your pointer finger to your first knuckle constitutes one serving, and there are 100 calories in that serving.

The food menu was wonderful, and even though I was eating fewer calories, I wasn't hungry because I was making

Mini-Meal Magic

Ready to give it a try? Think variety. You want to continue to eat from all the food groups – grains, fruits, vegetables, dairy and protein – throughout the day. But you don't need to balance your intake of food groups at every meal as you did when you were eating three meals. Instead, you want to achieve balance over the course of an entire day, which means about eight grains, three or four fruits, four vegetables, two or three dairy products and five lean meats or other protein foods each day.

better, more filling choices. It took me a while to learn what good choices are. The nutritionist would test our knowledge by giving us a variety of foods on our menu, and we were supposed to choose the right ones. One day my doctor walked in when my roommate and I were eating muffins. He asked why we were eating muffins, and we said, "Because they were on our menu." Obviously, muffins weren't the healthy choice.

After I got out of the hospital, I continued eating four to five mini-meals throughout the day. I have breakfast, lunch, supper, a night time snack of a rice cake or some sugar-free jelly and occasionally I have a mid-morning snack as well.

I eat smaller portions and make better food choices. I used to eat eggs and bacon for breakfast, but now I eat half a grapefruit, a serving of oatmeal with skimmed milk, half a bagel and, of course, coffee. I haven't eliminated any foods from my diet, except sweets because of my diabetes. I've just learned to recognise what serving sizes are, and I apply that knowledge to whatever I eat.

I have also kept up with my exercise plan, and now I walk 2½ to 3½ miles five times a week. Walking coupled with my new mini-meal habits have helped me maintain my weight at 9 stone for the past three years. And it has done wonders for my diabetes.

keep your eye on two different horizons: fat and calories. While fat reduction is the most important priority for good health and weight loss, you don't want calories to fall too low or climb too high.

Eat *Fight Fat* foods. That means foods high in fibre and low in fat and added sugar, which in turn means things like fruit, vegetables and whole-wheat bread. Avoid empty-calorie snacks like doughnuts.

Select a serving. Favour foods that are already portioned into individual servings, like a baked potato, a container of yogurt or a bagel. Eating a set portion ensures that you'll stop when you're full (or nearly full) because you'll run out of food, says Michele Harvey, R.D.

Choose no-risk foods. As you adapt, says Dubner, choose low-calorie foods.

Go to pieces. Mini-meals will be more satisfying if you eat them in small bites, says Dubner. So instead of one big rice cake, have a few of the bite-size variety. Instead of eating a big pretzel, have lots of small ones. You can even cut a biscuit into pieces and eat the pieces individually.

Here's the best advice from experts for getting into the mini-meal mindset.

Give your regular meals the split. Try dividing what you eat for breakfast, lunch and supper in half to create six meals, suggests Anne Dubner, R.D. If you usually eat a bagel for breakfast, for example, eat half when you get up and the other half later. If you have a sandwich for lunch, eat the halves at two different times. That way, you won't spend any more time preparing food.

Watch the fat and the portions. In determining your daily intake, it's important to

Don't tempt yourself. If you know that you have no resistance to certain foods – like biscuits, for instance – stay away from them. If you don't, you'll probably end up eating well beyond fullness. Choose mini-meal foods that you know you can control, says Donna Weihofen, R.D.

Watch out for fat-free. Most of the new packaged fat-free foods won't fill you up for very long. Also, many fat-free foods have added sugar to make up for the loss of fat, points out Weihofen.

Be a Time Machine

Eating mini-meals doesn't have to be time-consuming, according to Natalie Payne, R.D. Here are some timesaving strategies.

Take mini-meals on the road. Keep a snack stash in your car; carry snacks in your handbag when you go shopping; and stock your briefcase when you fly. Good portables include small boxes of raisins, mini-boxes of cereal, cans of low-sodium vegetable juice cocktail and whole-wheat hard pretzels.

Switch meals. Consider some easy-to-prepare, easy-to-eat (but somewhat unusual) choices for your meals. Make a turkey sandwich in the evening, for example, and put it in the fridge. Then grab it on your way out the door in the morning and eat it for breakfast on your way to work.

Keep it cold. If you don't have access to a refrigerator where you work, freeze a juice carton overnight and put it in the bottom of your lunch bag the following day. The frozen juice will keep easy-to-eat items such as yogurt and cheese cold.

Stash some safe bets. At work, keep a desk drawer stocked with canned fruit (in water or fruit juice), dried fruit, low-fat crackers and other non-perishable convenience foods. (And don't forget a can opener.)

Slice at night. When slicing up carrots and other raw vegetables for dinner, don't forget to slice some extras to take along and munch the next day at work.

A Mini-Meal Menu Sampler

It can be a little daunting to figure out how to eat all day and still lose weight, so we asked Anne Dubner, R.D., to put together a sampling of daily menus to show how satisfying mini-meals can be.

The trick to losing weight on mini-meals, she says, is to listen to your stomach. Eat when you start feeling a little hungry — don't wait until you're famished — and stop as soon as your hunger goes away, not when you're stuffed. That way you'll stay steadily satisfied.

Day One

Breakfast: Half of a whole-wheat bagel with puréed roasted peppers mixed with reduced-fat or fat-free cream cheese, a 250-ml glass of skimmed milk, and 90 g of blueberries

Snack: The other half of the bagel with roasted peppers

Lunch: Half of a turkey club sandwich (made with turkey breast, sliced tomato and lettuce) and a mixed garden salad with one tablespoon reduced-fat Russian dressing

Snack: The other half of the sandwich

Supper: About 250 g of pasta primavera (made with rotini pasta, frozen mixed vegetables, garlic, Parmesan cheese and one tablespoon of olive oil) and a slice of Italian bread topped with one teaspoon of reduced-fat margarine mixed with one teaspoon each of crushed fresh garlic and grated Parmesan cheese

Snack: An oatmeal raisin biscuit

Day Two

Breakfast: One slice of raisin bread with one tablespoon of peanut butter and a 125-ml glass of orange juice

Snack: A reduced-fat fig bar and a 250-ml glass of skimmed milk

---

Supper – Think Small

Supper can be the toughest time to eat a mini-meal. If you go out to eat, you're served too

Lunch: Half of a chicken salad pita sandwich (made with low-fat, cubed cooked chicken, toasted walnuts, raisins, small grapes and honey) and handful of raw vegetables such as baby carrots and celery

Snack: The other half of the sandwich

Supper: Cheese quesadilla (made with a fat-free flour tortilla, one tablespoon each of grated reduced-fat Cheddar and hot-pepper Monterey Jack cheese, 1½ teaspoons of chopped canned green chilli peppers, 1½ teaspoons of sliced black olives and salsa, chilli powder and sliced spring onions to taste) with 90 g of white rice mixed with two tablespoons of salsa

Snack: 250 ml of nonfat flavoured yogurt with three digestive biscuits

DAY THREE

Breakfast: A muffin with scrambled egg substitute, an orange wedge and a 250-ml glass of skimmed milk

Snack: A sandwich made with half of a banana and one tablespoon of peanut butter

Lunch: A small Greek salad (made with chopped tomatoes, cucumbers, sweet red peppers and onions, with feta cheese and a dressing of lemon juice and olive oil with oregano and garlic) and a slice of Italian bread

Snack: Six crackers with tuna salad (made with tuna, one tablespoon of reduced-fat mayonnaise and a squirt of lemon juice)

Supper: Potato skins (made with one quartered baked potato, 125 g of grated reduced-fat Cheddar cheese, some spring onions or chives and paprika) with 60 g of steamed broccoli

Snack: A moderately large bowl of reduced-fat popcorn sprinkled with two teaspoons of Parmesan cheese

much food. If you eat at home, you might linger at the table with the family and eat more than you planned. Here are some ways to think small at supper time.

Have an appetizer. Have a snack ready in the fridge for when you walk in the door after work, says Dubner. After you've eaten, change into comfortable clothes, take a shower or do whatever else you do to ready yourself for an evening meal with your family. Then you can spend as much time at the dinner table as you like, but you won't overeat because you won't be as hungry.

Don't stay on course. Switch back and forth between courses by alternating bites of your main dish (chicken or pasta, for example) with a bite of salad. If you do that, says Dubner, you won't finish eating before the rest of your family does.

Fill 'er up. Before ordering supper at a restaurant, drink a big glass of water to quiet your appetite, says Dubner. Then take a sip of water after every bite so that you'll eat more slowly.

Hold the bread. Ask the server not to serve the bread. Or take one roll and send the basket back, says Harvey.

Try a smaller portion. Ask the server for a smaller portion, says Harvey. You can request a meal that's half the usual size, for instance.

Don't entrée right away. When eating out, have a small bowl of non-creamy soup such as minestrone or a small salad before making a decision on your main course, says Dubner. That way, you won't be as hungry and you'll order a smaller meal.

Or don't order it at all. Instead of ordering a main course, order an appetizer, says Harvey.

Start low, end high. Eat your vegetables first, then the starches, such as potatoes and bread.

REAL-LIFE SCENARIO

Binge Today, Diet Tomorrow

For 20 years, Ann has been a chronic yo-yo dieter – up 10 pounds, down 5, up 5, down 10. Either she's dieting to starvation by existing on raw vegetables and canned tuna or eating all the wrong things. For Ann, there is no in-between. Lately, though, she seems to have more "eating days" than "diet days," and her weight just keeps going up. What's happened to her will power?

After so many years of dieting, Ann's body is probably tired from all the bouncing up and down on the scale. Like all yo-yo dieters, she has probably set unrealistic goals, and when she keeps falling short of meeting them, she loses her desire to diet. For women like her, a sensible weight loss of only a pound a week is viewed as failure.

Like many yo-yo dieters, she eats out of frustration for failing and promises to start all over again tomorrow.

It's going to be difficult for Ann to reclaim her will power, since it's been years since she's eaten sensibly. But she can do it if she changes her habits. First, she needs to set realistic weight-loss goals. She needs to realise that the only way she'll achieve long-term success is through gradual steps; if she doesn't lose weight right away, she shouldn't consider herself a failure.

Second, she needs to believe that all foods are allowed; otherwise, the foods she deprives herself of on her "diet days" are exactly the foods she'll want on her "eating days." Most important, she needs to get on a normal eating plan with three small meals a day, spaced fairly evenly, and enough snacks in between to keep her from bingeing later on. Once Ann quits playing yo-yo with her eating habits, her weight is bound to settle down, too.

Expert consulted
Rebecca Reeves, R.D., Dr. P.H.

Leave the highest-calorie and fattiest items like meat for last, says Dubner. That way you'll fill up on the lowest-calorie items and feel too full to finish the high-calorie foods.

Take it home. Before the server brings the meal, ask for a doggie bag. Then when he brings the dinner, immediately divide your food in half, putting part in the take-home container and leaving the rest on your plate. Or ask the server to do it for you. Store the take-home container under your chair so you won't be tempted to nibble from it, says Dubner.

Don't worry about detours. Every once in a while – at Christmas, for instance – you'll stuff yourself. Don't feel guilty. "You are not going to get lost when you take a detour, as long as you don't keep slapping yourself across the face," says Harvey. You will get lost, however, if you continually berate yourself, she says, because then you'll feel so bad about yourself that you'll keep eating.

Slimming Starts

Breakfasts of Champion Weight-Losers

If you skip breakfast, you can shave off 300 to 400 calories and maybe about 10 minutes or so of preparation and chewing time.

But you'll probably eat more, get fatter and lose time in the long run.

Studies have shown that thin people tend to be breakfast-eaters, while overweight people tend to be breakfast-skippers. There are plenty of reasons for this.

For one, if you don't eat breakfast, you're in for a crash around mid-morning. If you're lucky, you'll make it to lunch. Either way, you're likely to overeat or make poor food choices.

"When people skip breakfast, they get tired and irritable," says Bonnie Spring, Ph.D. "They also experience food cravings. Their hunger may become so intense that they overeat before they feel satisfied. Or they may grab something sugary or fattening to boost their mood."

So you actually end up making up for and well surpassing the 300 to 400 calories you thought you saved by skipping breakfast. And because you're energy-drained, it takes you longer to get things done, which means you lose

more time than the 10 minutes you thought you were saving.

Breakfast-skippers also risk slowing their metabolism. "Breakfast is the day's most important meal because it's your body's signal that it's time to fight fat," says Jan McBarron, M.D. While you sleep, your body stores food as fat so that you have energy to burn when you're awake. Eating lets your fat-burning enzymes know that it's time to get up and go to work. If you don't eat, your body will continue to store fat.

No More Excuses

What are women's two most common excuses for skipping breakfast? Number one: You don't have enough time to make breakfast. Number two: You're not hungry in the morning. It's time to stop the excuses and do something.

Stop eating at night. Women who tend to skip breakfast also tend to eat the majority of their food late in the day, usually after 6:00 P.M., says Diane Grabowski-Nepa, R.D.

WOMAN TO WOMAN
She Starts Her Day Off Right

Julie Hazy, a teacher from York, used to think that skipping breakfast would help her lose weight. Her logic: Why take in extra calories if she wasn't hungry in the morning? Now, hungry or not, Julie makes sure she eats breakfast, and she's lost over 3 stone since adding a morning meal to her diet.

I never used to eat breakfast; I'd have a cup of coffee to give myself a kick-start, and that was it. I'd read that to lose weight, you should eat breakfast. But I thought if I wanted to lose weight, and I'm not hungry in the morning, that would be a good time not to eat. The trouble was, because I wasn't eating breakfast, I was taking in the bulk of my calories late in the day. By supper time, I was so hungry that I was more likely to eat easy-to-prepare, high-calorie foods.

So now I make sure that I eat breakfast every day – usually a bowl of Rice Krispies with skimmed milk, a glass of orange juice and that good old coffee kick-start with nonfat creamer. Sometimes I will have a low-fat muffin or half of a bagel – but always with a cup of coffee and a glass of juice.

I've also been learning to choose healthier foods. I don't restrict my diet; I just cut portion sizes. For example, I love doughnuts. But no doughnut is worth 16 grammes of fat. I'd rather have a small piece of the doughnut, or better yet, a low-fat muffin.

I use substitution with other foods, too. I cook egg substitute or egg whites instead of whole eggs in the morning, spread light margarine instead of butter on my toast, and drink skimmed milk instead of whole milk. Food tastes better without all the fat.

Another trick I have learned is to write down everything I eat – what I eat, how much and when. I aim for the number of servings recommended in the Food Guide Pyramid – 2 to 4 servings of fruit a day, 6 to 11 servings of cereal, bread or other grains, 3 to 5 servings of vegetables and 2 to 3 servings of milk and of meat equivalents. I also exercise. I try to walk or ride my HealthRider for 20 to 30 minutes every day.

But it all starts with breakfast.

Such late-night eating keeps you from being hungry when you wake up. But it also contributes to weight gain because a sleeping body can't burn off the food as quickly as a moving body. It stores it as fat instead.

Gradually start eating more in the morning. If you are not hungry in the morning, start gradually. Your first few breakfasts might consist solely of a piece of fruit such as an apple or a banana, says Grabowski-Nepa.

"It's better to get something in your system than to go without it," she says. Other ideas for small breakfasts include yogurt or an oat bran muffin. Once you get into the habit of eating a small breakfast, move on to more substantial items like whole-wheat toast or bagels.

Go for convenience. Pouring a bowl of cereal and eating it takes less than 10 minutes. Yogurt, oat bran muffins, bagels and fruit are other good foods that you can eat on the go.

Do other things first. Some women, no matter how little they eat the night before, are not hungry when they first wake up. No problem. Instead of turning off the alarm and eating breakfast right away, take a shower first. Do your hair and get dressed, then have breakfast. Or drive to work and then eat. "There's no rule that says you have to have breakfast as soon as you roll out of bed," says Grabowski-Nepa. "You can wait for an hour."

You do, however, want to try to eat breakfast within the first couple of hours after waking up.

Be untraditional. No law forces you to eat traditional breakfast foods for breakfast. "Try beans and·rice wrapped in a corn tortilla, which is one of my breakfast favourites," says Grabowski-Nepa. Or consider left-overs or perhaps a turkey sandwich on whole-grain bread. Just make sure it's low in fat.

Blend a breakfast drink. If you really can't stand the thought of eating breakfast, drink it instead. Try a fruity, frosty shake, suggests Judith S. Stern, R.D. The night before, slice half of a banana and freeze it. In the morning, toss the sliced banana into a blender with about 60 g of sliced strawberries and 250 ml of skimmed milk. Add a drop or two of lemon juice to give the shake some extra flavour. If you forget to freeze the banana, you can still blend it, but add an ice cube. You can also try peaches and cinnamon instead of strawberries and lemon.

Turn in. One way to help yourself get up early enough to have time for breakfast is to go to bed earlier. Gradually start heading for bed a few minutes earlier than normal. Make no more than 15 minutes of change per week. Then set your alarm so that you get up a little bit earlier every day. You'll know that you have adjusted when you start waking up just before your alarm goes off.

WOMEN ASK WHY

Do I have to eat breakfast even if I'm not hungry?

Your body is like a furnace in that it needs to burn some kind of fuel – in this case, food. As with a home heating furnace, the most effective way for your body to use fuel is to burn it consistently rather than having the fire stoked up, burning a lot of fuel quickly, letting the fire go out and then having a huge fire built again. So just as a steady, consistent rate of combustion is best for your furnace, a steady, consistent source of energy is best for your body.

When you wake up in the morning, your fuel level is very low. If you try to get through your busy morning without breakfast, you'll be running on reserves.

Many women who struggle with their weight skip breakfast and skimp on lunch. By the time they finally do eat, they lose control over what and how much they eat. But skipping one meal and skimping on the next doesn't necessarily give you license to eat whatever you want come supper time. If you eat an adequate breakfast, followed by your usual lunch, you'll be in much better control – physiologically because you won't be so ravenously hungry at the end of the day, and psychologically because you won't have the sense that you're entitled to a double- or triple-size supper after running on reserves all day.

The way to convince yourself to eat breakfast, even if you're not ravenously hungry when you wake up, is to think of eating a morning meal as refueling your body. And you don't have to sit down to a big, heavy meal to stoke your fires. Have some fruit, cereal and skimmed milk, toast or a roll.

Another way to help make eating breakfast a habit is to avoid snacking too much late at night, which can leave you feeling full in the morning. Remember, eating at night is like stoking the fire when the demand for fuel is low.

Expert consulted
Abby Bloch, R.D., Ph.D.

The Best Breakfast

The best breakfasts are also the easiest to prepare.

What's the best?

In a word, oatmeal.

Oatmeal and other whole-grain hot cereals are the most filling and satisfying breakfast foods you can eat, says Grabowski-Nepa. "For a lot of people who don't have time, it might seem like too much work," she says. "But you can microwave it. It only takes a couple of minutes."

Running a close fat-fighting second is a low-sugar, high-fibre cold cereal, and whole-grain breads come in third.

Here are a few things to keep in mind when choosing breakfast foods.

Think fibre. High-fibre foods such as whole-grain breads, oatmeal and some cold cereals help to keep your blood sugar levels stable, which in turn helps you avoid cravings later. They also make you feel full faster and longer.

When picking out breakfast cereals, look for ones that have at least four to five grammes of fibre per serving, says Grabowski-Nepa. The more fibre the cereal has, the better. (You can find out by checking the nutrition label on the box.) You can get even more fibre by adding some blueberries, a sliced banana or other fruit to your cereal.

Avoid sugar. "A lot of women eat a really sugary cereal at 8:00 in the morning, and by 9:00 they're ravenous," says Grabowski-Nepa. That's because the high amount of sugar makes the body overproduce insulin, which then signals you to eat more. Look for cereals in which sugar is not the first ingredient listed on the label.

THE FAT-FIGHTER'S BEST BREAKFASTS

Some of the most seemingly benign breakfast foods can add up to a ton of fat and calories. Take pancakes or waffles. They don't look greasy, but because restaurants often make them with whole milk and then we slather butter and syrup on top, such breakfast choices can add up to more fat and calories than the greasiest three-egg omelette.

To help you make the best fat-fighting choices at breakfast, Tina Ruggiero, R.D., has provided a list of bad, better and best options. To qualify as a "best" breakfast, foods had to be more than just low in fat and calories. They had to contain fibre, which keeps you full through the morning. And they had to be rich in vitamins, minerals and other nutrients.

OMELETTES

Bad: Three-egg cheese omelette, served with three strips of bacon and two slices of buttered white toast (approximately 705 calories and 48 grammes of fat)

Better: Three-egg omelette made with egg substitute and filled with cheese and spinach, served with one strip of bacon and two slices of white toast with low-sugar jam (approximately 565 calories and 26 grammes of fat)

Best: Three-egg omelette made with 185 ml of egg substitute and cooked with non-stick spray, filled with 30 g of low-fat cheese, 30 g of chopped mushrooms, and 60 g of spinach, served with 125 ml of water-packed fruit salad and one slice of whole-wheat toast with one tablespoon of low-

---

Group your foods. Once you become a bona fide breakfast-eater, try to work a few different food groups into your morning routine. Think dairy, complex carbohydrates, and fruit.

To get your dairy, you could have nonfat yogurt, skimmed milk or nonfat cream cheese or sour cream. Dairy foods will give you the protein you need to help sustain your satiety until you eat lunch or a mid-morning snack. For carbohydrates, try hot or cold cereal, whole-wheat toast or a bagel or an oat bran muffin. For

sugar jam (approximately 392 calories and 10 grammes of fat)

PANCAKES

Bad: Short stack of pancakes (three) with butter and syrup, served with two sausage patties (approximately 564 calories and 35 grammes of fat)

Better: Short stack of pancakes with butter and syrup, served with two slices of smoked ham (approximately 436 calories and 19 grammes of fat)

Best: Short stack of pancakes with one teaspoon of margarine and one tablespoon of reduced-calorie syrup, served with fresh peach slices (approximately 355 calories and 15 grammes of fat)

SANDWICHES VS. OATMEAL

Bad: Ham, egg and cheese sandwich, served with hash browns and 250 ml of orange juice (approximately 609 calories and 27 grammes of fat)

Better: Muffin with fat-free cream cheese, served with hash browns and 250 ml of orange juice (approximately 441 calories and 12 grammes of fat)

Best: Hot oatmeal mixed with 60 g of assorted berries and skimmed milk, served with 1/8 of a honeydew melon and 250 ml of apricot nectar (approximately 440 calories and 2 grammes of fat)

germ, one tablespoon of honey or brown sugar, one tablespoon of chopped nuts and one tablespoon of raisins. Serve with 185 ml of apple juice.

❧ Try egg substitute scrambled with green peppers and onions and topped with some salsa. Serve with a fat-free flour tortilla and 185 ml of orange juice.

Figure on fruit. "Every meal should include a fruit or vegetable," says Cheryl Rock, Ph.D. Breakfast is no exception to this rule. Concentrate on deep yellow fruits like cantaloupe, which provides beta-carotene along with vitamin C. Or try a peach, a mango, 60 g of berries, a banana, half a grapefruit or 30 g of raisins. Or try 185 ml of 100 percent orange, cranberry or strawberry-kiwi juice.

Combine protein with carbohydrate. "If you eat all carbohydrates at a meal, you'll feel sleepy in an hour or so," says nutritionist Elizabeth Somer, R.D., author of *Nutrition for Women* and *Food and Mood*. A favourite power breakfast of Somer's is quick and easy: a tortilla with low-fat cheese, plus an orange. Or try a bowl of whole-grain cereal with skimmed milk and a banana.

fruit, have a banana, blueberries, strawberries or orange juice.

"People feel more satisfied when they have a variety of foods," says Grabowski-Nepa. "Plus, you eat more nutrients." Here are some energising multi-food-group breakfast ideas.

❧ Have a toasted whole-wheat slice of toast or bagel with a tablespoon of peanut butter, 250 ml of skimmed milk, and a banana.

❧ Try 185 g of oatmeal cooked with skimmed milk and topped with two tablespoons of wheat

Break Bad Breakfast Habits

There's a saying that's somewhat true: If you are going to overeat, you might as well do it at breakfast. That way you have all day to burn off the calories. But overeating calories and fat at any meal, including breakfast, can still hamper your fat-fighting efforts. And some breakfast foods are deceiving. They seem healthy yet are loaded with fat or calories. Here is what you need to know to avoid breakfast fat traps.

Watch your toppings. You can ruin plenty of otherwise healthy foods by putting the wrong things on top of them. As we mentioned earlier, for instance, cooked oatmeal is a great fat-fighting breakfast. But if you add 60 ml single cream and two teaspoons of margarine, the meal becomes 58 percent fat. To scalp the fat, leave off the margarine and replace the cream with skimmed milk.

You can save 19 grammes of fat by using 30 g of fat-free cream cheese instead of regular cream cheese on your bagel. And you can slash fat by 28 percent by replacing whole milk with skimmed on your cereal.

Make sure your muffins are low-fat. Many times, as soon as we see the words oat bran or whole-grain, we think "healthy." But that's not always the case. Some oat bran muffins, for instance, are loaded with fat, says Grabowski-Nepa. So be sure to check the label.

Use jam – in moderation. You may be fooled into thinking that all-fruit jams mean "all you can eat." They don't. (By the way, all-fruit spread doesn't even count as one of your daily fruit or vegetable servings.) Fruit spreads are made with real fruit – as well as fruit juice, which is just a nice name for sugar.

"Your body can't tell the difference between fruit juice and sugar," says Grabowski-Nepa. Sure, all-fruit jams are slightly more nutritious than other jams, which can be nearly all processed sugar and very little fruit. But they still have a lot of calories.

Be yogurt smart. When picking yogurt as a breakfast food, be sure to pick the right kind. Go for either nonfat or 99 percent fat-free yogurt. And look for one that's either sugar-free or sweetened with fruit juice, which often does not add as many calories as pure sugar.

Eat out with caution. Eating at a cafe/diner can be a fat and calorie nightmare. A typical waffle, for instance, has 550 calories and 21 grammes of fat. Just one slice of French toast has 150 calories and 7 grammes of fat. And a single pancake without butter and syrup has 165 calories and 5 grammes of fat.

So what can you order? Ask for an egg-white omelette loaded with mushrooms, onions, tomatoes, spinach or other vegetables. Forgo the cheese and ham. And get some whole-grain toast on the side, says Grabowski-Nepa.

No-Fat Noshing

Your Guide to Sensible Snacking

If you're trying to lose weight, you should snack for precisely the same reason that your mum told you not to as a kid: It'll ruin your appetite.

Snacks keep you from overeating at mealtime. That's a good thing. Any time you overeat, your body turns into a fat-storing machine. Snacking also will supply your body with the fuel it needs to keep calories on a steady burn. Without a small snack break every few hours, your stomach gets empty, signaling your metabolism to burn calories more slowly.

But snacking can be risky business. You can't lose weight eating chocolate bars, cakes and biscuits. The trick to snacking the fat-fighter's way lies in picking the right snack foods. Eating healthy snacks throughout the day that are full of nutrients and fibre and low in fat and calories can help you lose weight because you won't be hungry. You can resist temptation.

Redefining "Snack"

"There's a connotation that snacks must be bad," says Diane Grabowski-Nepa, R.D.

"I think women feel that way because of the foods they typically snacked on in the past. Usually they opted for something sweet or salty. But snacks can be so healthy. You can eat fruit. You can have soup or leftovers. You can have a baked potato. Snacking in itself is healthy. It just depends on what you eat when you snack."

Usually it's taste, not health or weight loss, that controls which snacks we tend to reach for, says Audrey Cross, Ph.D.

How we view taste is a product of upbringing. Most of us reach for snacks that we identify as comfort foods. "We might be bored or feel angry or depressed. Or we might feel we deserve a reward," says Marcia Levin Pelchat, Ph.D. "Then we turn to certain foods that, in our experience, make us feel better." Usually, this means fatty snacks like potato crisps and ice cream.

"Fortunately, you can find many snack items like biscuits, cakes and ice cream in low-fat, low-sugar, low-sodium versions," says Dr. Cross. "By choosing these – in moderation – our snack urge

WOMEN ASK WHY

Why are my fat-free biscuits making me gain weight?

Many times when you see "no-fat" in huge letters on a food package, your brain registers "no-calorie." It's easy to tell yourself that something fat-free is not going to count in your diet. Unfortunately, however, there are no freebies when it comes to fat-free snacking.

Low-fat doesn't mean low-calorie, and in many cases, those no-fat goodies are just as high in calories as the regular kind. After all, when the manufacturers take the fat from a chocolate biscuit, they have to put something back. What they substitute is often a whole lot of sugar, making up most if not all of the calories that went away with the fat.

Extra sugar is what makes your fat-free biscuits taste so good. Since the tendency with fat-free snacks is to eat as much as you want, it's easy to end up eating a large number of calories. The fat-free claim even makes some women think that eating fat-free snacks will help them lose weight. The problem is that eating more calories than you burn, no matter if those calories come from high-fat or nonfat foods, makes you gain weight and body fat. So much for the advantage of being fat-free.

The best way to deal with nonfat snacks is to read the fine print. Take a look at the nutrition label, especially the size of the portions and the calorie content of each. No-fat is no lie, but if you do a little extra detective work, you'll be able to make a much more informed decision about how much you really want to eat. Just remember that there can be too much of a good thing when it comes to no-fat noshing — especially if you have a sweet tooth.

Expert consulted
Barbara Whedon, R.D.

can be quelled without disastrous nutritional consequences."

Refine Your Tastes

Many women learn to retrain their tastebuds and thus lose interest in fatty, sugary snacks, Dr. Cross says. Does that mean that we can learn to appreciate the colour and crunch of a green pepper as much as the gooey richness of a Snickers bar?

"Yes, but for most of us it's not easy," says Dr. Cross. "It takes time. You may fall off the wagon occasionally, but you can do it." Here's how to get started.

Think nutrition. In planning your daily nutrition goals, factor in snacks. "Think of snacks as food eaten between meals instead of as treats or rewards," says Barbara Whedon, R.D.

"Make your snack an extension of your meal," she suggests. "If you plan to have soup, salad and fruit for lunch, for example, don't eat the fruit. Save it for your snack. The same with your dessert or bread at supper or your breakfast juice or muffin." (This will also pave your way to the method described in Mini-Meals on page 47.)

Don't try to be perfect. Denying yourself rarely works, says Margo Denke, M.D. One thing that does, she says, is cutting back on how much we eat when we do snack. Also, don't assume that every single snack you eat has to be nutritious. "Some can be just for fun.

It's the overall diet that counts in terms of nutrition," says Dr. Margo Denke.

Plan for temptation. Take your own snacks to work so that when everyone else is selecting an item from the snack trolley, you have dried fruit in your desk or nonfat yogurt in your office kitchen, says Dr. Cross. "That way you get something to eat, too," she says.

Look for healthier substitutes. If you crave a salty snack, for example, and you're used to appeasing that desire with a bag of potato crisps, look for the new low-fat brands, says Alice K. Lindeman, R.D. Just be careful not to eat more than you used to. An even better choice would be pretzels. "The big Dutch pretzels take a while to eat and can satisfy that desire for salt and crunch," she says.

Beware the Fat Trap

The fact that you eat low-fat snacks also doesn't give you license to eat freely of other foods. When Barbara Rolls, Ph.D., and her colleagues analysed the impact of such snacks on women's eating behaviours, they found that those who ate low-fat snacks tended to eat more at lunch than women who ate higher-fat snacks.

"We concluded that thinking a food is low-fat can be a trap because we may believe it gives us license to overindulge in other areas," says Dr. Rolls.

WOMAN TO WOMAN
Sensible Snacking Did the Trick

Valerie Groninger knows that nothing can ruin a perfectly good weight-loss plan like too many unauthorised trips to the fridge or cupboard. Snacking was one of the biggest obstacles that she overcame on her 3½-year path to fitness.

Like many women, after my children were born, I couldn't seem to lose the weight I'd gained during pregnancy. I was never happy with my weight gain, but I tolerated it – until I got laid off from work. With the extra time on my hands, I resolved to try to lose the extra pounds. Working towards my master's degree in education played a big part. I didn't want to go to college with all those 20-year-olds looking like a mum of two kids who goes home and eats bonbons while she studies.

I got myself into a pattern of eating the snack foods that I buy for the kids, like biscuits. I finally realised that I don't have my six-year-old son's metabolism, and I can't eat what he eats. So I began to cut back and count fat grammes religiously.

I actually snack more frequently now than before, and I'm down from a size 18 to a 12. I just choose snacks that are lower in fat, and I eat smaller quantities. For instance, instead of full fat ice cream, I buy low-fat and have two spoonfuls, right from the carton. I don't even get out a bowl because I know I will eat more. At first I was surprised that I really felt satisfied by the smaller portion.

My worst time for snacking is right before supper. When I'm cooking, I sometimes taste-test more than I should. In the winter, herbal tea gets me through to supper. In fact, I often find that drinking something is a good way not to snack. In the summer, I might have a fruit ice pop. I even make my own fruit bars by freezing juice in Tupperware moulds.

This is a wonderful time to lose weight: There are so many good-tasting low-fat snacks on the market. I can honestly say that I'm happy with my eating lifestyle, and I've never yet felt deprived.

A little maths reveals why low-fat snacks can be a trap. Thirteen reduced-fat mini-chocolate-chip biscuits may add up to only 130 calories. But if you eat the whole 250-g box, you'll take in an amazing 910 calories. It's awfully easy to do that while watching a favourite television show. As another example, you can have 22 low-fat tortilla chips for 110 calories, which sounds great, but the entire 220-g package would cost you 770 calories.

"Those grammes of fat add up quickly, and so do the calories," Whedon explains. "I tell my clients that eating 40 to 60 grammes of fat a day is reasonable. Dropping much below that greatly restricts your food choices and is difficult to maintain. You must make a decision about how many fat grammes you will devote to snacks."

Craving Control

To satisfy your tastebuds, intellectualise your choices, says Whedon. "Often we grab what's nearby. We feel hungry, so we hurriedly select something from the vending machine or have one of the biscuits served at a meeting, with no thought about what we feel a need for," she says.

Think texture. According to Whedon, what we often crave is a mouth-feel more than a taste. Snacks can be chewy, crunchy, smooth, creamy, cold, sweet or salty. Often we want a combination. "If you crave something creamy and sweet, for example, yogurt might be perfect," says Whedon. "If you desire cold and crunchy, try slices of green pepper. An ice lolly will take

SUPER NO-FAT SNACKS

Don't confuse "No-fat noshing" with "No-fat gorging." Run amok with snacks, even the low-fat variety, and you'll gain weight. Calories do count.

The secret of successful snacking is to be selective. Instead of snacking mindlessly, think about your choices. Here are 50 indulgences that, when eaten in the portions listed, can keep eating fun without packing on the pounds.

Food	Portion	Calories	Fat (g.)
Apple	1 medium	81	0
Applesauce, unsweetened	125 ml	53	0
Apricots, dried	5	83	0
Apricots, fresh	3 medium	51	0
Bagel	½	81	0
Banana	1 medium	100	0
Biscuit, devil's food, low-fat	1	50	0
Biscuit, Digestive	¼	59	1
Biscuit, pecan, low-fat	1	70	3
Blueberries	250 g	82	0
Bread, sourdough	1 slice	70	1
Butterscotch sweets	4 pieces	88	1
Cantaloupe, cubed	185 g	57	0
Carrot	1 medium	31	0
Celery	1 stalk	6	0
Cereal, frosted, shredded wheat	4 biscuits	100	0
Cottage cheese, low-fat	125 g	81	1
Crackers, Ritz	5	60	1
Crackers, whole-grain, fat-free	5	60	0
Crackers, whole-wheat	6	96	3
Cucumber	1 medium	16	0
Dill pickle	1 medium	12	0
Fig bars, fat-free	2	100	0

Food	Portion	Calories	Fat (g.)
Fruit juice bar, frozen	1	25	0
Fruit roll sweet	1 roll	81	1
Grapefruit	½ medium	37	0
Grapes	155 g	58	0
Honeydew melon, cubed	1 cup	60	0
Jelly Babies sweets	3 pieces	20	0
Jelly beans	8 large	83	0
Life Savers sweets	1	9	0
Orange	1 medium	65	0
Peach, dried	1	62	0
Peach, fresh	1 medium	37	0
Pepper, green or sweet red	1 large	20	0
Pineapple, cubed	155 g	77	0
Popcorn, caramel, low-fat	90 g	100	0
Popcorn, light	90 g	45	3
Potato crisps, fat-free	30	110	0
Pretzel, whole-wheat	1 small	51	0
Pretzels	10 thin	70	0
Pudding, chocolate	125 g	100	0
Raisins, seedless	2 Tbsp	55	0
Rice cake, plain	1	21	0
Strawberries	185 g	45	0
String cheese, low-fat	1 piece	60	3
Tortilla chips, baked, low-fat, with salsa	10	90	1
Tuna, light, packed in water	60 g	65	0
Yogurt, nonfat	125 g	60	0
Yogurt bar, frozen, nonfat	1	45	0

care of cold and sweet, while Jelly Babies are chewy and sweet."

Plan ahead. "Understand that snacking can be a spontaneous behaviour and be prepared," says Dr. Lindeman. "Keep some items like rice cakes, dried fruit, or cereal mix in a desk drawer, or find a vending machine with healthy selections."

Practice damage control. Don't fall for the notion that if one tastes good, two taste better. Filling a small bowl with potato crisps instead of diving into a full bag helps will power do its work.

Avoid triggers. Boredom can lead to unnecessary snacking. Nutrition experts advise keeping busy when you feel like having a snack. Food commercials and being around people who are eating can also trigger the urge to indulge. Finally, bypass the supermarket aisles loaded with finger foods and the checkout lanes stocked with chocolate bars, suggests Dr. Cross.

Take slip ups in stride. If you do overindulge, forgive yourself, forget about it, and get back on course.

Treat yourself every once in a while. "If you're counting calories, save enough of them to give yourself an occasional treat," says Whedon. "That way you won't feel deprived, and that vastly increases your chances of success."

Control your servings. It's easy to overeat on snacks, so choose foods that come in single-serving portions, such as yogurt in 250 ml cups and pieces of fruit. For low-fat crisps and unsalted pretzels, make your own single servings using snack-size plastic bags.

Think of snacks as golden opportunities to eat the foods you often avoid. For some of us, that's vegetables and fruit. Some ideas: broccoli florets with low-fat sour cream dip, a baked sweet potato drizzled with fat-free caramel sauce, low-fat tortilla chips with salsa, frozen grapes or bananas and grated carrot salad with low-fat mayo and raisins.

Top your popcorn. Air-popped popcorn minus the butter can seem bland. But with a little creativity, it can be a taste treat. Try sprinkling on a little grated cheese or hot spices like pepper or chilli powder. You can even toss in some cinnamon or a handful of raisins.

Guilt-Free, Fun-to-Eat Snacks

Tired of pretzels? Bored with low-fat biscuits? Can't look at another carrot? Don't revert to cupcakes just yet. Here are some other tempting snack choices that won't pack fat on your thighs.

❧ Keep sliced turkey breast in the fridge for sandwiches. (When freshly sliced, it will keep for two to five days.) Line a pita pocket with lettuce and tuck in the turkey.

❧ Layer nonfat frozen yogurt with chopped fruit and roasted and cooled chestnuts in a sundae dish. Try vanilla yogurt with chopped bananas or strawberry yogurt with sliced strawberries.

❧ Toss leftover fresh pasta with a smidgen of olive oil to keep it from clumping, then store it in a sealed plastic bag in the fridge. You can use it to make instant pasta salad by tossing one tablespoon of nonfat dressing with 185 g of pasta. Toss in some leftover vegetables, too.

❧ Make ice cream sandwiches by spreading slightly softened nonfat frozen yogurt between two low-fat oatmeal biscuits or digestives. Store them, tightly wrapped, in the freezer.

❧ Peel and section a variety of citrus fruits. For a quick treat, mix grapefruit sections with oranges and tangerines.

❧ For delicious potato-skin snacks, bake extra potatoes and stash them in the fridge. When you're ready, halve the potatoes and scoop out the insides with a spoon, leaving about 6 mm of flesh. Sprinkle with grated reduced-fat Cheddar cheese and minced chives. Grill about 14 cm from the heat until the potatoes are warmed through and the cheese has melted, about four minutes.

❧ Heat a frozen waffle according to package directions. Top it with maple yogurt, made by folding together equal parts of maple syrup and plain nonfat yogurt. Add sliced bananas or apples.

❧ For an easy and delicious dip, combine 125 g nonfat ricotta and 125 g nonfat natural yogurt. Stir in one to two teaspoons of your favourite herbs, such as basil, dill and tarragon. Enjoy with slices of fresh vegetables or reduced-fat whole-wheat crackers.

❧ Nibble on strips of low-fat cheese and strips of sweet red, yellow and green peppers or chunks of carrots.

❧ Keep chunks of mangoes and nectarines, plus some seedless grapes and stoned cherries, in plastic bags in the freezer. They're quick refreshers, and they're as good as ice pops.

❧ Choose some new raw vegetables and keep them in bite-size pieces in the fridge. Eat them either with or without a low-fat dip. Cherry tomatoes, sugar snap peas, cut-up swede, whole white mushrooms, Jerusalem artichokes, cut-up fennel bulb, Chinese cabbage ribs, sliced celeriac, sliced mooli and some jícama chunks can perk up your palate.

Leaner Lunches
Midday Strategies Away from Home

esides packing some extra padding on your thighs, a lunch that's high in fat can make you tired in the afternoon, when you should be mentally alert. So lunch is the perfect meal to eat lean.

In addition to being low in fat, the ideal lunch, whether you are packing it yourself or eating out, should be balanced, says Kathy Dimoff, R.D. That means one fruit, one vegetable, two breads and a small meat or dairy serving. What's that in real food terms? An apple and a sandwich made with two slices of whole-wheat bread, one or two slices of turkey, and some lettuce, tomatoes, sprouts or even sliced green peppers.

This means that the bulk of your meal will consist of grains, fruits and vegetables – the hallmark of healthy eating. But there are plenty of ways to get this nutritional balance into your lunch without resorting to a turkey sandwich every day.

Packed Lunch Basics

Packing lunch in these days of hectic living takes time, but would you do it if it would earn you £1,000? When Dimoff asks a group of women at her diet centre if they would pack their lunches if they were paid £1,000 a day, everyone raises their hands.

"It proves that finding time for packing lunch is just a matter of priority," she says. So put it at the top of your to-do list with the help of the following advice.

Mondays are for stocking. Put together your lunch staples on Monday mornings. That means taking foods like bananas, canned soup, pretzels, apples, small cans of applesauce and dry cereal to work and storing them for the week to come.

Build a good sandwich. Just one sandwich can contain everything you want to eat for lunch: bread, vegetables and protein, points out

Dimoff. Here's her advice for mastering sandwich-making.

✦ Choose more flavourful whole-grain bread or pitas. Because they have more fibre, whole-grain breads will fill you up faster than their white counterpart.

✦ Skip the usual deli meats and choose lean cuts of chicken, turkey or roast beef. Your serving of meat should weigh no more than 90 g.

✦ Go wild with vegetables. Pile on any combination of sprouts, sliced cucumbers, green pepper rings, shredded carrots, onions, sliced mushrooms, cos lettuce and shredded cabbage. The vegetables will add moisture to your sandwich, eliminating the need for mayo.

Have a pita party. For something a little more festive, make some bean dip or buy ready-made hummus and pack it in a plastic container. For dipping, slice a pita and wrap it separately.

Bring on the soup. A vegetable-based soup can also be a perfect lunch if you round it out with some bread or fat-free crackers and fruit. Plus, it has a bonus: You'll eat less. A study at an obesity research centre showed that when people have soup for lunch, they eat less at that meal and feel more satisfied.

Because soup is hot, you eat it more slowly, explains Judith S. Stern, R.D. So your brain has the time to tell your stomach, "I'm full." Homemade soup is ideal, but canned soup is fine, provided you check the label to make sure the fat count is low, she says.

Have supper for lunch. Here's a real time-saver: Lunch on the leftovers from last night's supper. "If you are making salmon steaks, for instance, prepare an extra one," says Marie Simmons. "Salmon is good cold, and you can

---

REAL-LIFE SCENARIO
Escape the Salad Bar Fat Trap

Sue Grant wanted to drop a few pounds, so she gave up soup and turkey sandwiches for lunch. Now she eats a salad every day – a big pile of lettuce, a little cheese, turkey, egg, croutons, a mound of crunchy veggies and a few crackers on the side. Her favourite topping is Russian dressing, although she often opts for Italian Caesar. The problem is, Sue is gaining, not dropping, pounds. What's up?

Salads are the staple of dieting women, and rightfully so – they can be both healthy and filling. But by adding regular salad dressing and a lot of cheese, eggs and croutons to her plate of lettuce, Sue has herself stuck in the salad bar fat trap.

Say that Sue typically makes a turkey sandwich with two slices of cracked-wheat bread, two slices of turkey and a little lettuce and tomato. Add about two teaspoons of regular mayo to her sandwich, throw in 250 ml of vegetable

---

round it out with a salad of cooked potatoes and cucumber slices drizzled with a little lemon juice and olive oil."

Break tradition. There's no reason you can't have a totally non-traditional packed lunch. How about a single-serving box of your favourite whole-grain cereal topped with nonfat yogurt or skimmed milk, along with some cut-up fruit?

Lunchtime Survival

Packed lunches may be the best way to go, but let's be realistic: You probably won't make your own lunch every day.

Whether you're venturing out to a restaurant or heading to the company cafeteria for lunch, these strategies can help you achieve both.

soup on the side, and you have a lunch with about 375 calories and 14 grammes of fat. Not bad. Now if you get out a big salad bowl and pile up some lettuce along with all of Sue's favourite fixings and two tablespoons of Caesar dressing, you have a lunch with about 596 calories and 36 grammes of fat. So much for her hopes of dropping a few pounds.

Salad can be a healthy way to go, especially when you add a lot of veggies as Sue does. It's just not going to help her lose weight, though, unless she cuts back on some of those high-fat salad bar fixings.

The key to making a leaner lunch is to pay attention to portion size. When you're trying to fight fat, soups, salads and sandwiches are all satisfactory choices; you just have to avoid serving up anything with fattening frills on a huge plate.

Expert consulted
Neva Cochran, R.D.

Start off with a snack. Before lunching out, have a snack from the low-fat stash in your desk drawer. This will take the edge off your hunger so you won't be dipping bread into olive oil while waiting for your food.

Be a leader. When lunching with friends, be assertive and voice your restaurant preference. Have two or three alternatives in mind, places where you know they serve at least one reduced-fat meal.

Get familiar with the menu. Go to restaurants you're familiar with whenever possible so that you can make up your mind before leaving the office. That way you can order without having to look at a menu that's just begging you to change your mind.

Dine alone. It may be kind of lonely, but you'll eat less. Psychologists theorise that you linger over your food and eat more when you're with company. Researchers found that when people eat with one companion, their consumption rises by 28 percent. With two companions, they eat 41 percent more and with six or more companions, they eat 76 percent more food.

Go to a deli. With tons of fattening stuff like corned beef, ham, cheese and pepperoni, delis may at first seem like the last places you'd want to eat lunch. But a deli is actually one of your best options, says Toni Ferrang, R.D.

Why? Because you have more choices and more freedom to custom order than at any other type of restaurant. You don't have to order the six-different-kinds-of-meat-and-cheese mile-high sandwich slathered with mayo and oil. Instead you can get a turkey sandwich with tomato, lettuce, and mustard on whole-wheat bread.

Do a balancing act. There will be times when you simply won't be able to choose what you eat. At a conference, for instance, the menu may be a predetermined mix of fatty foods. Just eat modest portions, says Dimoff.

Take a taste of temptation. Ah, the smell of those wonderful hot dogs you love so much is luring you into temptation. Well, let it – once in a while. Sure, the dogs are full of fat, but if you make smart food choices the rest of the day, you'll stay out of fat city. Just round out each of your meals with a piece of fruit or a vegetable, says Ferrang.

Svelte Suppers

Please Yourself While Pleasing Others

Supper: It's the meal most likely to destroy a diet.

After a day of calorie- and fat-watching, you're good and hungry by the time you get around to making supper. You nibble while you cook – and what you're preparing is most likely something that suits your family but not necessarily your weight-loss goal. But that's okay, because you're going to ignore the fattening stuff.

The meal goes on the table. Everyone digs in, including you. And why not have a second helping, while you're at it? And dessert. Your appetite turns into the Energiser bunny: It just keeps going and going, all the way till bedtime.

If your diet is going to take a dive, there's a good chance it's going to happen at supper time. The average woman eats almost half her daily calories – 46 percent – after 5:00 P.M.

The Supper Knell

In reality, the problem is not supper. Women who splurge during or after supper usually can trace their true food problem to much earlier in the day. "Their biggest problem is breakfast and lunch, because they skip them or eat very little," says Toni Ferrang, R.D. "By the time supper comes around, they're so hungry they're all over the food."

If you're a night eater and you want to lose weight, you're going to have to turn your eating habits nearly upside down. Night eating is the worst thing you can do, says Ferrang, because what you overeat at night will very likely follow you to bed. And since your body goes on slow burn while you sleep, those calories will look for a cosy place to rest, too – right in your fat cells. So you have to toss some of those extra supper calories towards your breakfast and lunch, spreading your calorie intake more evenly throughout the day, says Ferrang. Here's what she suggests.

Satisfying His Meat-and-Potato Yen

Once you start eating more during the day, you'll have solved more than three-quarters of your supper dilemma, says Ferrang. What's the remaining quarter? Your dining companions.

"Many women complain that supper is their downfall because they have families to feed or husbands who are looking for a hunk of meat," says Marsha Hudnall, R.D.

Putting smaller, low-fat suppers on the table can get dicey when you have a meat-hungry man to feed. It's even trickier when you have picky kids who cringe at the sight of vegetables, whole grains and just about anything low-fat and nutritious. With some communication, compromise, and even sheer trickery, however, you can stick to your food plan while keeping your husband and kids happy.

Tell your husband your intentions. If you are watching what you eat but your husband keeps tempting you with second helpings, take him aside and explain how you are trying to eat and why. Chances are, once he understands, he'll be more supportive, says Ferrang.

If he still complains, try to strike a compromise, suggests Joyce D. Nash, Ph.D. Maybe your husband can take the kids out for pizza, burgers or hot dogs once a week, for instance. Or get him to cook meals for himself and the kids a couple of nights a week while you fend for yourself.

Remember: You have the right to eat whatever you want, even if your family doesn't want the same things. You can strike a balance between the meals everyone likes and the meals you need. You don't need to please everyone all the time. Sometimes it's good to just not worry what they say.

Fill up on vegetables. You can continue to cook the meat your husband loves while at the same time cutting back on fatty foods. Just be sure to cook up a bunch of vegetables and whole grains, says Hudnall. If he's craving steak, for instance, go ahead and cook it. Just make sure it's a lean cut, limit yourself to a 90-g portion (that's about the size of your palm) and fill the rest of your plate with broccoli, brown rice and steamed carrots, she says.

Cook up an optical illusion. A small amount of meat looks like a lot when you cut it into small pieces and mix it with a bunch of stir-fried vegetables, says Hudnall. Similarly, try fixing a stew with lots of vegetables, a delicious broth, and only a little meat, says Diane Woznicki, R.D. Or try making a pasta or rice dish and garnishing it with thinly sliced beef or chicken. The same goes for fajitas: Use lots of peppers and onions but only three strips or so of meat. That way your husband will feel like he's getting a treat while you get food that meets your weight-loss requirements.

Pull a disappearing act. Kids – and even grown men – who hate vegetables can't complain if they don't know what they are eating. Try finely chopping or puréeing vegetables and hiding them in family favourites such as meat loaf and tacos. To make tacos, for instance, Hudnall stretches a small amount of lower-fat minced beef by mixing in tomato paste and finely chopped celery and onions. "The tacos end up having a lot of vegetables, but the kids don't know it," Hudnall says.

Tempt with colour. If you teach your youngsters to think of food in terms of colour – the more colourful the better – they will automatically start eating the healthier meals you are making, says Pat Baird, R.D., author of *The Pyramid Cookbook*. "I often tell people to cook by colour and to include a variety of vegetables that are red, green, yellow and orange," she says. And orange doesn't restrict you to oranges. There are cantaloupes, apricots, papayas, mangoes, winter squash and orange peppers. Younger children can make a game of listing how many different foods of various colours they can name and find in the supermarket fruit and vegetable section.

Persist for 10 suppers. You know how people talk about having an "acquired taste" for beer, coffee or caviar? The same thing can happen with vegetables. Once your husband or kids eat a food about 10 times, they'll learn to like it, says Hudnall. (And so will you.) So have faith. And keep introducing those new, filling, low-calorie vegetables to the supper table. Have your family try just a bit until they want more.

Switch to fruit. Let's face it: Some kids are vegetable sleuths. No matter how much you dress up or hide vegetables, their microscopic vision spots them every time. Almost as soon as you put the meal on the table, you hear a symphony of "E-w-w-ws." What to do? Serve up a healthy, low-fat, low-calorie children's favourite: fruit. A fruit side dish or dessert can give you a weight-loss option for the supper table while sparing you another night of "Yuck!" and "Gross!"

BEWARE OF SUBTLE EATING CUES

What do your place mats, wall colour, compact disc player and remote control have to do with how much you eat? Quite a bit. Here are some simple changes that you can make in your eating environment that will help you to eat less – without even thinking about it.

Set a dark table. Bright colours such as orange, red and yellow will make you hungry, according to research. But darker colours such as grey, black or brown won't, says Maria Simonson, Ph.D. Although your kitchen won't look as warm and festive with a dark tablecloth, dark napkins or dark walls, they could help your weight-loss efforts, she says.

Eat from small packages. If a food comes in a large package, you will most likely use more of it, according to research. Researchers tested how people use different-size bottles, boxes and bags of cooking oil, spaghetti and Smarties, among other foods. The researchers suspect that we may consume more food from a larger package for three reasons. One, we perceive the food as less expensive. Second, we don't have to worry about running out. And third, we may try to use up the whole box just to keep it from taking up so much cabinet space. The moral is that the smaller the bottles

---

Low-Fat Cooking Secrets

Want another effective way to serve low-fat suppers without getting a lot of lip from your husband or kids? Make sure that they taste spectacular. Low-fat food doesn't have to be tasteless and rubbery.

You can discover new delights, not grim restrictions, on a low-fat supper eating plan, says nutrition counsellor Michelle Berry, R.D. "If you think about getting variety – in flavours, ingredients and preparation styles – then healthy eating can be a delicious, satisfying adventure," she says.

In fact, if you concentrate on making small changes, you can slowly eliminate fat from your favourite dishes. And your husband won't even notice, says Kathy Dimoff, R.D. Here are ways to cut the fat out of your suppers without sacrificing flavour or satisfaction.

Take fat from your favourites. Most women use the same 10 or so recipes over and over again. So pull together your regulars, look them over, and find ways to eliminate fat. "You can often make very subtle changes that another person will never notice," says Dimoff. Changes could include substituting extra-lean minced beef or turkey for the higher-fat variety, using lower-fat dairy products and mixing in more spices and less oil.

of cooking oil, packages of sweets and boxes of food you buy, the less you'll have to eat during each sitting.

Munch to Mozart, not syndicated sitcoms. Listening to gentle music while you dine forces you to concentrate on what you are eating, which means you'll eat more slowly and eat less. You'll also be more satisfied with what you eat because slowing down allows you to taste it. On the other hand, if you eat while watching television, eating becomes automatic, so you eat more.

Channel-surf away the commercials. Eating or drinking while watching television is dangerous to begin with. But be extra careful if a diet commercial pops up on the screen. In fact, flip to another station. In one study, 86 women dieters drank a milkshake and then watched a sad movie with either no commercials, neutral commercials, or ones featuring successful dieters. All of the women were supposed to test bowls of peanuts and Smarties during the flick. The women who saw the diet commercials ate nearly twice as much as the other women. Researchers suspect that the thin women in the ads reminded the women who watched that they had gone off their diets, which removed their inhibitions about eating.

Investing in a quality non-stick frying pan means that you won't have to add as much oil to sauté food, says Ferrang.

Try broth. Instead of sautéing in oil, try using vegetable or chicken broth, says Ferrang.

Fry without the fat. Generally, frying is the worst way to cook anything. That's because your food is simply sitting in butter or oil, having a gay old time absorbing all that pure liquid fat and delivering it straight to your belly.

Two fried favourites, chicken and french fries, can be made without the grease, says Dimoff. To make fries, slice baking potatoes into wedges, sprinkle with cayenne pepper, and roast in the oven until brown. You'll save 12 grammes of fat

per serving. To make chicken, dip skinless breasts in egg whites and roll them in breadcrumbs, then bake.

Let it soak. Marinate your fish or meat in soy or teriyaki sauce ahead of time to add flavour. That way you won't feel tempted to fry it, says Ferrang.

Get the best cut. When it comes to red meat, choose leaner cuts such as loin and top round. A top round steak contains 3 grammes of fat per 90-g serving, while a rib-eye steak contains 10 grammes per 90 g.

Cut the fat. Always trim visible fat from meat before cooking. It can make a big difference. 90 g of beef chuck steak, for example, has 18 grammes of fat. Trimmed, the same cut has 6 grammes.

Spray. Use a non-stick spray instead of oil or butter. You'll save on fat no matter what you're cooking.

Turn the dial first. If you heat the frying pan before adding oil, less fat will be absorbed by the food. Warm oil cooks more efficiently, while cold oil tends to soak into meats and vegetables.

Learn pseudo-sautéing. Instead of letting your food swim in a puddle of oil, cook it with its own natural moisture. Begin with the tiniest quantity of oil and add water – no more oil – as needed for moisture.

When you roast meat, use a rack. A rack allows fat to drip off so the meat doesn't steep in it, reabsorbing all the bad stuff.

Know your marinades. When grilling chicken, try this oil-free marinade: Combine 750 ml of apple juice and two cloves of garlic, minced, with 250 ml of reduced-sodium soy sauce. Experiment with making other marinades without fat. Try flavoured vinegars, fruit juices and a variety of spices and herbs.

Have some spicy low-fat chicken wings. Instead of using regular chicken wings, use skinless chicken breast fillets to make "buffalo wings." Marinate them overnight in the refrigerator in a mixture of hot-pepper sauce, olive oil, lots of garlic powder and red wine vinegar. (Experiment with the amounts to suit your taste.) Then roast the chicken wings at 200°C, Gas 6 for 15 minutes. Your kids will love them.

Be a low-fat loafer. Make a better meat loaf using a mixture of one-third cooked brown rice or oatmeal, one-third minced turkey (breast meat only) and one-third extra-lean beef. Splash on Worcestershire sauce, barbecue sauce or ketchup, and your family won't miss the missing fat.

Make chicken à l'orange. If you have a can of frozen orange juice concentrate, you have a great way to add flavour to stir-fried chicken or beef and vegetables without adding fat. Just a few spoonfuls will do.

Perk up your sweetcorn. Stir salsa into frozen sweetcorn while you heat it through; the spice eliminates the need for butter. When you're boiling corn on the cob, add some cayenne pepper to the water for butter-free Cajun corn.

Slim down your pasta sauce. If you're making your own spaghetti sauce, look for the seasoned, stewed varieties of canned tomatoes. They tend to be lower in oil than those labelled pasta-ready. You can also use frozen veggie-burger crumbles instead of minced beef.

If it's Friday, this must be pizza. Pizza is

WOMAN TO WOMAN

Her Supper Slimmed Down – And So Did She

Carol Seda, an executive coordinator for a public relations and advertising firm in Exeter, lost 5 stone in eight months by slimming her suppers. Here's her story.

During my teenage years I was practically underweight. When I turned 23, my whole life changed. Recently married, I was anxious to demonstrate my cooking skills for my husband and friends. My weight crept up. Then I was diagnosed with ovarian cancer, and I underwent an emergency hysterectomy. Afterward, my weight zoomed to 15 stone. Overwhelmed by the situation, all I did was eat. I'd get mad and eat. I'd get happy and eat. I'd get depressed and eat.

Throughout these upheavals, food was my constant comfort. I especially loved cooking suppers for my husband. He likes food and bragged about my good cooking. Eager to please, I prepared meaty dishes like steak, and I whipped up cakes and fudge. We never dreamed of eating grilled chicken or minced turkey. If I bought a hefty roast for supper, we'd eat the whole thing. A loaf of bread lasted only three days in our house. For supper, I could eat a whole pizza by myself.

I was in denial about my size. Five years later, I was

one of those foods that men crave almost as much as meat, so you probably won't hear any complaints about this meal. Try homemade pizza that boasts a low-fat crust topped with low-fat cheese and steamed vegetables. It can go a long way towards meeting your remaining nutritional requirements for the day, says Cheryl Rock, Ph.D. Or try a fruit pizza. Start with a low-fat, whole-wheat pastry crust. Mix fat-free cream cheese with low-fat or non-fat ricotta and spread it over the baked crust. Add kiwi or other fruits – peaches,

shocked when I saw a picture of myself. I resolved to regain my previously slender figure and take control of my life. My doctor gave me a food planner that explained how to count calories and watch fat.

I embarked on my new eating plan with a vengeance. If something had more than two grammes of fat per serving, I wouldn't buy it. I wrote down everything I ate in a food diary. I measured out portions on my food scale. It was very hard, but I stuck with it. My husband and I also started exercising – walking and working out at a gym.

Five stone lighter now, I've tempered my eating habits. I've learned what a correct portion is, so I don't have to measure everything. Now I eat many different foods in moderation. I've developed some great strategies to avoid overeating at supper, which had always been my biggest problem meal. Before supper, I drink two to three glasses of water to fill me up and soothe my hunger. At supper, I fill up on vegetables and starches like rice and have just a small portion of meat. I completely avoid fried foods, and I don't miss them a bit.

I know that I never again want to look like I did in that picture. I keep a close eye on my weight, and if it starts floating up, I go back to my strict eating plan, if only for a while, until my weight falls back in line.

Losing the weight was tough, but if I can do it, anybody can!

berries and so forth – as if they were pepperoni. Heat some marmalade in the microwave and brush it on top with a pastry brush, then enjoy.

Portion Control

Even if you successfully get your husband and kids to jump on your low-fat supper wagon, you still have one more obstacle to tackle – portion size. Your family may be able to eat serving after serving, but you can't. Just watching them down forkful after forkful can be a powerful temptation to overeat. But you can put down your fork and step away from the table before eating yourself into a food coma. Here are some strategies.

Sigh. Really. Take a deep breath before actually picking up your fork for the first bite. It will help you to relax, eat more slowly, and stop before you stuff yourself.

Cover your plate. Many women often overeat at supper because they skimp on their initial servings. They put only a little of this and a tiny bit of that on their plates. Then they eat that tiny bit. "They feel like that was nothing, so they go back for more," says Hudnall. But serving number two is larger. And serving number three is still larger. Eventually, they end up stuffed but still unsatisfied.

Instead, fill your plate up the first time, making sure the majority is covered by the lower-calorie vegetables and grains. The simple act of covering the dish can mentally make you feel satisfied, Hudnall says. And you won't be tempted by seconds. "At Green Mountain we serve food on smaller plates. People are always saying, 'Oh, my God. This is so much food,' " she says. "It's really not a lot of food. But it sure looks like it."

Stay seated. Try this supper exercise: Set your kitchen timer for 20 minutes. Then don't allow yourself to get up from the table until it goes off, says Dimoff. This exercise will make you realise how quickly you eat, she says. It takes about 20 minutes for the brain to realise that you have swallowed food. So if you eat more slowly, you're less likely to accidentally stuff yourself.

Focus on food. Focusing on tasting and

WOMEN ASK WHY

Why do so many men love meat-and-potato meals?

Many men will say they crave protein. They'll say that a vegetarian meal just can't satisfy their hunger like a good juicy steak and a nice buttery baked potato can. While it's true that a low-fat meal based on plant foods will be digested more quickly and leave you feeling hungry sooner than a meal with more protein and fat will, most men who think a meal isn't a meal without meat and potatoes think so because their fathers were also meat-and-potatoes men. If a woman comes from a household where supper was always dictated by her father's appetite, she could conceivably be a meat-and-potato-lover, too.

It's all about foods that we considered familiar in the past — "comfort foods." For someone who was raised on the stuff, roast beef and mashed potatoes are not only gastronomically satisfying but they're also emotionally satisfying.

To deal with a husband who turns up his nose at anything you prepare that doesn't hark back to his father's tastes, start by choosing alternatives to meat that men are likely to respond to. Chances are practically nil, for instance, that serving tofu seven days a week will fly. But there's room for compromise — say, a supper of pasta with vegetables or fish or poultry with rice.

Enlist your man in the process of buying and preparing food, cut down on meaty meals gradually, and maybe even promise one "real" meal a week. The key, however, is to convince him that meat-free meals are real meals. After all, he'll get plenty of protein with these foods, too, and maybe he'll find a few new "comfort foods" to pass on to the next generation.

Expert consulted
Jeanne Goldberg, R.D., Ph.D.

smelling what you eat will help you to eat more slowly, which will help you to eat less. To help focus on your food, remember to sit down, turn off the television, and put your fork down between bites, says Ferrang.

Have a happy ending. Remember when you were a kid and you had to ask to be excused from the supper table? Take a tip from childhood. Sometimes we dive into second and third helpings at supper only because we haven't given our brains the "this meal is over" cue, says Hudnall. So once you finish your first helping, put down your fork, put your napkin on your plate, and mentally put an end to the meal.

Taking Your Diet Out to Eat

Little Things That Make a Big Fat Difference

Restaurants are famous for serving portions that only King Kong could finish. Or heart-attack-on-a-plate steak suppers. But that doesn't mean that you can't find sensible meals outside of your own kitchen. If you master four simple fat-fighting strategies, you should be able to eat out whenever you want, enjoy your food, and not gain a pound, says Elizabeth Brown, R.D. The fat-fighting strategies for eating out, feeling satisfied and fighting fat? Thinking, choosing, ordering and eating – in that order.

Dining-Out Art No. 1:
Think Ahead

Much of the secret to eating out lies in what you do before you set foot out of your house. You want to be in control when you arrive at the restaurant. That means already knowing that you are going to order a healthy, low-fat meal. Here's how to plan.

Wear something nice – but form-fitting. A precision-fitted waistband will remind you to practice portion control. It sounds crazy, but it works, says Susan Olson, Ph.D. "Your focus shifts from the sensations of the taste, smell and sight of the food to your body and how you want to look," she says.

Ruin your appetite. Yes, it's perfectly okay – in fact, it's smart – to have a low-cal snack or beverage at home before leaving for the restaurant. The snack will tame your hunger pangs so you don't gorge later on. Good choices include a few crackers with low-fat cheese or a small green salad with a bit of fat-free dressing. "This technique works on the same principle as not going to the grocer's when hungry," says Dr. Olson. "If you eat a little before you leave the house, you'll be able to make rational choices in the restaurant instead of just eating out of hunger."

Visualise yourself eating wisely. Mentally rehearse what you will order. "What you put in your mind is what your brain will follow," says Dr. Olson.

Work off the calories. If you know there's a bigger-than-usual meal in your future, exercise will help burn those extra calories. And there's a bonus: If you take your brisk stroll or quick run before dining out, you'll remember the effort that went into the workout and you'll be less likely to overdo it at mealtime.

Jot down tomorrow's menu today. Think of a restaurant meal as one of 21 healthy meals you expect to eat this week. To help you see this meal in perspective, write down what you plan to eat tomorrow and realise that you're not going to be happy if you have to cut back on tomorrow's food because of today's splurge.

Think about the trip home. How are you going to feel later as you're dabbing your lips with your napkin and getting up from the table? Satisfied or fat? You should feel pleasantly satisfied, never unpleasantly stuffed.

Dining-Out Art No.2: Make the Right Choice

Even though restaurants still feature large portions and numerous fatty dishes, owners have become increasingly sensitive and responsive to the public's growing demand for low-fat, low-calorie meals. Many have adjusted their menus accordingly. This is why you see more and more restaurants, especially those that cater to business people, who dine out much more than most of us, offering special "heart-smart" and weight-conscious dishes prepared with fewer saturated fats, less sugar and more fresh fruits and vegetables.

You'll want to make careful choices about where you'll eat and what you'll order. Here are some factors to take into consideration.

Pick the right kind. It's wise to steer clear of old-fashioned or homestyle restaurants as well as classic French establishments, which will have pretty rich dishes, and Continental restaurants, which usually feature heavy sauces and big portions of starches and meats, says Aliza Green,

a restaurant consultant and former chef. Her recommendation? Ethnic restaurants, including Thai, Chinese, Italian, Mediterranean, Greek, Turkish, North African and the like. "In most ethnic places you can get a lot more vegetables and grains and lighter sauces, and the more authentic the restaurant, the better." Of course, she warns, "you still have to be careful. In some Italian restaurants, for example, the most popular dish is fettuccine Alfredo, which is loaded with cream and butter."

Get the lower-fat main courses. From fast food to Chinese, just about every type of restaurant has at least one edible lower-fat dish. According to nutritionists, here are some safe picks.

Mexican: Chicken fajitas and chicken burritos, but skip the guacamole and soured cream

Fast food: Salad with low-fat dressing, the grilled chicken sandwich, or the smallest burger without mayo and special sauce

Deli: A turkey breast or lean roast beef sandwich with mustard

Italian: Spaghetti with red or white clam sauce

Chinese: Szechuan prawns, stir-fried vegetables, prawns in garlic sauce, or chicken chow mein. And request that they be prepared with just a little oil.

Pizza shop: Pizza with vegetable toppings instead of pepperoni, sausage, or extra cheese and the thin crust instead of the deep-dish version

Know the language. There are particular key words and phrases on a restaurant menu that generally spell trouble for dieters. Here are some menu words to stay away from: buttery, buttered, butter sauce, sautéed, fried, pan-fried, breaded, glazed, crispy, creamy, creamed, in cream sauce, in its own gravy, au gratin, Parmesan, in cheese sauce, escalloped, au lait, á la mode, au fromage, stewed, basted, prime, hash, pie, Hollandaise, deep-fried, dipped in batter, batter-fried, tempura, bisque, Alfredo (butter-and-cheese sauce), carbonara (butter-and-cheese sauce plus bacon), casserole (could contain undetermined, and often rich, sauces or other fatty ingredients), stuffed with cheese or meat, large, extra-large, jumbo, piled-high or stacked and – last but not least – all you can eat.

Does it sound like there's nothing left? There is. Here's a list of words to eat by: pickled, tomato sauce, cocktail sauce, steamed, poached, in broth, in its own juice, garden fresh, roasted, stir-fried, chargrilled, grilled, roasted, braised or baked, Florentine (spinach), primavera (with vegetables; this is fine if it's not in cream sauce), marinara (tomato sauce) and stuffed with vegetables or herbs.

Try many restaurants. While one deli may make a sandwich with plenty of whole-grain bread, lots of relish and sauerkraut, and beef with excess fat trimmed off, the next might make one with fatty beef, high-calorie Thousand Island dressing, and mounds of cheese. Rather than avoid all of one type of restaurant, shop around. Do a little menu investigating. You can check out all of the Mexican places, for example, and then decide on the healthiest. Just avoid the obvious fry pits where the restaurant counter is a window on the side of a trailer and the cashier wears a stained paper hat.

WOMAN TO WOMAN

Inside Tips from a Restaurant Reviewer

Describing Joan Zoloth as just another restaurant-goer is a little like saying the Grand Canyon is only a hole in the ground. As a restaurant reviewer, Joan does battle with mouthwatering appetizers and scrumptious desserts on an almost daily basis. And she knows how to handle the hazards in a menu and maintain a healthy weight.

I really have two styles of eating out: one for work and one for pleasure. As a restaurant reviewer, I have to eat foods that aren't conducive to weight management. I eat out about four times a week, and each time I have to try an appetizer, a main course and dessert. I know other reviewers who only take a taste of each dish, but I like food too much to do that.

I've heard lots of great eating-out tips, but there are only a few that I follow. When eating out for pleasure, I stay away from appetizers and desserts, unless it's something too good to pass up. Usually, that means it's something I can't make at home. If I must have dessert, I always try to pick a fruit one. Or I split desserts and appetizers with someone.

Many menus now use some kind of key or symbol to indicate healthier items, which helps diners choose wisely. I used to think that pasta was automatically healthy. But if it's covered with Alfredo sauce, that's not so. Most often, I order fish as my main course. Even then, I finish the vegetable portion of my meal and leave part of the main dish.

Coupled with ordering smart menu choices, I also exercise – in part to work off the calories. So when I eat out, I find myself thinking, "Now I'll have to run X number of miles to make up for this."

I'm convinced that exercise and smart menu choices are the reasons that I'm far from fitting the portly image that people have of restaurant reviewers.

Appetise lightly. Generally, you want to stay away from fried veggies and cheese. Instead, opt for clear broth soups, fresh vegetables, or prawn cocktail. Vegetable and bean soups are often good choices because they are filling. Just avoid any soup with a name beginning with "cream of," says Brown.

Know your salads. Don't let the word *salad* on the menu lull you into thinking that it's automatically a wise choice, says Green. Caesar salad, for example, is a very popular salad in Italian restaurants. "But it's one of the worst things you can order," she says. "Chefs use mayonnaise and cheese in the dressing, and plenty of it. And the croutons are fried in oil." Similarly, salad bars may look like safe havens for dieters, but watch out. Ladling on those creamy, high-fat dressings, sprinkling on handfuls of croutons or bacon bits, and gobbling down mayonnaise-packed potato and macaroni salads can turn your light meal into a caloric nightmare.

Watch the sidelines. Sometimes the fattiest part of a restaurant meal isn't the main course or dessert, it's the side dish. Be sure to order vegetables that are steamed, not cooked with butter or cream sauce. And watch what you put on your vegetables once they arrive at the table. You're better off using sour cream rather than butter on your baked potato, for instance, because a tablespoon of butter has over four times more fat than a tablespoon of sour cream. Other options include a little low-fat ranch dressing or some grated Parmesan cheese.

Have dessert. You don't have to say no automatically when the dessert trolley is wheeled over, says Hope S. Warshaw, R.D. "Depending on the restaurant, you can opt for various sweets that are kind to your waistline. Try sorbet. Or lemon ice, which is offered in some Italian

restaurants." Other options, says Warshaw, are fresh raspberries or strawberries with a bit of liqueur. "Also, some family-style restaurants offer low-fat frozen yogurt," she adds.

Bypass the buffet table. Try to steer clear of those one-price, all-you-can-eat places. If at some point you get stuck at one of these places, don't begin filling your plate until you first look

YOUR RESTAURANT SURVIVAL GUIDE

This handy cheat sheet can help you make the best choices in any tempting out-to-eat situation. Column A lists 10 fattening foods and behaviours, and column B lists better

Column A

You leave the house famished.

Your dining companion says, "How about French food (or pizza or ribs)?" You say, "Sure."

The moment you're seated, you attack the bread basket.

You order a glass of wine to start.

Somebody orders something that sounds good, and although you hadn't intended to order it yourself, you do.

You recite your order to the waiter, no questions asked.

You eat and eat and eat.

You finish everything on your plate.

You order a slab of cheesecake.

You get in the car and lean against the door, moaning, "I'm so full!"

alternatives. Picking options in column B more often will add to your dining experience while reducing the numbers you see on the scale.

Column B

Before you leave for the restaurant, you drink a glass of water and have a celery stalk or a carrot to take the edge off your hunger.

You say, "Hmmm, how about seafood (or vegetarian or Thai food) instead?"

You drink the water poured for you and, with your companion's okay, ask the waiter to remove the bread and butter.

You continue to drink water or order tomato juice or mineral water.

You ignore what everyone else is ordering and just focus on your own meal. In fact, you don't even open the menu – you know what you can eat.

You're unsure about how a dish is prepared. You ask the waiter about it and possibly ask to have it changed – say, from fried to baked, or with the sauce on the side.

You eat and talk and eat and talk.

You leave about half of your meat or fish and ask to have it wrapped so you can take it home.

You order some sorbet and have a forkful of a companion's cheesecake.

You walk home (or take a brisk walk once you get there).

over all the selections. Then choose the lower-fat items. Be sure to start your meal with a broth soup to fill up. Then limit yourself to one trip to the buffet, says Brown.

Cut loose occasionally. As a general rule, dining out doesn't mean leaving your diet at home. However – and this is not a contradictory statement – everyone, including someone who's trying to lose weight, is entitled to have exactly what she wants in a restaurant from time to time. If you're going out to celebrate your 25th anniversary or your son's college graduation, have that piece of chocolate cake or a glass of champagne. As long as you're mindful of your weight-loss programme and return to it immediately, you can have a "sinful" restaurant meal occasionally.

Dining-Out Art No. 3: Customise Your Order

To fight fat, you'll want to give the server detailed instructions on how you want to have your food prepared and served. At first you may feel like Meg Ryan in the film *When Harry Met Sally*, who ordered her food as if she were describing how someone could navigate a car from one end of London to the other without getting stuck in traffic. But as you get used to being specific about the food you order, it will feel less awkward and more like second nature. Here are some special instructions that you should never be ashamed to voice.

Take it on the side. Never let the server ladle dressings, sauces or gravy onto your food. "Salad dressing is the largest source of fat in a woman's diet," says Jayne Hurley, R.D. If a salad comes with avocado, grated cheese, bacon bits and blue cheese dressing, for instance, you can ask the server to leave off the cheese and serve the dressing on the side. Then add just a little bit of dressing for taste. Also, ask for some vinegar on the side to water down the dressing.

If you don't see it, ask for it. "Don't be

REAL-LIFE SCENARIO

Her Weight Climbs with Her Career

Alisa can trace her weight problem back to her last promotion. As vice-president of a major advertising agency, she spends most lunches and often a few suppers a week dining with important clients. Alisa's careful about what she orders, but it's her job to portray the firm as generous, so starters, wine, and dessert are often served. Even though she religiously does aerobics four days a week, she's started to put weight on her tiny, 7.5-stone frame. What can she do to prevent weight gain?

If Alisa eats and drinks only half of what she orders, she can feel comfortable saying, "I'll have what she's having" while making clients with heartier appetites feel comfortable, too.

A couple of glasses of wine or some other alcoholic drink, however, can undermine your resolve to eat less. If Alisa is sitting with clients at a business supper, she's going to have a hard time abstaining from wine, which will weaken her resolve not to indulge. But if she drinks slowly, alternates her wine with a few sips of water, and munches on a few bites of an appetizer in between, the alcohol will be absorbed by her blood much more slowly. So drinking less alcohol will not only save her the calories from the drinks but also the calories from food that she might consume as she becomes less inhibited.

Alisa can also be smart about her main course. The simpler the preparation, the better. In other words, a simple piece of grilled fish is better than a slab of triple-layer lasagna. Dessert can also be a trap. Alisa may want to scope out the menu for good meal finishers like fruit cups, which often appear under "appetizers" instead of "desserts." If she wants to order a piece of cake, she should decide in advance that she'll leave some on her plate.

Expert consulted
Marsha Hudnall, R.D.

afraid to make special requests," says Carole Livingston, a frequent restaurant-goer and author of *I'll Never Be Fat Again*. Nine out of ten restaurant owners surveyed by the National Restaurant Association said that if customers requested it, they would happily serve dishes with sauce or dressing on the side and cook with vegetable oil or margarine instead of highly saturated butter, lard, or shortening. And eight out of ten of these eager-to-please restaurateurs added that they would gladly bake or grill chicken or fish rather than fry it.

"If you don't see a simple pasta dish on the menu, for example, but you do see that the restaurant serves other dishes that contain pasta or tomatoes or vegetables, ask for pasta prepared with vegetables in a tomato-based sauce," says Livingston. "Ask the chef to put things together. Often, the better the restaurant, the easier it is to make alternate choices."

Ban the butter. Ask your dining companions if it's okay to move the complimentary bread and butter to their side of the table. Better yet, have the server remove them altogether.

Be wise about size. Don't think that just because you paid for the food, you have to finish every morsel. "Restaurant portions are unisize and unisex, so they're usually too big for most women," says Green. Ask for a doggy bag and take the rest of the food home for another meal. In fact, have the server put half of your meal in a take-home container before the food is actually served. That way you won't be tempted to eat the whole thing.

Order first. By doing so, you'll be less tempted to have some of the other, more fattening dishes that your companions may choose.

Ask questions about the menu. To avoid confusion, some people are better off not looking at the menu. If you've been watching what you eat for any length of time, you already have a pretty good idea of what you can have and what you can't. Ask for specifics about the specials; even if they don't have exactly what you want, at the vast majority of restaurants you can still get baked or grilled poultry or fish, a simple pasta dish, steamed vegetables, and fruit for dessert. Remember, the menu is there to tempt you, but you're there to make choices.

Milk it. Ask the server to bring you skimmed milk for your coffee. Unless you ask, you can expect to be served single cream.

Make a side dish your main course. You don't have to order an main course. Instead, try appetizers or side dishes as a main course.

Dining-Out Art No. 4: Eat with Pleasure

Once your food arrives on the plate, you can still take some steps to ensure that you won't take fat home on your thighs. Here's how to dine like a fat-fighter.

Look around. Remember to take in the atmosphere. Is there a fireplace? Do you like the artwork on the walls? What kind of flowers are on the table? How's your conversation going? All these things can enhance your dining pleasure as well as help you eat more slowly. The end result? You'll eat less.

Breathe deeply. Often when we go out to eat, we focus our attention on how long it's taking the server to bring us our meal. Then, when it finally comes, we devour it without tasting it. This time, when the server puts your food on the table, don't pick up your fork right away. Instead pause and enjoy the appearance and aroma of the food for a few seconds, then remind yourself to relax and eat slowly.

Satisfy your thirst. Drink plenty of water throughout the meal, and you'll eat less. Order a bottle of mineral water for the table, or ask the server to bring a jug of tap water.

Go native. In a Chinese or Thai restaurant, use the chopsticks (especially if you don't use them well). It will slow you down, and you'll get full before you can eat the whole meal.

Lose the race. Have an unspoken competition with your dining partners to be the last person to finish eating. Men and women with weight problems tend to eat fast and are usually the first ones in any given group to be finished.

Focus on chatting, not chewing. Talking more and eating less is the secret to enjoying your meal without overindulging, says Dr. Olson.

Dare I Do Dessert?

Selections You Can Live With

Over the millennia, women have added umpteen foods to their "forbidden" list: cheesecake, chocolate, pudding, ice cream, cupcakes and biscuits. Indeed, today's forbidden list usually consists of desserts. And it sets us up for trouble, says Susan Olson, Ph.D.

"The minute a woman says she can't have something, it becomes especially appealing," says Dr. Olson. "Then, if she does eat it, she'll probably binge, thinking that she should get it while she can. On the other hand, once she knows she can have that food, she won't want it as often."

So instead of banning particular foods from your diet, isolate your true passion foods. Then be sure to work those passions into your diet and cut back on other foods that you won't miss, says Toni Ferrang, R.D. If chocolate is your passion, for instance, pick a satisfying portion – say, two or three good quality chocolates – and be sure to have it on selected days, says Dr. Olson. (Ever think you'd be forcing yourself to eat chocolate?)

Sampling what you like most helps to avoid binge eating. But eating small amounts of dessert on a regular basis can also cut down on unnecessary snacking, says Dr. Olson. When you eat something sweet after a meal, you provide your brain with the signal it needs to know that the meal is over. Without something sweet, you may not feel satisfied. And you'll be searching through the kitchen all night looking for something to munch on.

Halving Your Cake and Eating It, Too

When you're working desserts into your fat-fighting plan, you need to pay attention to the portion size and fat content. Here's how.

Follow the law of fours. Ask yourself, "Do I need dessert every day? Do I physically crave it that often?" The answer is probably no, says Denise T. Garner, R.D. So instead of having dessert every day, aim to have it four times a week, she says. Then make your dessert days coincide with your exercise days. That way you won't feel guilty about indulging.

Don't eat fat you don't need. Just as you

don't want something sweet every day of the week, you probably don't physically crave the sweetest, fattiest dessert you can think of as often as four times a week, says Garner. So on the dessert days when your tongue isn't telling you to eat cheesecake, chocolate chip biscuits or fudge, go for lower-fat sweets such as fig bars, fruit, fat-free frozen yogurt, sorbet, angel food cake or ginger snaps, she says. Try making a fresh fruit sundae with low-fat iced milk or frozen yogurt and berries, for instance.

Satisfy your sweet tooth with fruit. Few things taste as refreshing as fresh, seasonal fruit. You can purée fresh fruits like strawberries, then pour the mixture into ice cube trays and freeze it. Or you can make a fruit shake by mixing sliced bananas, skimmed milk, cinnamon and vanilla in a blender. To make it easy to whip up fruit shakes quickly, keep peeled, sliced fruit in plastic bags in your freezer. When you crave a shake, you can just purée the fruit in a food processor until smooth.

Bake a less-fattening cake. One trick to creating wonderful, light desserts without sacrificing taste is to take a favourite recipe (or one that catches your eye) and make a few clever substitutions for high-fat and high-sugar ingredients. Fruit juice, for example, can add considerably more flavour than plain old white sugar. Cocoa powder is a fill-in for full-fat chocolate. And marshmallow cream, used instead of butter or margarine, makes a rich, creamy, low-fat frosting. Puréed prunes will moisten any chocolate recipe so you won't need as much butter or shortening. (If a recipe calls for 250 g of butter, use 150 ml of prune puree and 155 g of butter. If you don't want to purée the prunes yourself, you can buy prune butter or baby-food prunes.) And if your recipe includes nuts, toast them first at 180°C, Gas 4 to intensify their flavour and then use less than the recipe calls for. Here's a list of quick and easy substitutions.

- 250 ml of evaporated skimmed milk instead of 250 ml of double cream
- 250 ml of skimmed milk instead of 250 ml of whole milk
- 60 ml of fat-free egg substitute instead of one medium whole egg
- Three tablespoons of cocoa powder dissolved in two tablespoons of water and mixed with one tablespoon of prune purée instead of 30 g of baking chocolate
- 125 ml of fruit purée plus 125 g butter instead of 250 g of butter (for baking)
- 125 ml of applesauce or 60 ml of applesauce and 60 ml of buttermilk instead of 125 ml of oil (for baking)
- 250 ml of plain non-fat yogurt instead of 250 ml of sour cream
- 125 ml of marshmallow cream instead of 125 g of butter (for icing)
- 90 to 125 g of chocolate chips instead of 185 g of chocolate chips
- One teaspoon of coconut flavouring instead of 125 g of shredded coconut

Do three bites. On days when you crave the likes of Death by Chocolate, take your chosen dessert – yes, any dessert – and have three normal-size bites. When you take the first bite, don't swallow right away. Hold it in your mouth. Let it slowly melt on your tongue. Enjoy it. Really taste it. Then take two more bites exactly the same way. Wrap up whatever is left and save it for tomorrow. "I always tell people to pick whatever they want because it satisfies them more. Then limit the portion," says Diane Wilke, R.D.

Fine-tune your portion vision. Pre-packaged desserts will often tell you how many servings make up a cake or pie. When most women slice one piece at a time from a cake,

WOMEN ASK WHY

Why do women crave chocolate and men crave meat?

Women sometimes indulge in chocolate because they feel lonely or sad. If you're looking for the perfect mood food, chocolate fills the bill. Like all melt-in-the-mouth, high-carbohydrate foods, chocolate is both soothing and stimulating. The active chemical compounds in chocolate, similar to one of the chemicals found in marijuana, can actually improve your mood. On top of that, chocolate causes your brain to produce the same feel-good chemicals it produces when you're in love.

It's no big surprise, then, that we women crave a couple of pieces of chocolate once in a while. It's no surprise, either, that so many women are self-described chocoholics.

Men have their own addictions. If a man eats in response to an emotion, it's anger that is most likely the trigger. Meat is the perfect mood food for working out anger or frustration because it takes effort to chew. Guys are going to want a couple of cheeseburgers or (even better) a big, juicy steak that they can really sink their teeth into. When you chomp down on food like that, your jaw is tight. Unlike chocolate, which melts passively in your mouth, meat has to be chewed aggressively.

When women feel anger or other strong emotions, we also feel the need for something really chewy. It may not be meat, although we sometimes crave that, too, but certainly something crunchy like crackers, crisps, biscuits or nuts.

In light of all that, it's pretty tough to cut something that tastes as good as chocolate out of your diet. So don't do it. Eating small amounts of chocolate may actually prevent you from overindulging later on. If you do get the urge to eat a whole bag of Smarties, though, it may be a sign that you need to take a look at how you're feeling.

Expert consulted
Susan Olson, Ph.D.

however, they end up with fewer servings than the package says because they cut the slices too large, says Garner. So instead of cutting one piece at a time, slice the cake or pie into exactly the number of portions that the package indicates and then remove your slice.

Wash down cake with coffee. Coupling a dessert with a flavoured coffee, which only adds about 10 calories, can bring your meal to a very satisfying close.

Freeze away temptation. You want to eat just one small serving of dessert a day, especially if you've chosen the most fattening of desserts as your passion food. At home, remove the temptation of eating more than your share by cutting your daily allotment and then storing the rest in the freezer. That way, the food isn't as readily available to eat.

Resisting Temptation

Sometimes you'll be tempted to eat way more chocolate chip biscuits than your eating plan could ever call for. Here are some ways to help you avoid overindulging.

Shroud the Godiva chocolates. You bought them as a hostess gift. But you're contemplating eating a few, then probably a few more. Instead put the box in a brown paper bag. When a study team headed by Maria Simonson, Sc.D., put all of the doughnuts on a coffee trolley in brown paper bags, the rate of purchase by factory workers fell by 50 percent. What works for doughnuts (about 58 percent fat) should work for chocolate (about 63 percent fat).

Post-it to yourself. If you often eat dessert late at night and you want to kick the habit, stick some notes to your refrigerator door. Here are some ideas.

- Closed for the evening.
- Breakfast comes soon.
- Drink iced water.
- Have a mint.
- Toothpaste your palate.
- Walk around the block.
- Are you really hungry, or just bored?

Save dessert for later. If you're an evening snacker and you usually eat dessert at supper, Dr. Simonson advises saving the dessert for later. Gradually cut back on the size of the portion, and eat it early in the evening.

Charm your mouth. Avoid having your dessert late at night, because the calories will slowly make their way to your thighs while you sleep. So if you are a 10 o'clock snacker, suck on a mint or fruit-flavoured sweet instead of opting for biscuits, says Dr. Simonson. "It helps alleviate the need for something to chew and taste," she says. If you want something to sip late at night, Dr. Simonson recommends iced water. "It can fill you up and eliminate your craving. Many people always keep a glass of iced water by the bed." Or try low-fat

WOMAN TO WOMAN

She Challenged Her Cravings and Won

Lesli Hicks, a technical writer in Leicester, loved dessert and yearned for it all the time. Cakes, pies, pastries and sweets were staples in her diet. With some lifestyle changes, she curbed her cravings, reprogrammed her tastebuds, and lost nearly 2 stone. This is her story.

A trim 7.5 stone in school, I was pushing 10 stone by my 10-year class reunion. I wasn't obese, just pleasantly plump. But it wasn't comfortable.

Looking back, it's hard to believe I didn't weigh more. Often I'd eat dessert – cakes or pastries – right after work. My biggest weaknesses were desserts containing chocolate or icing sugar, such as cakes, pastries and custards. But I regularly gobbled an entire bag of peanut butter cups. The cravings overpowered me.

Faced with my 10-year reunion, I needed to regain control.

I bit the bullet – and the apple, substituting fruits and vegetables for doughnuts and cakes. It worked. The healthy foods provided more energy, so I started exercising, doing a session of abdominal crunches three times a week, 100 jumping jacks at a stretch, weight lifting and hiking.

Nearly 2 stone lighter, I'm more alert and have more energy than ever. Now and then I have a peanut butter cup, but the chocolate company's sales probably have dropped noticeably.

If someone gives me a dessert gift, I give it away or share it at work. Now I go for weeks without dessert. I've changed my life, not just my diet.

or skimmed milk, she says.

Make up for it tomorrow. So it's your birthday. Someone cuts you the largest piece of cake you've ever seen – and you eat it. Don't get discouraged. Just put in some extra time exercising that week, says Garner.

Be Beverage Aware
Calories and Fat Are Too Easy to Swallow

Water. About 70 percent of the world's surface is covered by it. It makes up almost 65 percent of your body's total weight. It's pretty much everywhere but in our glasses. Given a choice between a plain glass of water and fizzy drink or fruit juice, most of us will choose the fizzy drink or fruit juice.

If you want to drop a few pounds – or a few dress sizes – water can be your new best friend. It's far too easy to consume a lot of calories from other beverages. A 375-ml can of regular cola, for instance, has about 150 calories. Besides calories, other diet saboteurs lurk inside the festive-looking containers of fruit juices, fizzy drinks and wine coolers – saboteurs such as caffeine, high-fructose corn syrup (sometimes labelled "fruit sugar") and alcohol. So your choice of beverages can sometimes pack on as many pounds as your favourite ice cream.

Wet Your Whistle with Water

Water is, without a doubt, the best beverage choice for losing weight. Not only is it fat- and calorie-free but it can also help you eat less. Here's why.

You'll feel full. "If you drink water or have a bowl of broth-based soup before a meal, it takes up the space in your stomach that you would otherwise fill with food," says Felicia Busch, R.D. Research shows, she says, that filling up on liquids decreases the number of calories you eat in a meal.

You'll burn more calories. Drinking enough water helps your body operate under optimal conditions and may help you perform at peak metabolism. This in turn means that you may be better able to burn off fat. Drinking iced water burns a few more calories because the body heats the water to its own temperature.

Your hands and mouth are busy. If your hands and mouth are already occupied, you're less likely to eat. This trick works well at parties, where people congregate around the buffet table while stuffing themselves with hors d'oeuvres. If you have a glass of water, you can sip, not eat.

Get Your Fill of H₂O

Camels can go for long periods of time without water, but people can't. Water is an important part of every cell in your body, and it acts as the base in which all chemical reactions, like digestion, take place. It also plays a significant role in regulating your body temperature. So it's important to drink adequate amounts every day. "People who want to lose weight should drink more than 2 litres of water a day," Busch says. She recommends drinking 130 ml of water for every 10 pounds of body weight. Thus, a 12-stone woman should drink almost 2.25 litres of water. That's more than a half-gallon a day. Seem a little hard to swallow? Here's how to make water more appetizing and get your daily quota.

Buy bottled. If tap water doesn't appeal to your tastebuds, buy bottled water, suggests Busch. Drinking water that's already measured in bottles also makes it easier to gauge your daily intake.

Make citrus your main squeeze. If plain water doesn't float your boat, try adding a twist of lemon or some lime juice, says Ann Dubner, R.D.

Perk it up with fruit juice. For even more flavour, dilute a quarter of a glass of fruit juice with water, says Donna Weihofen, R.D.

Drink all day. Keep a glass of water nearby all day and take a sip every 15 minutes. "You'll be

WOMEN ASK WHY

If alcohol has no fat, why is it so fattening?

While there isn't any fat in alcohol, when you consume too many calories, you're going to store that excess energy as fat. In other words, you don't need to eat fat to get fat: Just as when you overindulge in carbohydrate and protein, you're going to pack on the pounds if you drink too much beer, brandy, or bourbon. With alcohol, the propensity for gaining body fat is even greater since gramme for gramme, alcohol supplies more energy than either carbohydrate or protein: One gramme of fat provides nine calories, alcohol has seven, and carbohydrate and protein each have four.

If alcohol itself can be fattening, the *effect* of drinking alcohol can be even more fattening. As you drink, your body's natural food intake regulators tend to be blunted and you become less and less inhibited around food. Psychologically, alcohol can really reduce the amount of control you have over what you put on your fork and into your mouth. This disinhibiting effect is another reason that drinkers can put on weight.

One way to avoid the fattening aspects of alcohol is to limit how much and how often you drink, thereby limiting the number of calories you consume from alcohol or food. One way to avoid the temptation to overindulge is to drink non-alcoholic beverages first, preferably drinks low in calories such as water or vegetable juice (fruit juice is a little higher in calories). Filling up on finger foods like vegetables and crackers before and while you drink will slow absorption and the disinhibiting effects of the alcohol you do drink, thus helping you to cut out a lot of calories.

Expert consulted
Johanna Dwyer, R.D., D.Sc.

surprised by how you can end up drinking a litre of water throughout the day without even realising it," says Dubner. And if you prefer cold water, simply fill a water bottle halfway and put it in the freezer overnight. The ice should provide cool water all day long as you refill your bottle.

Drink before you eat. Drinking a glass or two of water before meals helps take the edge off hunger so you eat less, says Dubner. Also, since many people mistake thirst for hunger, try having a glass of water the next time you want to snack.

The Diet Soft Drink Myth

Calorie-conscious women and diet soft fizzy drinks seem to go together like hot summer days and lemonade. And it seems to make good sense. After all, diet drinks have no calories, just like water. And taste better. So they should be right up there with water as great fat-fighting beverages, right?

Not quite. Researchers found that women who drink beverages loaded with artificial sweeteners such as aspartame may actually eat more food. Researchers compared the food intakes of women who drank slightly less than four drink cans' worth of aspartame-sweetened lemonade over the course of a day to those of women who drank the same amount of sugar-sweetened lemonade. The women who had the artificially sweetened lemonade ate more during the day following the test than those who had regular lemonade.

WHAT YOU GET IN LATTE LAND

Skimmed milk or whole?

Whipped cream or not?

Those gourmet coffee shops that are popping up on street corners across Britain have given us more than just a new place to meet and make friends. They've given us a whole new way to filter fat into our diet.

Going from plain, ordinary coffee to gourmet renditions has taken us from a modest 10 calories and no fat per brew to as much as 300 calories and 21 grammes of fat.

Is it necessary to add all those calories and fat grammes to make a great-tasting coffee drink? We decided to find out. A group of coffee connoisseurs (six of our colleagues) took it upon themselves to sample the choices at a typical coffeehouse, trying to discern which fat and calories were expendable and which were absolutely essential to the full coffee experience. Here are our tasters' choices. (The following beverage information comes from Starbucks, one of the new chains of coffee shops in the country; the nutrition information is based on a 375-ml "tall" serving.)

Caffè latte. A shot of espresso mixed with warm milk and 1 cm of foamed milk. Here's the comparison when it's made with different ingredients.

➤ With whole milk: 210 calories and 11 grammes of fat

➤ With reduced-fat (2 percent) milk: 170 calories and 6 grammes of fat

➤ With skimmed milk: 120 calories and less than a gramme of fat

The tasters found that the latte with whole milk had a slightly creamier, heavier consistency; with skimmed, it had a stronger coffee flavour. The froth lasted longer on the latte with whole milk. The consensus was that a latte could be served with skimmed milk with little noticeable difference.

Caffeine makes you hungry by lowering your blood sugar, and it causes thirst by increasing your urine output. "Drinks loaded with caffeine are nutritionally worthless," says Busch,

Cappuccino. A shot of espresso, steamed milk, and foamed milk. Here are the differences.

🍂 With whole milk: 140 calories and 7 grammes of fat

🍂 With reduced-fat (2 percent) milk: 110 calories and 4 grammes of fat

🍂 With skimmed milk: 80 calories and <1 gramme of fat

Tasters found the difference between whole and skimmed milk even less noticeable in the cappuccino than in the latte. As with the latte, the foam did not last as long with skimmed milk. And whole milk offered a creamier consistency, but the skimmed allowed the coffee taste to come through.

Caffé mocha. A shot of espresso mixed with 45 g of chocolate, warm milk and whipped cream. First we tested the coffee with all three types of milk and with whipped cream. Here are the results.

🍂 With whole milk: 340 calories and 21 grammes of fat

🍂 With reduced-fat (2 percent) milk: 300 calories and 16 grammes of fat

🍂 With skimmed milk: 260 calories and 12 grammes of fat

Without whipped cream, there were some big differences. Here's what we found.

🍂 With whole milk: 260 calories and 12 grammes of fat

🍂 With reduced-fat (2 percent) milk: 220 calories and 7 grammes of fat

🍂 With skimmed milk: 180 calories and 3 grammes of fat

Some of the tasters really missed the whipped cream, which gave the drink a sweet, rich, dessertlike flavour and consistency. With whipped cream, few of the tasters found much difference between a mocha made with whole milk and one made with skimmed. They offered two suggestions: If you skip the cream, at least treat yourself to whole milk. Otherwise, opt for a smaller amount of whipped cream with skimmed milk.

Coffee, Fat, and Calories

African tribal warriors first used ground coffee beans mixed with fat to heighten aggressiveness before going into battle. Like other caffeinated beverages, coffee makes you feel hungrier and thirstier. Plus, after a caffeine "rush," you may feel tired and less able to make wise food choices.

Caffeine aside, coffee drinks are often harmful to weight-loss efforts because of what we add to them. A plain cup of coffee has between 5 and 15 calories, depending on the brew, and no fat. While we may not be as bad as the African warriors who mixed fat with their coffee beans, we come close with the cream, whole milk, whipped cream, chocolate, honey and almost anything else that we put in coffee. One cup of Irish coffee, for instance, has more calories than a slice of chocolate cream pie. And adding two tablespoons of single cream to a cup of coffee increases the calories by 59 and the fat by about six grammes.

Here are a few guidelines to help you make sure those cups don't go straight to your hips or cause other health-related problems.

Drink no more than two cups a day, tops. "Sometimes when people drink too much coffee, they feel that they need to eat something to settle their stomachs," says Christina Stark, R.D. Caffeine stimulates stomach acid secretion in some people, which can cause nausea and stomach aches.

Lighten up the lighteners. Instead of adding whole milk or cream, to your coffee, opt

"so the less you drink of them, the better."

If you must drink diet fizzy drinks, however, don't drink any more than two diet beverages a day, Dubner says.

for skimmed or low-fat milk. Replacing whole milk with skimmed will save 7 to 11 grammes of fat.

Try flavoured beans. Using fruit-, vanilla-, or dessert-flavoured coffee may be a good way to get added flavour without calories or fat.

Spice it up. For great taste without added calories or fat, dust your coffee with cinnamon.

Break the pastry connection. Some people make it a habit to have their coffee along with something fattening such as cake or doughnuts, says Stark. If coffee is your cue to reach for the baked goods, she says, you have to find a way to disassociate coffee and food. In this case, switching to decaf may not help.

"Start by substituting a low-fat treat, such as digestive biscuits, for the piece of pie or cake that you would normally have," says Elizabeth Brown, R.D. Then gradually try to wean yourself from the habit of having an accompanying treat. Adding a little milk or cinnamon to your coffee might help you to think of it as dessert so you'll still feel satisfied, she says.

Give Alcohol the Push

Trying to save calories by skipping lunch so that you can indulge at happy hour doesn't work (although many try that strategy). Studies show that very few people decrease their food intake when they drink alcohol. It's easy to drink many more calories than you would ever consciously

---

DECEPTIVE DRINKING

Few calorie-counters are surprised to learn that a cheeseburger has 359 calories and 20 grammes of fat. They may even be prepared for the news that an accompanying shake has 340 calories. Yet they may very well be astonished to learn that a bottle or can of their favourite beverage can contain nearly as many calories as a cheeseburger or a shake – even though the information appears on the container.

Why do otherwise-savvy dieters get duped? Because many containers hold two or more servings, not one, and beverage labels often list the calorie content for only one serving, which is usually 250 ml.

Who drinks only half of a bottle of juice or other beverage and saves the other half for the next day? Hardly anyone. So in essence, we are fooled even though the information is right before our eyes, albeit not readily obvious.

Here you'll find the calorie totals for some of the most popular canned and bottled beverages – the whole thing, not just 250 ml.

---

consume from food, and high-fat bar food, such as peanuts, nachos and crisps, does little to help the diet cause.

Second, as you probably could guess by the way your mouth feels the morning after, alcohol dehydrates you. So you can't count alcoholic drinks as part of your daily liquid intake, Busch says. Instead, you'll need to drink even more water to counteract each alcoholic drink you down. No one knows how much, though, as there haven't been any studies yet, she says.

If you don't drink, count yourself ahead of the game. If you decide to indulge, these tips can help you make the best choices for your waistline.

Go with one. Don't exceed one standard serving of alcohol a day. You can take your pick

Drink	Portion (ml)	Calories
McDonald's shake (chocolate, vanilla or strawberry)	425	340
Ocean Spray cran-grape	500	340
Coca-Cola	625	250
Fruitopia Strawberry Passion Awareness	500	240
Snapple kiwi strawberry cocktail	500	220
Bartles & Jaymes original wine cooler	375	200
Snapple lemon iced tea	500	200
Special Recipe Natural Brew draft root beer	375	180
Celestial Seasonings Raspberry Zinger tea	500	160
Beer	375	146

The higher the proof, the more calories it contains. So for weight-watchers, it makes sense to order the brand of liquor with the lowest proof, Payne says.

Make it skimmed. If you like drinks such as white Russians or Kahlúa and cream, ask for skimmed milk, not whole milk, as the base, Payne says.

Go halvesies. For drinks made with a shot of alcohol and soda water or mineral water, get a half-shot of the alcohol and more mineral water to reduce the calories, says Payne. Be careful, though, that the bartender doesn't use a high-calorie mixer like 7-Up.

The Truth about Fruit Juice

What do a glass of orange juice, cranberry juice and grapefruit juice have in common? (a) They all have tons of vitamin C. (b) They're good for your health. (c) They can make you fat.

The answer: All of the above.

Some fruit juices have more calories than sweetened fizzy drinks. A 500-ml bottle of Ocean Spray cran-grape juice has more than 300 calories, while a 375-ml can of Fanta has about 150. Many fruit juices contain high-fructose (fruit sugar) corn syrup. Despite this, 100 percent fruit juices are still better choices than the Fantas and colas because they have nutrients, Busch says. And unlike the fizzy drinks, you can reduce the calories from fruit juice. Here's how to do it.

Water it down. You can easily make fruit juice a diet drink by adding more water to it, Busch says. If you're making juice from concentrate, try making two jugs of juice from one can of concentrate. You'll cut your calories in half, and you'll get more for your money. If you like

of either a 375-ml beer, 50 ml of hard liquor, or 16 ml of wine. If you enjoy an occasional drink, you can still have it without doing too much damage to your diet.

Begin with a virgin. Since we often gulp down our first drink most quickly, start with a non-alcoholic beverage, says Natalie Payne, R.D. Then, when the lower-calorie drink begins to fill you up, have your alcoholic beverage.

Big is better. Order a tall glass with more mixer. The bartender can then dilute the high-calorie alcohol with more soda water or diet ginger ale. Also, the larger drink will last longer, so you may not be as likely to order a second, says Weihofen.

Ask for a lower proof. Here's a simple rule:

the fizz of carbonated drinks, another alternative is to make juice with sparkling water instead of tap water, Weihofen says.

In fact, diluted fruit juice doubles as a great low-calorie sports drink.

Swilling Secrets

As you venture out in pursuit of beverage variety, these additional guidelines may help you make smart choices.

Milk does a diet good. If late-night eating is your downfall, you might want to try drinking a glass of low-fat or skimmed milk instead of eating, says Maria Simonson, Sc.D. It's a good, low-fat alternative to the cake, biscuits or other treats we might otherwise consume.

Check the label. Although some people believe that any clear beverage is good for you, "white doesn't make it right," says Busch. Many clear beverages sold as sparkling or flavoured water are really sweetened fizzy drinks in disguise. So read the label to make sure there are no added calories.

November December January

Holiday Helpings
No Time for a Guilt Trip

Many women can gain about five to seven pounds between Christmas and New Year's. But if you had to guess when we are most likely to put on those pounds, would you pick (a) New Year's Eve Party, (b) Christmas supper, (c) Hanukkah celebrations, (d) all of the above, (e) none of the above.

The answer? None of the above. "It's not one meal that adds on the five to seven pounds that you pick up during the holidays," says Denise T. Garner, R.D. "It's all of that extra nibbling day after day."

For many women, this nibbling starts as early as Halloween, when there are often tons of sweets at home and at work, says Garner.

"There's more access to food around these celebrations; it tends to be a very social time," says Ronna Kabatznick, Ph.D. "Neighbours invite you for drinks, family members invite you to supper, co-workers invite you to office parties, and there are sweets on people's desks at work. These ongoing food temptations make it much harder to stick to your regular eating habits," she says.

Party Training

You can avoid that slow, steady holiday weight gain while still having a good time. Here's how to participate in the party atmosphere without gaining weight.

Don't starve ahead. Many of us skip a few meals to leave room for a big eating event. While your appetite may be stronger, your enjoyment of the experience won't be improved. "By supper, you'll be starving, so you won't make good decisions about what you eat," says Barbara Whedon, R.D.

Load up with lean before the party. Instead of cutting back on meals before a big event, appease your appetite with some low-fat food beforehand. "If you curb your appetite, you can make better choices," says Whedon. Some good pre-party fare includes soup or a few pieces of fruit. By taking in at least some calories before the big event, you'll take the edge off your appetite and help keep yourself from going overboard.

Pick just four. Whether it's hors d'oeuvres or

desserts, limit yourself to four samplings, says Garner. That means fresh vegetables with one tablespoon of dip, one spinach ball, one mini egg roll and one cube of cheese. For dessert, you can have a taste of pecan pie, one forkful of cheesecake, a bite of fudge and one biscuit. If you feel awkward taking such small portions, give the rest to a friend. This way you can taste the four foods you really want without loading up on calories.

Talk more. The more you talk, the less you'll eat, says Garner.

Begin with the buffet. While this is usually where a party's heartiest – and heaviest – fare resides, you should be able to scavenge at least a few good-tasting items that don't contain fat in the double digits. "Some good choices are things like prawn cocktail, fruit salad and any vegetable that's light on the dip," Whedon says. A large steamed prawn has only about 5 calories, with just a trace of fat. At 45 calories per tablespoon, you can even have some cocktail sauce.

And don't forget the pretzels, which are also low in fat. "If there's a cold-meat platter, stick with turkey or lean roast beef," Whedon adds. By contrast, other meats, such as bologna, salami and pepperoni, and most cheeses are extremely high in fat.

Favour the hostess with something fat-free. Take a light alternative, such as a vegetable platter or fruit plate, to the party. Even non-alcoholic beer or sparkling grape juice makes a nice offering. These make warm and generous gifts to the hostess, and they give you something to nibble on or sip that you won't feel guilty about.

WOMEN ASK WHY

Why do I feel so tired after a big Christmas meal?

The common need for a postmeal snooze can be traced to several factors, depending on what you eat and when. A traditional Christmas meal, for example, includes not only turkey but also a lot of carbohydrates that are quickly metabolised. The roast potatoes, stuffing, breadsauce and white bread are all easily broken down during digestion, leading to a rapid rise in blood sugar (glucose) levels. In response, insulin (a hormone released by your pancreas) rises to clear the bloodstream of glucose and most amino acids, but it does not substantially reduce the concentration of a particular amino acid called tryptophan, which is the precursor to the sleep-promoting neurotransmitter serotonin. With the bloodstream clear of most competitors, tryptophan can easily cross the blood/brain barrier, speeding up the brain's synthesis of this natural sleeping potion.

The time of day when you sit down for your feast can also affect how tired you feel when you polish off that last piece of Christmas pudding. Because we naturally experience a wave of drowsiness during the midafternoon, which is a likely

Give temptations the brush-off. After a few hors d'oeuvres, sneak off to the bathroom and brush your teeth. You'll be less likely to eat more cocktail sausages if you know they're going to taste like spearmint.

Pass on the plate. Instead, opt for a dainty cocktail napkin. Carry your finger foods one small portion at a time, and that's how you'll eat.

Or use a fork. When at Christmas parties, you really should be wary of most finger foods. The best foods to eat with your hands are prawns, vegetables and fruit.

time for a Christmas dinner, you'll feel the urge to nap then even if the meal itself doesn't lead to drowsiness. Our natural circadian rhythms – the cycles of waking and sleeping – trigger a drop in alertness and performance at midafternoon regardless of what we eat. And if your Christmas meal also includes alcoholic beverages such as wine – which are, after all, depressants – you're going to feel even sleepier.

One way to re-energise after a postmeal slump is to take a short walk before surrendering yourself to that coma in your recliner. But you can avoid the slump in the first place by balancing the carbohydrates in your meal with protein and a little bit of fat (the amount found in the gravy or stuffing will suffice) and by politely refusing that sleep-inducing wine and extra bread. Since many other factors, such as your sleep patterns, age and level of fatigue, can affect whether you fall asleep after a holiday meal, you can also prepare for the holiday and help to reduce the need for an afternoon nap by catching up on your sleep beforehand.

Expert consulted
Lynne Brown, Ph.D.

Use your other hand. This is a surprisingly effective and simple trick that works well at any party where finger foods are a fixture. Keep your drink in your dominant hand so that if you do reach for a snack, you'll have to think about it a bit more than usual.

Learn to say no. Have trouble turning down another serving of deep-fried cheese balls? Here are some suggested polite-yet-firm responses to the persuasive entreaty "Have some more...I made it just for you!"

- "No, thank you."
- "I'm full."
- "I appreciate all of your effort, and I've enjoyed every bite."
- "If you want to give me more, I can take another portion home."

"If you keep saying no, the person doing the coaxing will soon lose their power over you," says Dr. Kabatznick. When all else fails, use the medical excuse. "Many people with serious weight problems tell me that the only way they've ever gotten people to stop pushing food is by saying that they have an allergy or that they're concerned about their cholesterol or that their doctor advises against something," says Ronette Kolotkin, Ph.D.

Always keep something on your plate. During the Christmas season, an empty plate tells the host that you are hungry for more. "No one believes you're full if your plate is empty. But if your plate still has a bit of food on it, that sends the signal that you've had all you can possibly eat," says Whedon. Make sure what you leave behind is your least favourite dish. Otherwise, you might eat it, thus devouring your anti-fat shield.

Tighten your belt. Wearing something snug to the party can serve as a restraining device for your stomach, says Mindy Hermann, R.D.

Keep your hands full of anything but food. Baby pictures, a sprig of mistletoe and a camera are all good items to take with you to seasonal gatherings where food is the focus.

Visualise. "When you do a mental dress rehearsal, it's like going through the experience, so when you actually experience the event, it's easier and you make better choices because you've already practiced them," says Judy E. Marshel, R.D.

Less Seasonal Nibbling

Many of the extra calories that we swallow over Christmas are eaten unconsciously. As we bake, we may sample the dough. We try free samples at the supermarket. We have a slice of pizza at the shopping mall while looking for Christmas gifts. And we have a few too many biscuits everywhere we go. Here's how to keep those calories from turning into pounds.

Bake in the morning. You'll be less likely to sample dough, nuts and chocolate chips just after breakfast than in the afternoon or evening, says Garner. Another good trick: Try chewing gum while you bake.

Practice sweat equity. Keeping up with your exercise programme during the cold, dark winter months will go a long way towards keeping off winter weight gain, and it will help to control holiday stress as well. Do aerobics to cable exercise shows, get an exercise bike or join a gym.

You can even be active on the actual days. "If you're spending the time with children, consider going sledging or ice-skating; these are non-food-centred ways of spending time. If you're with adults, go hiking or visit a museum," says Dr. Kabatznick.

"Exercise is the best single thing you can do during this season," Dr. Kabatznick adds. "It's a tension-reliever, plus it gives you food credits so you can overindulge a bit. Swim extra laps. Walk an extra mile or two a day. Enjoy your body in

REAL-LIFE SCENARIO
She Can Escape Seasonal Weight Gain

For Carla, a January diet is as certain as fireworks on the Fifth of November. Her "rite of celebrations" starts on Christmas Eve and doesn't let up until the last sip of champagne on New Year's Eve. She's so used to gaining weight that she now buys her Christmas clothes a size larger. Is there a way for Carla to eat, drink and be merry without gaining her typical 10 pounds?

Carla probably feels like seasonal weight gain is inevitable. After all, she's gained weight during this season for as long as she can remember. So has practically everyone else she knows. The national average weight gain for Christmas time is five to seven pounds. Eating an extra 500 calories every day from Christmas Eve to New Year's is all it takes to put on five pounds. That's the equivalent of a piece of pumpkin pie and a serving of roast potatoes a day. Carla shouldn't, however, throw in the towel. She can have all of her favourites and still maintain her weight as long as she practices some strategic eating.

Carla can start by abandoning her habit of buying larger-size party clothes. That's only an invitation to gain weight. Instead, she should party in clothing that fits — perfectly. That way, once she starts eating, she'll be only too aware of her expanding belly. Her clothes will remind her to put down her buffet plate and step away from the table.

ways that don't have to do with food," she suggests.

Eat before you shop. If you fill up before you shop for gifts, you'll be less likely to munch on sweet rolls, slurp shakes and contemplate a plate of nachos.

Don't cook on empty. You know that food shopping when you're hungry is a no-no. The same advice applies to cooking festive suppers. If

To get the most out of the festivities, Carla can go for the best of the best. That means surveying the dinner table or buffet, picking out the foods that look the tastiest, and omitting foods that look ho-hum. She can opt for foods that she can only get during this time of year, such as Christmas biscuits, mince pies and fruitcake, and avoid foods that she can have at other times of the year, such as cheese, nuts and crackers. Christmas food really connects us to our families and friends. That's why our favourite foods are so valuable. So instead of saying, "I shouldn't eat any of this because it's too fattening," Carla is much better off zeroing in on seasonal, wonderful foods.

How can Carla eat such fattening stuff without gaining weight? Simply by mastering portion size. By controlling the size of the portion, she can control the number of calories she consumes. If she loves Christmas biscuits, for instance, she can designate a portion – say, two biscuits a day – and hold herself to it, as part of a well-balanced eating plan. At parties, she can try taking just one serving of all the foods she finds most appealing and holding herself to one dinner-size plate. That means not putting so much food on the plate that she has to struggle to balance it while she walks around. Also, if she samples a food on her plate and realises that it's really not as great as she imagined, she doesn't have to eat it; she can just leave it on the plate and concentrate on eating only foods that are truly delicious.

Expert consulted
Colleen Pierre, R.D.

Charlie Brown, either, since such TV dates are usually accompanied by bowls and bowls of couch-potato food. Instead, get on your stationary bike and ride from Nazareth to Bethlehem (about 70 miles as the dove flies) over the 12 days of Christmas. Or play holiday tunes on your headset while you exercise. If you just can't drag yourself away from that favourite holiday rerun, replace the snacks on your lap with those holiday cards that you've been meaning to address.

No More Stuffing Yourself Silly

Why don't we gain extra weight around summer holidays? Because we're outside cycling, walking on the beach, tossing horseshoes and playing catch with the kids. We're burning more calories, and we're not eating as many of them. A typical barbecue menu of BBQ chicken, pasta salad and watermelon doesn't pack quite the same fat and calorie punch as typical Christmas or New Year's fare, says Garner. But you can keep those three winter feasts from turning into body fat. Here's how.

Eat the chow, skim the fat. While not all Christmas calories can be easily trimmed away, you can limit the damage. If you're eating turkey, for example, a serving of white meat has less than half the fat of a comparable serving of dark meat. If you're having a roast, trim away the visible fat, including the crispy bits – they're burned fat, but they're still fat.

you're hungry and you surround yourself with food, you're bound to nibble through the preparation, and you'll probably make more food than you really need. Take the edge off by having a light but satisfying snack, such as non-fat or low-fat yogurt or digestive biscuits, before you begin to cook.

Break your date with Frosty. And don't hang out with the Grinch, Jimmy Stewart or

(continued on page 100)

HELP YOURSELF TO BETTER HOLIDAY CUISINE

Even just one helping of a typical Christmas dinner can pack more than 1,000 calories and 50 grammes of fat. (Just imagine the big fat damage when you eat seconds or thirds!) Yet you can slash half of those calories and fat grammes from these meals and still eat your favourite festive foods.

"Decide what food is most important to you, or what food is only eaten or available during that particular holiday season, and enjoy a moderate amount," says Mary Pat Bolton, R.D.,

There are also easy cooking strategies to remove fat and calories from your typical holiday fare without sacrificing flavour. Here's a holiday-by-holiday breakdown of some fat- and calorie-slashing secrets.

CHRISTMAS I

Traditional

> 155 g of roasted turkey, white and dark meat, with skin (291 calories and 14 grammes of fat)

> 185 g of bread stuffing made from a mix (356 calories and 7 grammes of fat)

> One slice (⅛ of a 23-cm pie) of homemade pumpkin pie (316 calories and 14 grammes of fat)

Slimmed-Down

> 155 g of turkey breast without skin (238 calories and 7 grammes of fat)

> 185 g of cornbread stuffing made outside the bird with chicken broth instead of lots of eggs and drippings (265 calories and 8 grammes of fat)

> One slice of pumpkin pie made with non-fat and reduced-fat dairy products (288 calories and 8 grammes of fat)

CHRISTMAS II

Traditional

> 185 g of boneless cured ham (303 calories and 15 grammes of fat)

> 250 g of mashed potatoes made with whole milk and butter (223 calories and 9 grammes of fat)

> Three homemade sugar biscuits (198 calories and 10 grammes of fat)

Slimmed-Down

> 90 g of ham (151 calories and 8 grammes of fat)

> 250 g of mashed potatoes made with non-fat soured cream and garlic (169 calories and 2 grammes of fat)

> Three gingersnaps (87 calories and 2 grammes of fat)

NEW YEAR'S DAY

Traditional

> 250 ml of eggnog (341 calories and 19 grammes of fat)

> Six to eight nachos with cheese, beans, minced beef and peppers (569 calories and 31 grammes of fat)

Slimmed-Down

> 125 ml of eggnog (171 calories and 10 grammes of fat). After you've had your eggnog, stick with sparkling water (0 calories and 0 grammes of fat) or have a glass of hot mulled cider made by simmering 1.5 litres of fresh apple juice, one cinnamon stick, three whole cloves, three allspice berries and strips of orange rind in a saucepan over medium heat for 10 to 15 minutes. Strain before serving. (63 calories and 0 grammes of fat per 250 ml).

> Twelve homemade nachos made by cutting 12 corn tortillas into quarters and topping them with low-fat Cheddar cheese, salsa, beans and

peppers (hold the beef). This makes 48 nachos (351 calories and 7 grammes of fat per 12 chips).

VALENTINE'S DAY

Traditional

- 45-g chocolate bar (207 calories and 14 grammes of fat)

Slimmed-Down

- 125 g of frozen strawberry yogurt with two tablespoons of chocolate syrup drizzled over it (192 calories and 3 grammes of fat)

EASTER

Traditional

- A basket of chocolate bunnies and eggs (143 calories and 10 grammes of fat per 30 g; for 10 30-g bunnies and eggs, 1,430 calories and 100 grammes of fat)
- 155 g of roast leg of lamb with 90 g of steamed asparagus and 90 g of boiled potatoes (456 calories and 23 grammes of fat)

Slimmed-Down

- A 30-g chocolate treat per basket, with the rest of the space filled with jelly beans (104 calories and a trace of fat per 30 g of jelly beans – about 10; for 30 g of chocolate plus 50 jelly beans, 663 calories and 10 grammes of fat)
- 90 g of lamb with 185 g of steamed asparagus and 185 g of boiled potatoes (399 calories and 15 grammes of fat)

BANK HOLIDAY PICNIC

Traditional

- Two pieces (about 185 g total) of cold, fast-food fried chicken, white meat from the breast or wing (494 calories and 30 grammes of fat)
- 250 g of potato salad (358 calories and 21 grammes of fat)

- 250 g of baked beans (382 calories and 13 grammes of fat)
- One 7.5-cm-square packaged brownie (227 calories and 9 grammes of fat)

Slimmed-Down

- Two pieces (about 250 g total) of cold, oven-fried chicken breast without the skin, baked without oil (318 calories and 8 grammes of fat)
- 250 g of potato or pasta salad made with fat-free mayonnaise (304 calories and 5 grammes of fat)
- 250 g of low-fat vegetarian baked beans (236 calories and 1 gramme of fat) or 250 g of low-fat non-vegetarian baked beans made with low-fat turkey sausage and reduced-sodium chicken broth (272 calories and 2 grammes of fat)
- One wedge of watermelon (92 calories and 1 gramme of fat)

MID-SUMMER'S BBQ

Traditional

- A 155 g barbecued hamburger (426 calories and 23 grammes of fat)
- A 90 g barbecued Italian sausage (268 calories and 21 grammes of fat)

Slimmed-Down

- A 155 g barbecued turkey burger made with lean minced turkey, minced onions, garlic, red peppers, celery and a small amount of tomato paste (289 calories and 3 grammes of fat). You can add lots of nearly fat-free toppings such as tomatoes, lettuce, pepper rings and onions.
- One-half (about 90 g) barbecued skinless chicken breast (142 calories and 3 grammes of fat)

Be careful with add-ons. Don't cover your plate with a whopping serving of stuffing and a pool of gravy. Both gravy and stuffing are often made with butter or meat drippings, which are extremely fattening.

Create borders. As you fill your plate for a festive feast, maintain a little margin of space between portions of food – just enough room so that you can still see some plate. The result? You'll automatically keep portions at a more reasonable size. A plate with 220 g of turkey, 350 g of stuffing, 125 ml of gravy, 185 g of candied sweet potatoes, 125 ml of cranberry sauce, and 185 g of green beans all smashed against one another with no space to breathe would come to 1,422 calories. The same foods on the same-size plate, but with portions cut in half to allow for space between the foods, would amount to only 711 calories.

Take off the turkey's coat. Without the skin, a 100 g serving of white turkey meat has only 157 calories, with 18 percent of that from fat. Dark meat is fattier: A 100 g skinless serving has 187 calories, with 35 percent from fat. The same-size serving of white meat with skin has 197 calories, with 38 percent of that from fat; dark meat with skin has 221 calories, with 46 percent from fat. So as long as you skip the skin, you'll do fine.

Say yes to yams. Canned candied yams have only 240 calories per 125 g serving, and many brands have no fat. Check the label to be sure. Adding butter to canned or fresh yams made at home obviously adds calories and fat.

Add a twist to Christmas baking. Make lower-fat meringue biscuits or gingersnaps instead of chocolate chip or sugar biscuits.

Be selective. When you think about it, many of the foods that we enjoy at holiday time, such as roast turkey, sweet potatoes and hot mulled apple cider, are perfectly healthful when prepared simply and eaten in reasonable quantities, points out Marshel. Focus on the peas, broccoli and lean meat, and go easy on the gravy, butter, au gratin dishes and pie.

Take it – and leave it. Chances are there's so much going on at the dinner table that few people will really notice what you have or haven't eaten. So if what you do or do not put on your plate becomes an issue, just take what's served. "If worse comes to worst, you can take the food and not eat it," says Dr. Kabatznick.

Have dessert for supper. Most Christmas meals are eaten between the normal lunch and supper hours. So there's no real reason to have another full-fledged meal around 7:00 P.M. Instead, save your dessert for that time, suggests Garner.

Practice recovery. What happens if you go completely AWOL from your fat-fighting plan? The trick to emerging from the Christmas food fest without permanently losing your weight-loss motivation is to accept the fact that you've slipped a bit and then get on with your wholesome new way of low-fat living. Immediately resume your usual food and fitness programme, no matter how many days you've been away from it.

Every Woman's Eating Plan
Strategies for Special Situations

When it comes to sticking to a weight-loss plan, not all women are created equal. Some of us have incredible demands on our time, making regular exercise difficult to fit in. Others have a harder time resisting food, mainly because it seems to be ever-present. Some of us have careers that require us to eat out nearly every day. And still others work such odd hours that breakfast becomes supper and supper becomes breakfast.

Considering the differences in lifestyle, it's no wonder that a 1,200- or 1,500-calorie eating plan may work for some women but not others. Similarly, while some weight-loss tips could change your life forever, they could be no help at all to someone else.

So when it comes right down to it, every woman must in part design an eating plan that fits her personal lifestyle, says Kristine Napier, R.D., author of *Eat to Heal*. Napier came up with the 10 most common types of women who struggle with weight. Here she offers the most up-to-date, realistic and beneficial advice on how each type of woman can modify a fat-fighting plan to fit her lifestyle.

Midlife Crash-Dieters

You may have developed the weight-loss technique way back in school. You went out with some friends. You finished off half a pizza. Then you downed the largest hot fudge sundae the ice cream place could make. And then you felt fat.

So you didn't eat anything the next day. At the end of the day, you happily looked down at your flat belly and the gap between your waist and your jeans and you knew that fasting for a day did the job. So crash dieting became the norm for you.

The problem is, sometime during your thirties, the technique stopped working as well. In your forties, it doesn't seem to work at all, at least not permanently. No matter what diet you try, from cabbage soup to eating nothing at all, you lose only a few pounds and then gain back more. As soon as you splurge on an evening of appetizers, wine, pizza and one double-scoop ice cream cone, you gain two pounds. And sipping mineral water and eating salads for a few days doesn't seem to get rid of the weight the way it used to.

It's time to get off the calorie roller coaster.

You need to take a challenging but important step: Start eating real food in realistic amounts. That's hard for chronic crash-dieters, who are used to eating what they consider "forbidden" foods and then later purging themselves of the damage with intense exercise, starvation, or a combination of the two. Here are some solutions.

Consult a nutrition savant. If you can, consult a registered dietitian to help you determine how many calories you need to eat to maintain or lose weight based on your body size and activity level. You'll probably be surprised by how much food you actually should be eating. And having a dietitian tell you so will help cement your trust in this new eating lifestyle. Don't be tempted to resume your past vicious cycle, which gradually helped you pick up an extra 30 or so pounds. For you, getting on a regular eating plan is essential to proving to yourself that you can eat somewhere between 1,500 and 1,800 calories daily and lose weight.

Find portion control. You need to meticulously measure food and discover healthy portion sizes. That way, you'll never feel overloaded, as if you were going to burst, or so empty that your stomach growls. Try to plan to include a favourite food in a healthy portion daily – preferably early in the day – to help you stick to your eating plan.

Eat breakfast. You're probably used to skimping on breakfast in an attempt to cut calories. But starting the day with an energy-packed meal will keep you satisfied through the morning as well as boost your job performance. Most important, you'll eat less later in the day.

Satisfy snack attacks. Plan two snacks each day that satisfy your tastebuds as well as your hunger. Don't make the mistake of talking yourself into something like carrots when you really crave chocolate chip biscuits. Chances are, you'll fill up on carrots, then you'll have the biscuits anyway. Instead, plan to have a snack of one chocolate chip biscuit and one glass of skimmed milk in the midafternoon. In the long run, you'll eat fewer calories.

Have a real supper. Do you usually prepare a big meal for the family but make yourself a salad to save calories? Such deprivation only leads to binge eating later on. Eat a regular supper with your family.

Living with a Man Who Eats Heartily

The scenario is all too common: A woman tries to keep her husband and teenage sons in food. Breakfast amounts to no less than a whole loaf of bread for French toast and three-quarters of a gallon of milk. After-school snacks rival banquets with Henry VIII. Although Mum eats just a fraction of what the guys in her household consume, she gains a couple of pounds a year. The menfolk, especially the boys, complain that they can't gain weight.

How can Mum feed her family the incredible number of calories they seem to need while not gaining weight herself – without cooking two entirely different sets of meals?

Plan, plan, plan. You can eat the same foods as your husband and sons do as long as you cook lower-fat meals and dish out a smaller helping for yourself than you do for them. They can serve themselves in more generous double or triple portions. Plan menus carefully to make sure that you cook fat-fighting foods. You will not only be fighting fat yourself but you'll also be doing the men in your life a favour, reducing their risk of heart disease and other conditions associated with high-fat diets. Try roasting a chicken with new potatoes, carrots, onions and brussels sprouts, for example, for a low-fat meal that also provides your children with the nutrition their growing bodies demand.

Study portion sizes carefully. While your 1,500- to 1,800-calorie level really does accommodate a lot of food, it's half of what your teenage sons can eat. While they might easily put away two to three cupfuls of rice at supper, your calorie budget can only afford half a cup to a cup. Similarly, while they may be able to handle 155 to 185 g of roast beef at supper, you need just 90 g. Measure portions a few times and then periodically check on your ability to eyeball them.

Put margarine on the table, not on the food. While the men might be able to use two to three teaspoons of margarine on their rice, for example, you can get by with less.

Buy things you don't like. When it comes to snacks, you have a couple of options, depending on your will power. If your will power is of stellar quality, buy snacks for your family that you'll declare off-limits to yourself. (Don't go overboard, though, with items that aren't very nutritious or that are heavily laden with fat, especially saturated fat.) If, on the other hand, your will power is less than mighty, you could at least consider purchasing things you don't like. They love fig bars and you hate them? Great! Fig bars are a great, nutritious snack, anyway, so you'll be doing your boys a favour. Nacho cheese-flavoured tortilla chips are one of your downfalls? Just don't bring them into the house,

WOMAN TO WOMAN
Food Is Her Bread and Butter

For Bonnie Reith, kitchen manager at an award-winning restaurant in Portsmouth, food is her craft. Luscious meals are a constant temptation, but she's able to pursue her culinary passion and exercise healthy self-control with a few tricks of the trade.

My mother didn't force us to clean our plates. I was never made to feel that I had to eat everything that was set before me. I was always encouraged to eat healthy food only when I was hungry. I think this practice prepared me well for a field in which I am surrounded by food eight hours a day, five days a week. Of course, professionally, I have to try lots of different foods. I have the "unfortunate" task of tasting a sample of everything I make before it ends up on the customer's plate to make sure that it's nothing less than delicious. You don't need to try half a loaf of bread, though, to make sure it's up to par; a sliver will suffice. The same is true of soup: A spoonful will do — you don't have to eat a bowlful.

One of the few advantages of working in a hot kitchen is that I must drink lots of water to prevent dehydration. As a bonus, drinking so much water dampens my appetite. And when the temperature soars to a sweltering 110°, a slice of cool pineapple has more appeal than a slice of chocolate cake.

The most nutritionally challenging times are days when the restaurant is especially busy. If I don't take time off to eat a balanced meal before a rush of orders hits, I'm more prone to random nibbling all day. So I try to make time to eat my meals before the crowds arrive.

I love watching our customers savour the flavours and textures of our dishes. And if there's too much of a good thing, we send them home with a doggie bag. Mum would be so proud!

no matter how much the guys like them. If they can't live without their favourites, tell them it's up to them, not you, to restock. Of course, there occasionally will be leftover temptations: Your son or husband leaves a half-eaten bag of tortilla chips out in full view. Without blinking an eye, through out the bag and pat yourself on the back. (And ask them not to leave their leftovers.)

Eat vegetables. If you find yourself tempted to take second helpings along with your masculine dining companions, try cooking yourself an extra vegetable at supper, and make it something that you really love. Are you crazy about asparagus with freshly squeezed lemon juice? Don't hesitate to add it to the menu frequently. Or maybe baby carrots cooked with brown sugar and cinnamon strike your fancy. Whatever it is, having another vegetable to eat while the men continue to eat up will keep you from having another portion just to be sociable.

Choose desserts carefully. Tell the family that you have a new kitchen rule: Dessert will be served not nightly but on Wednesdays and Saturdays only (or whatever days are convenient for you). When dessert night rolls around, serve yourself a small portion and enjoy every bite. For the rest of the week, make fresh fruit the family dessert, splurging on raspberries, strawberries or whatever your family likes. To make it special, buy low-fat or non-fat frozen dairy toppings and serve yourself one generous dollop. Let the men finish the container.

Slim down when they're not around. Make a point of eating lean when you're alone, such as at lunch. But don't starve yourself, either. Sitting down to the supper table ravenously hungry with men who shovel it in like steam engines may be your undoing. In fact, you might try having a glass of vegetable juice or fruit juice an hour or two before supper to turn down your appetite.

Empty Nesters

As midlife approaches, many women go from

WOMAN TO WOMAN
She Made Time to Exercise

Rhonda Matthews, an primary school substitute teacher, Weight Watchers International leader, fund-raising director, and mother of three in Dorchester, doesn't have time to exercise. Or so she thought. But she found ways to squeeze it in, and she lost over 2 stone in five months. Here's her story.

I didn't have a problem with my weight B.K. – before kids. I taught at a primary school, so I had time in the afternoons to attend aerobics classes and play ball games. I was free to drink a beer after a game or stop off for pizza. But because I was always busy, the calories didn't catch up with me.

Then I had two kids – and gained over 2 stone.

People said, "You have two toddlers; you must be so busy. The weight will just fall off!" I'd laugh. Yes, I was busy every minute. And I didn't have time to exercise. But I always had time to sit and eat the crust off my kids' pizza or make biscuits and eat most of them myself.

When I first had kids, I thought I'd put them in the playpen while I did my workout. That was unrealistic. They were good kids, but they weren't happy to be cooped up while I danced around the room.

Between not eating right and not exercising, it's no wonder that I never lost the weight I gained during pregnancy. Two extra stone might not sound like a lot, but I didn't feel good about myself. My clothes didn't fit well, and I didn't feel attractive. As a 28-year-old mother of two, I didn't expect to look like a model, but I didn't want to look matronly, either.

I tried to lose the weight on my own, mainly by cutting back on food, but I wasn't seeing any results. One day at the barber shop, watching my son get his first haircut, I overheard people raving about a woman close to my age who looked great after having joined Weight Watchers. I was shocked. I thought Weight Watchers was for older women — my mother's generation. Nevertheless, I decided to give it a shot.

They taught me to eat right, balancing grains, a little protein and lots of fruits and vegetables. Most important, they solved my exercise dilemma, suggesting that I get up a half-hour earlier to exercise.

I thought they were nuts. I was already getting up at the crack of dawn with my kids. But I set my alarm for 5:30 A.M. and crawled out of bed. I made a deal with my husband — if the kids woke up while I was exercising, he promised to tend to them.

I reached my goal weight in five months. Walking and aerobics tapes, both great things for people with little time and money for exercise, were the keys to my success. I wasn't afraid about putting weight back on when I became pregnant with my third child. I did gain weight, but I lost it all while I was still breastfeeding my baby — in six months!

Exercise has given me control over my weight, my body, and my life.

Mothers often think about feeding their children (and husbands) as a means of not only filling their stomachs but also healing their hurts and rewarding their accomplishments. With the children gone, food often takes on a new meaning for the women; it can (at least temporarily) fill the emotional void and heal their own loneliness. In addition, it's hard to get used to making less food. If you have poured an entire box of spaghetti into a pot of boiling water for the past 15 or so years, for instance, you'll need to give yourself time to adjust to making less pasta. Here's how to make the transition.

Plan a daily menu. From that menu, make a shopping list and stick to it when you shop. This will keep you from overbuying. Are you tempted to buy crisps, biscuits and ice cream just in case the kids stop buy? Don't. You may feel obligated to eat them just to get rid of them.

Stash the money you save on groceries. Watch it grow and promise to buy yourself something special with it. Having another incentive not to overbuy groceries can be a big help.

Spoil the kids when you see them. Having the kids over for supper? Take this opportunity to make their favourite dishes, then send the leftovers home with them.

Find new interests. Do you continue to bake because you love to do it but then eat the biscuits, cakes and pies yourself? If so, find another hobby.

Go to a gym. Do you get lonely at mealtime, either because you live alone or because your

having no time to themselves due to the demands of a growing family to suddenly having too much time. In addition to learning how to fill the physical and emotional voids left by departing children, "empty nest" mums must learn how to shop and cook for two (or sometimes one) in ways that will prevent weight gain.

husband travels frequently? Find an exercise class that meets late in the day. It will take your mind off making and eating a big supper, and it may reduce your appetite.

Make your own frozen suppers. Find items that freeze so that you can make a full batch and put some away for another meal. Or at least cook something that you can warm up later in the week for a second meal. Believe it or not, you'll come to enjoy not having to cook for every supper.

Working Odd Hours

In nursing school, no one seemed able to keep weight on, recalls Napier. The class schedule was grueling and left little time for sleeping or eating.

Fifteen years later, the schedule doesn't seem that much easier, but now it seems to promote weight gain instead of weight loss. The same is true of other jobs where the hours change from day to night and night to day. All-night supermarket cashiers, police-women and others who do shift work have unique weight-related problems. Women who work odd hours seem to pick up a few pounds whenever they switch shifts. Yet changing sleep patterns alone don't generate weight gain. What's going on?

Indirectly, the fatigue that accompanies shift changes is probably to blame. Many women respond to that fatigue by eating, because munching helps them stay awake. Losing track of regular mealtimes also adds calories. When you're up at odd hours, you often eat at odd times and may have four or five good-size meals without even realising it. In addition, many

WOMAN TO WOMAN
From Crash-Dieter to Fitness Fan

Anne Bolin, Ph.D., associate professor of anthropology in Cambridge, crash-dieted for years, losing the same 2.5 stone dozens of times. Then she discovered bodybuilding at age 39, stopped dieting, and lost the weight for good. Here's her story.

I started dieting at age 13, beginning my 26-year stint as a yo-yo dieter. I was a great dieter – I could white-knuckle it for weeks, and the weight would come off. Then I'd reward myself, relax my eating rules, and give in to my cravings, and my weight would float back up. My wardrobe was filled with clothes from size 6 to 18.

As an anthropologist, I was looking for a new group to study. I became intrigued by a film on women bodybuilders. No one in my field was writing about this, and these women were doing something that was very non-traditional. They wanted to have muscles.

When an anthropologist studies a group, she doesn't just post out a survey. She asks dozens of questions, of course, but she also establishes personal relationships with each person and ideally becomes one of the group. I decided to take that a step further and learn everything I could about bodybuilding, not only by lifting weights but by competing in the sport as well. Never mind the fact that I had never lifted a weight, and I used to smoke four packs of cigarettes a day.

women are captive victims of vending machines or midnight cafeteria fare, neither of which is conducive to eating on the lighter side. Here's how to fight fat while surviving shift changes.

Pack your food. Pack snacks and a lunch for your shift. In addition to carrot sticks, take a fresh orange (peeled and sealed in a resealable plastic bag so that you can't use the I-don't-have-time excuse) and a sandwich with good-quality protein (like turkey on whole-wheat bread) and a juicy tomato slice to make lunch interesting.

Unfortunately, bodybuilding played right into my crash-dieting lifestyle. During the training and competition season, I winnowed my body down to just over 8 stone-competition size. During the off-season, however, I binged, and my weight soared back to 11 stone. I'm only five feet three inches tall, so I walked around in tent dresses and fat clothes most of the time.

Then a beach experience changed my life.

I was sitting on the beach in a two-piece bathing suit without a cover-up, which I rarely did. I went into the ladies room and looked in the mirror. I was disgusted – I knew I needed to change my crash-dieting ways.

I started to educate myself about healthy eating as a way of life, balancing proteins with carbohydrates and limiting fat. It was a slow process, but each year my off-season weight gradually lowered from 11 stone down to 9 stone now.

I've learned to eat six small meals a day, so I'm never hungry. I switched to low-fat or no-fat milk products, and most often I choose turkey, chicken or fish for my protein rather than red meat. Most important, I now have a healthy relationship with food. Plus, I have tons of energy.

My most important secret is that crash diets don't work. I don't deprive my body any more, so I no longer get gnawing cravings the way I used to. I feed my body good, nutritious food. I'm worth it, and so are you.

Also pack a small helping of your favourite treat. Do you love chocolate because it helps you get through those interminable nights? Pack one or two small chocolate pieces which are just a few grammes each.

Leave your money at home. Even if you've packed a lunch, you might not be able to resist a co-worker's offer to bring you a treat from the cafeteria. So don't take money to work. To keep you out of range of the food concession, pack your own diet soft drink or sparkling water.

Invest in a good thermos so you can make gourmet coffee for yourself. If you have things to do on the way home from work, lock whatever money you'll need in the glove compartment of the car.

Wait until you are awake to think about supper. Plan your at-home meals carefully, too, and do it when you are not hungry or tired. Do you generally arrive home in the morning hungry and tired after an all-nighter? Each night before you leave for work, make yourself a meal and then heat it in the microwave when you get home. Or set out the cooking utensils and at least some of the ingredients before you leave for work. Yet another option is to buy healthy frozen meals and heat them in the microwave.

Plan regular eating times. Develop an eating schedule for your odd hours, trying to include three small meals and one to two small snacks. Work out when you like breakfast and then plan healthy breakfasts for those times. Ditto for lunch and supper. Maybe you like to have your big meal while you're working. If so, take a serving of lasagna or low-fat meat loaf and a baked potato with steamed broccoli to work and heat them in the microwave, if one is available.

Don't play hooky from food. Avoid skipping meals because you are tired. You'll only make up for it later, as it will eventually make you ravenously hungry and set you up for a binge.

Don't fall into the fast-food trap. Fast food is famous for hidden calories and fat. If you have steel-reinforced will power, however, you can occasionally stop at fast-food places and choose their lower-fat fare such as a grilled chicken breast sandwich, fajitas or a salad with low-fat dressing.

On-the-Job Wining and Dining

In many professions, doing business over breakfast, lunch, or supper is routine. Financial planners, lawyers, publicists, and others often need to meet their clients when they are available, which often includes mealtime. In some professions, meeting over lunch or supper gives you an opportunity to forge good relations by treating your companion to a nice meal.

As more and more women go into business for themselves or fill the ranks of management, business meals become a fact of life. Even if you are careful, in just four years at such a job, you could pick up as much as 12 pounds. Two extra teaspoons of butter per day, for example, is about 68 calories. If you work 50 weeks a year and dine out three times a week, that adds up to 10,200 calories, which in turn equals about three pounds a year. You think you're being careful: You ration the butter to just one pat on a lunchtime roll. Most nights you hold yourself to a salad or choose grilled fish in a light sauce or a grilled chicken breast sandwich. And if you order dessert, you don't finish it.

Even so, you simply cannot account for all the hidden calories. That single pat of butter, for instance, is really nearly two teaspoons instead of the scant one you'd use at home. Then there's the "light" sauce for the grilled fish. Skillfully prepared with lemon juice and herbs, it looks and tastes low-fat, but it's usually loaded with butter and cream. And when you chose those grilled chicken breast sandwiches, you probably didn't know that the chef soaked butter into the bun (no wonder they often taste so moist).

No matter how much you have to eat out, though, you can maintain your figure and fight fat. Here are some dining-out secrets.

Get to know the food servers. When you can, frequent the same restaurants and get to know the staff. If possible, arrange to speak with the chef at off-peak hours and ask what he can do to cut calories for you. Then order the same type of food there, instructing the server to tell the chef who is requesting the food.

Don't even think about opening the menu. Once you open the menu, temptation kicks in. Instead, be committed to ordering grilled chicken, fish or lean beef. Grilled tenderloin, for example, is very lean and often excellent-tasting. Just ask the waiter or waitress to serve it without sauce.

Take some home for later. Restaurant portions are overly generous. Usually you'll eat more than you need just because the food is sitting in front of you. Size up the portion when it comes (use a scale at home to really learn healthy portion sizes), take what you would for a normal, healthy-size portion, and ask the server to remove the rest or pack it up for you to take home. Rest assured, it's no longer a sign of poor manners to avoid wasting food.

Eat low-calorie foods first. Fill up on salad or a broth-based soup, and then just sample the main course you chose.

Work in some fruit. Like most people who eat out frequently, you probably don't get enough fruit and vegetables in your diet. Get into the habit of ordering a fresh fruit cup for an appetizer and fresh berries for dessert. If you'd like, order the berries with cream, but have the server give them just a dab or two.

Aim for two super-healthy meals a week. Promise yourself at least one or two meals of steamed vegetables per week. Any restaurant can do this for you. In some, you might even be able to get the chef to accent them with freshly chopped basil or another favourite herb. Planning ahead can be a huge fat-saver.

Working at Home

Your friends may think you are so lucky: You have a full-time career, and you can still be at home for the kids. Or if you don't have children, you can make your own hours and take breaks to get outside when the weather is beautiful.

In theory, working at home is great. But, just as with a regular office job, work-related stress makes you turn to food, which is only too available just down the hall in the kitchen. Food is just too handy, and you can always go back for more. You don't even have to search in your purse for change.

What's the answer? If you have a home-based office, you must counter several things to control excess calorie intake. You'll need to put away food reminders, define the line between home and work and find an alternative to stress-induced eating. Here are some thoughts on how to tackle the problems.

Try not to work in the kitchen. Working all day around constant temptation is more than even the most virtuous people can handle.

Do the dishes, then start work. Before you start to work, let the answering machine take your calls and clean up the breakfast dishes. Later, do the same with the lunch dishes. Working around food and dishes is another powerful reminder to eat.

Take a lunch break. Eat meals at a set time, away from your work. Carrying food to your desk blurs the line between work and home, making eating too accessible.

Set a time to start supper. Leave work behind you for that specified time. Again,

mixing meal preparation with work tends to let eating spill over into your work life and leads to overeating.

Prepare for dealing with stress without food. Do you have room in your home office or somewhere nearby for an exercise bike or other type of equipment? Rather than getting up from your desk for a biscuit when stress and frustration strike, take a two-minute exercise break.

Stressed-Out Meal-Skippers

For women with hectic schedules, eating becomes a catch-as-catch-can affair. The day begins in such a whirlwind that you usually don't have time for breakfast. For whatever reason, you also end up skipping lunch most days or you grab something on the run from a vending machine. Having skipped the first two meals of the day, you usually grab whatever you can when you walk in the house after work, shoving things into your mouth as you prepare a meal for the rest of the family. Then you're not hungry at supper, and you only toy with your food. An hour or so later, when the junk-food fullness wears off, you ransack the kitchen for snacks.

True, you can't change your busy schedule. But you can change your response to it. Here are some suggestions.

Make breakfast at night. When you clean up the kitchen after supper, pack breakfast and set it next to your handbag or briefcase. A cereal bar, a banana and an apple are great on-the-go breakfast foods.

While you're at it, make lunch, too. If you're going to be away from home at lunchtime, pack something the night before that doesn't need to be refrigerated. If you're going to be home, make something – a sandwich or salad, perhaps – and pop it in the refrigerator. Having something ready takes at least some of the rush out of lunchtime and keeps you from grabbing junk food.

Make a super bowl. Each night when you clean up the kitchen, prepare a fruit bowl for the following day. It should have no less than one piece of fruit per family member, and at least two for you. When you walk in the door famished at the end of the day, reach for a piece of fruit, and encourage everyone else to do the same.

Fill up with liquids. As you prepare supper, pour yourself a tall glass of sparkling water, iced tea, vegetable juice or fruit juice. Not only will this keep you from eating but it will also hydrate you. If you've been running all day, you probably haven't had nearly enough to drink.

Set kitchen hours. After you've fixed the next day's fruit bowl and your portable breakfast, close up the kitchen and turn off the lights. This serves as a physical reminder that food is off-limits until the next day. Even if you are hungry, the dark kitchen should turn you away and encourage you to start off the next day on the right track.

Women Who Can't Exercise

Women who have a chronic condition will most likely need to modify their exercise programme. Certainly, a gentle swim may be in the cards for some, or perhaps an easy stroll. But for many, working up a sweat just might not be possible.

WOMAN TO WOMAN
Faster Meals without Fast Food

Stephanie Raquel, an associate at a public relations agency in Bath, often puts in 50-hour work weeks and devotes another 15 hours a week to church and community activities. Her husband works in marketing. Their world spins at two speeds – fast and frantic. Stephanie's time-saving ideas shaved hours off her schedule, freeing up time for healthier cooking, and she lost 2.5 stone. Here's her story.

I barely have time to eat, let alone cook. I'm so busy I often don't even have five minutes to stop for a toilet break, so healthy eating just went out the window. Often I had to choose between taking time to seek out something nutritious and grabbing a quick, not-so-healthy snack. It was too easy to pick the chocolate or crisps and get back to work. Plus, my job requires high energy, which was an easy excuse for me to eat as much as I wanted.

Extra weight piled on gradually. One day I noticed that my wedding ring didn't fit, and I told my husband I would need to have it resized. He looked at me with sad, loving eyes, and said, "Maybe the ring is not the problem." I knew it hurt him to say that, but it hurt even more to hear.

I needed to do something about my weight. First, I tackled my eating habits. Being an organised person, I wanted a plan. My husband and I began designing our menus a month in advance and consolidating our grocery shopping to one major trip a month. I no longer waste 20 minutes after a long day at work figuring out what to cook. Knowing what I'm going to make for supper also makes it easier to resist the McDonald's, Pizza Huts and other tempting take away places I pass on my drive home. Also, we prepare everything we

In addition to physical restrictions on exercise options, you may take medication that slows your metabolism or increases your appetite. Or perhaps you have no chronic ailment but are dead set against exercise for some reason. Either way, read on. The following information will

can in advance. Thank goodness for our freezer. We often chop up vegetables on the weekends and freeze them in plastic bags. We freeze everything we can, actually — grated cheese, sliced green peppers, bananas (for quick shakes) — so that it's all ready to go when we need it. If we cook too much pasta one night, we freeze the rest for another quick meal. I'd love to get a bigger freezer, but then I'd need a bigger flat.

We structure our suppers around healthy, quick foods such as pasta, stir-fries and sandwiches. The goal is to get supper on the table quickly.

I've made changes to my other meals as well. I have oatmeal for breakfast; it's quick and healthy. I often pack my own lunch so that I can steer clear of the fast-food restaurants in the vicinity of my office building. I keep healthy snacks like baby carrots, oranges and chocolate rice cakes in my office for stress-induced eating episodes. I also carry fruit and low-fat crackers in my car to munch on during my half-hour commute.

With my healthier eating habits I began to see changes in my weight, but not quickly. I started going to the YMCA to exercise. I noticed that if I exercised three times a week, I lost weight. If I went once a week, I maintained it, and if I didn't go at all, I gained some back. Three days a week became my goal. I've learned to combine exercise with other tasks to make better use of my time: I read trade magazines on the treadmill and defrost chicken or boil pasta while I do aerobics tapes.

Now I'm 2.5 stone lighter and my life is as hectic as ever, but I've realised that the leaner, healthier me responds more quickly to life's stresses. I feel great.

work for anyone with limitations.

To slim down, you must maximise nutrient density. In other words, since there's a limit to how many calories you can burn off with physical activity, every calorie you consume must be packed with vitamins and minerals. Premium ice cream, for example, has low nutrient density: The few nutrients it contains (like protein and calcium) are accompanied by loads and loads of calories from fat and sugar. Non-fat yogurt, on the other hand, has a higher nutrient density with six grammes of protein in just 100 calories.

Here's another example. Strawberry shortcake isn't devoid of nutrients, since the strawberries supply some vitamin C and folate, an important B vitamin. But once you pile the strawberries on the cake and hide them underneath whipped cream, those vitamins "cost" lots of calories, so the caloric cost of 50 milligrammes of vitamin C in strawberry shortcake is 352 calories. In contrast, a heaping bowl of strawberries alone is extremely nutrient-dense. You harvest 50 milligrammes of vitamin C as well as lots of folate and fibre for just 50 calories. What's more, you have lots more calories to spend throughout the rest of the day.

Here are other ways to harvest nutrient density without sacrificing flavour.

Fashion dessert from a rainbow of fresh fruits. Combining kiwifruit with strawberries and bananas, for example, creates the explosion of flavour you're looking for and also satisfies even the sweetest sweet tooth and the most discerning tastebuds. If it's creamy texture you want, try fat-free or low-fat frozen whipped toppings.

Buy exceptionally great cuts of meat. Generally you'll find them in the free range or organic section of your supermarket's meat department. No matter what your budget, though, you'll be able to afford them because you'll be buying so much less. You'll select just 90 to 125 grammes of uncooked meat for yourself, for example, instead of the 250 grammes or more that's customary. You'll harvest lots of protein, iron, vitamin B_{12} and zinc in that lean and luscious meat.

Choose hearty, whole-grain breads. The best-tasting breads come fresh from the bakery. You can preserve bakery freshness by freezing the bread in individual portions the day you buy it. Just slice the bread (if it didn't come that way) and close it securely in resealable bags. The whole-grain goodness is not only exceptionally satisfying but it's also quantum leaps more nutritious than white bread. You'll find it so satisfying that you won't need (or even want) butter or margarine on it. When you use it to make a sandwich, you'll be loading your meal with lots of minerals, B vitamins, and fibre.

Have a mixed medley. Just as you combine fruits to create a flavour explosion, you can blend many vegetables together. Accent tomatoes with sweet onions, basil and portobello mushrooms, for example, splashing everything with flavour-loaded balsamic vinegar and virgin olive oil (just a touch). Add crunchy chopped cucumbers to leafy cos lettuce, deliciously satisfying sweet red peppers and smooth mushrooms in a lunchtime salad that you've also loaded with smooth, slightly nutty chick peas. The flavour is intense, and the nutrient density can't be beat.

Have what you crave. Use some high-fat, high-calorie ingredients to lend interest and satisfaction (sometimes more psychological than physical) to your meals. But use them wisely and sparingly. Use a teaspoon of melted butter, for example, (yes, real melted butter – it's a great way to use your total and saturated fat allowance for the day) to top fresh fish, but load it first with plenty of sautéed fresh herbs. Fresh rosemary, for example, sautéed in a teaspoon of butter with fresh garlic, adds an absolute flavour explosion to even the driest, most boring white fish.

Stay-at-Home Mums

Children are like non-stop vacuum cleaners. Their small stomach capacities prevent them from eating enough food at one sitting to keep them full for a long time. Yet they need to eat a phenomenal number of calories to fuel their active, growing bodies, so they're constantly searching for snacks, drinks and more snacks.

The problem is, it seems as though the more your children eat, the more weight *you* gain. You're a grown-up. You're no longer growing (at least, not vertically), so you can't eat that many calories if you want to stay thin. Yet along with the kids, you're having a taste of peanut butter here, half of a biscuit there and maybe a glass of juice several times throughout the day. And then there are the last bites of food you clean up after you've already eaten your share. If little Marissa leaves a clump of macaroni cheese and pint-size Tommy stops eating with a third of his hot dog to go, you end up finishing their meals. It may not seem like a lot of caloric damage, but it adds up.

Let's tally up those last few bites. The last little bit of hot dog, for instance, has about 80 calories and the last few spoonfuls of macaroni cheese about 100. If you ate just that much extra food a day, you'd gain a pound in 20 weeks and somewhere around 12 pounds in five years. Just 125 ml of apple juice (most adults drink more) adds another 60 calories, and an extra biscuit packs 50 to 100 calories. It's easy to understand, then, how weight creeps on with all of those extra "bites."

To counteract this weight gain, you first need to distinguish between "mummy" food and "kiddy" food. By design, children's foods pack a lot of calories for their punch. That's because kids need to stuff their tiny stomachs with those calories so they can grow. As adults, though, we need to do the opposite – feel satisfied on relatively fewer calories. So, even if it seems that you're wasting food, you'll want to incorporate the following into your fat-fighting plan.

Picture a rubbish disposal unit. You can even put a picture of one on your refrigerator. Now tell yourself that that's where leftover food should go, not in your stomach.

Eat mummy food. Make yourself a gorgeous salad while the kids are eating lunch, with several vegetables and a good source of lean protein such as lean ham, chick peas, reduced-fat cheese, tuna or leftover roast chicken. Once you put the kids in for their afternoon nap, settle down with classical music playing, a goblet full of sparkling water and your salad set on a pretty place mat. You'll feel special – and satisfied.

Switch to better snack food. Start your children's healthy eating habits early. Instead of double-fudge biscuits, offer them simpler shortbread biscuits. Or try apple slices, a banana, popcorn or yogurt. These are things that you can snack on, too, without breaking your calorie budget.

Set eating hours. Open the kitchen just twice – once in the morning and once in the afternoon – for planned snacks rather than letting the kids snack whenever they like. This helps them develop healthier eating habits and also keeps you away from temptation. Plus, the kids will be more apt to eat quality foods at supper if they're not full from nonstop snacking.

Drink with them. Get into the habit of drinking milk when you pour it for the kids (skimmed for you and kids over age two). The high-quality protein is a great appetite-quencher, not to mention bone-strengthener.

Working Mums

It's a schedule that rivals the president's: You get up at 6:00 A.M. to throw a load of laundry in before work and fix lunches before the family starts crowding the kitchen. Then you have just enough time to shower, do your hair, and make it back to the kitchen to referee breakfast. After dropping off three children at two different schools, you arrive at work just on time. Compared to the flurry of morning activity, a day at work seems almost calm. The race starts again after work, with a marathon of driving to pick up the children. Making supper, cleaning up and helping with homework leaves you crawling into bed around 10:30, with thoughts of the next day's demands looming in the place where dreams should be.

Fortunately, you can accumulate exercise in short snippets throughout the day. It does you just as much good as a 30-minute block of activity.

The key to working exercise into a busy life is to give yourself lots of options and opportunities for brief periods of activity – 5 minutes here and 10 minutes there – for a total of 30 minutes a day. In other words, turn your knack for doing three things at once to your advantage. Here are some strategies.

Get up 10 minutes earlier each day. Before you go to bed, lay out trainers and exercise clothes appropriate for the weather. Use the same admirable discipline that gets you through those monster days to rise quickly and slip into your workout clothes. You should be out the front door in three minutes flat. Walk as briskly as you can for just five minutes and then turn around and head back.

Park five minutes further away from the

entrance. Sure, you've heard about this trick before, but you've always brushed it off, thinking that it couldn't make that much of a difference. Change your attitude. Parking further away from your destination really can help you lose weight. Parking 10 minutes from work will add 20 minutes of exercise to your day just coming and going.

Turn your lunch break into an exercise break. No doubt you've seen other working women headed out over the lunch break with their tennis shoes on. If you'd like, slip into the ladies room and swap your work blouse for a T-shirt. Also, keep trainers under your desk to make changing into them easy. When you pack the kids' lunch in the morning, pack one for yourself so that you can eat when you're back at work.

Delay supper by 10 minutes each day. Grab your husband (the guy you don't see often enough) and head out the front door again. Walk at a brisk pace for 5 minutes, then turn around and return. Use the time not only to connect but also as your second or third exercise installment. When you can, steal an extra 5 minutes, creating a 15-minute walk.

Invest in an exercise bike. Or buy a treadmill, a rowing machine, or a stairclimber – something on which you can read or watch television as you exercise. A recumbent bike is particularly well-suited to reading and is one of the most comfortable pieces of exercise equipment. When you can't steal 10 minutes before supper, grab 15 afterward to read the paper or a chapter of a novel or to watch the evening news, but do it on your exercise machine.

PART THREE

Stoke Your Fat-Burning System

Exercise Reality

You've Got to Get a Move On

Ask any group of women how many know they should exercise, and chances are, everyone will raise their hands. Ask the same group how many exercise regularly, and maybe only one hand will go up. Ask how many women *like* to exercise, and the odds are that no one will respond positively.

The scenario is typical. Some surveys show that fewer than 1 in 10 of us exercises as much as we should. And each year after age 40, the typical woman becomes less active.

If, like most women, you know that you should exercise but don't, you probably fall into one of two categories, says Catherine Brumley, certified trainer. Maybe you've never exercised and you think it's too demanding, complicated, or time-consuming. Or you have tried exercise and you didn't like it, got bored or dropped out for some other reason.

None of those reasons is good enough to justify avoiding exercise. You can overcome every one of them.

What's more, you should. Good intentions alone don't burn calories. If you want to lose fat and keep it off, you have to exercise. Fortunately, starting an exercise programme and sticking to it aren't nearly as difficult as you might imagine. Exercise need not be complicated or time-consuming. You can even learn to enjoy it.

The *Fight Fat* Exercise Prescription

To fight fat and keep it off, you must wage a two-pronged exercise strategy, according to Maria A. Fiatarone Singh, M.D..

Strategy No. 1. Do some form of aerobic exercise – enough to burn off 1,600 calories a week. According to research, that's how much you need to exercise to ensure that the weight you lose will stay off. That doesn't mean that you have to spend hours a day at a gym. Taking a walk every day or so can do it. If you weigh 10 stone, for example, you'll burn 1,600 calories by walking for an hour five times a week at a four-mile-an-hour pace.

You can burn 1,600 calories in less than five hours by choosing something more strenuous, such as aerobic dance or jogging. Or you can break up your activity into multiple 10- to 20-minute sessions throughout the day, such as walking for 15 minutes after breakfast, 20 minutes during your lunch break and 15 more after work. Throw in 5 minutes in the morning and afternoon as breaks and you've walked for an hour.

Strategy No. 2. Each week, on non-consecutive days, spend 20 to 30 minutes lifting weights. Follow the routine in The Weight You'll Want on page 123; it was designed for the women who come to renowned health spas. With fewer than 10 easy moves, you can do the routine at home or at a gym.

Give Yourself the Aerobic Edge

The word *aerobics* was coined in 1968 by Kenneth H. Cooper, M.D. In technical terms, *aerobic* means "living with oxygen." So Dr. Cooper categorised exercise that makes people breathe harder, thus taking in more oxygen, as aerobic.

Aerobics caught on big-time. Today when people hear the word *aerobics*, they often think of doing dance moves to music. But any type of physical activity that makes you breathe harder − running, walking briskly or swimming, for example − can be aerobic. Besides protecting against disease, aerobic exercise helps you fight fat in numerous ways.

❧ Aerobic exercise will raise your metabolic

WOMEN ASK WHY

I'm exercising and watching what I eat. Why am I getting slimmer but gaining weight?

When a woman tells me that she's getting slimmer but either gaining or just not losing weight on the scale, I assume that she's lifting weights.

First, weight lifting will stimulate calcium absorption in her bones. This means she's building a heavier skeleton. Second, she's building muscle. Muscle tissue weighs more than fat tissue. It's also much more compact. If you think about your muscle as the leanest cut of beef and picture fat as the grease that you pour from the pan when you cook bacon or chicken, you can get an idea of the difference in size. Fat is bulky while muscle is dense. So a woman could shrink from a clothing size 12 to a size 8 while her weight on the scale goes up or stays the same simply because she's building heavier, compact muscle and losing lighter, fluffier fat. She has changed her body composition. She's literally a smaller person.

A woman who drops a clothing size or two but doesn't see much of a drop in her weight on the scale should be happy. She's built muscle and burned off fat. Muscle cells require more oxygen and use much more fuel than fat cells, so muscle burns more calories. The more muscle a woman has, the more calories she burns. The more fat a woman has, the fewer calories she burns.

For that reason, nutritionists no longer care too much about what a woman weighs on the scale. We're more concerned with how much body fat she has.

Expert consulted
Kristine Clark, R.D., Ph.D.

rate during and after your workout. So you continue to burn extra calories after you exercise, says Janet Walberg-Rankin, Ph.D. When researchers compared women who exercised regularly with others who did not, they found that the first group had significantly higher metabolic rates. More than 10 hours after they'd finished exercising, the exercisers were burning calories 6 percent faster than the non-exercisers.

➧ You'll eat less if you exercise aerobically. When researchers measure the number of calories burned by aerobic exercisers, the results are surprising: The exercisers lose more pounds than can be accounted for by the burned calories. Why? One theory is that exercise reduces anxiety and depression, so exercisers eat less.

➧ You'll also eat less fat because you simply won't crave it as much. "Research indicates that exercise may enhance your preference for fruits and vegetables," explains Diane Hanson, Ph.D.

➧ You'll handle stress better, which also helps fight fat. Studies have found that physically active people handle stressful situations better than couch potatoes. Research also has shown that stress increases blood levels of the hormone cortisol, which seems to make your body store fat in the abdomen. So less stress means less pouch.

➧ You'll store less body fat. Aerobic exercise increases fat-burning enzymes, which break down fat and use it for energy in cells.

Ready for Liftoff

Lifting weights is one of the most important

WOMAN TO WOMAN
Exercise: Not Just a Job, an Adventure

For the first 20 years of her life, Barbara Press hated exercise. At 17.5 stone, she was too big to enjoy anything that required much effort. These days Barbara, otherwise known as Petty Officer Barbara Press, weighs 11 stone, and she loves exercise. What's more, her active lifestyle landed her new responsibilities as the physical fitness coordinator for her employer, the Navy

The only exercise I used to get was walking to the fridge to get more food. I was too big to do much else. When I had finally had enough of being overweight, I read everything I could get my hands on to educate myself about diet and exercise. I spent the first year learning to control what I ate and how much – how to measure portion sizes and make healthy choices.

I dropped 4.25 stone. Then I began to focus on an exercise programme. I started walking three times a week, slowly building myself up until I was walking five miles every day. Soon I was addicted to walking, and my day wasn't complete without a good workout.

I was pleased with the progress I was making, and I knew that if I quit, I'd be disappointed with myself. I was so curious

things you can do to fight fat. With weight training, you won't burn as many calories during a workout as you do with most aerobic exercises, but you will build muscle. That's significant, because muscle tissue burns more calories than fat tissue does, all day long. When your body is composed of proportionally more muscle and less fat, your metabolism runs higher.

Suppose you weigh 10 stone, for example, and 20 percent of your body is fat. Your twin sister also weighs 10 stone, but she has 30 percent body fat. Every day, you'll burn at least 120 calories more than your twin does simply because your body has 10 percent more muscle than hers.

to see the final results and what I would look like thin. I had always been told that I had a beautiful face, and I was sick of hearing that…I wanted to be a beautiful, healthy person.

Right now I'm maintaining my weight, so I don't work out seven days a week anymore; it's usually five days – or six, at the most. When I work out on my own, I do a walk/run routine: I walk a hard 3½ miles, and then I run 2 miles. Some days I go for a 4-mile run.

Whether I walk/run or run, I stretch afterwards, do abdominal exercises and then weights. I rotate my weight programme to work my upper body one day and my lower body the next.

To some degree, my job provides a workout. As a physical fitness coordinator in the navy, I have to run the troops three times a week. Their fitness level is different from mine (they only run 1½ miles), and when I run with them, I don't feel as if I've had a workout. So after I run the troops, I hop on the StairMaster for 45 minutes and then the bike for 15 minutes.

Losing weight was a long and difficult battle. It took me 20 years to put the weight on, and I didn't lose it overnight. But I always knew there was a better world for me. Because of my weight loss and new love of exercise, I've found it.

Metabolism also plays a role in fat loss during weight training. In one study, researchers found that metabolism revved up 15 percent after just 12 weeks of weight training. It's the equivalent of getting fewer calories without dieting or eating 15 percent more just to maintain your weight.

Building muscle mass is critical to fighting fat, because after age 30, you may lose ½ pound of muscle per year even if you exercise aerobically. And, not coincidentally, you may gain about 1½ pounds of body fat per year, with much of it deposited around your middle. The less muscle you have, the lower your resting metabolic rate. So when you lose pounds of muscle over the years, calories aren't burned the

way they should be and fat accumulates. Of course, there are several ways to compensate for a sluggish metabolism. To maintain your weight after you've reached 30, you'd need to cut your weekly intake by 105 calories every year. That means that in 10 years, you'd have to shave 1,000 or more *additional* calories a week.

Barring starvation, your other option would be to add a mile a week over and above your regular walking workout every year, beginning at age 30. But by age 40, you'd have to walk an *extra* 10 miles per week just to maintain your 21-year-old body.

The best option is to add about 60 minutes of resistance training per week. That's it. You don't have to starve yourself. And while you do still need to exercise aerobically, you don't have to exercise endlessly. In other words, resistance training is the most practical, effective way to prevent the loss of muscle and maintain your 21-year-old metabolic rate.

A bonus for women is that in addition to helping to build calorie-burning muscle, weight training helps to maintain your waistline, avoiding the apple shape that so many of us tend to develop after menopause. In one study, when 14 postmenopausal women completed a 16-week resistance training programme, all were delighted to notice that they lost fat from their abdomens.

No one is sure why resistance training targets the tummy. One theory is that belly fat is somehow different from fat deposited on the hips and thighs. It seems to respond quickly to any activity that boosts calorie burn, whether it's aerobic exercise or resistance training. The study found that while aerobic exercise melts away superficial fat around the waist, resistance training dissolves fat below the surface, around the internal organs, where it can be more of a threat to your health.

No matter what your age or how out of shape you are now, you can benefit from resistance training. If you follow the programme recommended by health spas, you can build about two pounds of muscle every eight weeks for the first six months. Female hormones will prevent you from building excessive muscle, so you'll never look as muscle-bound as the Incredible Hulk. But to maintain the muscle, you have to continue to lift weights.

Jump In to Exercise – And Stick with It

Chances are, if exercise has never worked for you, you've told yourself that it's because of one or more of the following reasons.

➤ You don't have the time.

➤ Your husband or kids (or both) get in the way.

➤ You're not really motivated.

If you've used any or all of those excuses, you're not alone. A survey conducted by the Sporting Goods Manufacturers Association found these three excuses to be among the top reasons for not exercising.

Although excuses may be universal, they shouldn't thwart your exercise programme. Here are some ways to overcome barriers to working out.

Give exercise a trial run. Try to stick with the effort for one month, suggests Brumley. The hardest part of any exercise programme is getting started, she explains. In the beginning, you sometimes tend to overdo it, so your muscles may ache. Or you feel somewhat awkward. But

---

YOUR PERSONAL MOTIVATION COACH

Yes, exercise helps you fight fat. But if you want to stick to your programme, you'll want to also focus on many of the other powerful benefits exercise offers women. Here's additional motivation to get off the couch.

Benefit No. 1. Exercise can reduce your risk of breast cancer by keeping oestrogen levels low.

Benefit No. 2. Among women, coronary heart disease outpaces everything else, including breast cancer, as the leading cause of death. Fortunately, heart-smart workouts help make costly, risky medical procedures like coronary bypass operations unnecessary by lowering levels of artery-clogging blood cholesterol. Research shows that women who exercise have 25 percent more HDL (high-density lipoprotein), the good cholesterol, and 20 percent less LDL (low-density lipoprotein), the bad cholesterol, than those in the low-fitness category. The HDL is desirable because it transports LDL away from the artery walls, where it tends to accumulate and slow or block the flow of blood to the heart.

Benefit No. 3. Exercise improves the way you breathe and builds muscle. That makes shopping easier to carry, jars easier to open and babies easier to hoist. It makes walking easier. It makes climbing stairs easier. It even makes chores like pushing a vacuum cleaner easier.

---

after a month, you have more energy and better self-esteem. "If you look at exercise as, say, 'Oh, for the rest of my life I have to do something that I hate,' you won't want to do it. But when you think of it as a trial run, exercise becomes more palatable. Usually once women get into the habit, it becomes something they like."

Tick off each day's progress. Mark the days off the calendar with a big, thick red marker so that you can see yourself getting closer to your goal. Tell yourself, "If I still hate to exercise when this month is over, I can try something different

Benefit No. 4. Exercise is one of the most effective ways to shake off a bad mood. If you've just had a run-in with your boss, for instance, a brisk walk can help you recover from the stressful encounter. Performed regularly, exercise will help keep your moods from swinging dramatically whenever stressful events occur.

Benefit No. 5. Exercise relieves menstrual discomfort by taming surging hormones, regulating ovulation and reducing associated discomfort such as tender breasts, bloating and anxiety.

Benefit No. 6. Exercise eases changes associated with menopause. Experts aren't sure exactly why, but one study showed that menopausal women who exercise moderately on a regular basis have more energy and less moodiness, anxiety, depression, sleep difficulties, night sweats and hot flashes than those who don't.

Benefit No. 7. Exercise strengthens bones. As our bones age, they lose calcium and other minerals, a process known as osteoporosis. The slowdown in oestrogen production that occurs at menopause can accelerate this process. The mineral loss makes the bones more porous, and porous bones break easily. Hip and wrist fractures are hallmarks of osteoporosis, as is a curved spine. Exercise can prevent or forestall the development of osteoporosis because it helps maintain and stimulate bone development and growth.

next month." Once you've made one month, you probably won't quit, says Brumley.

Exercise your right to an option. If you feel like a klutz in an aerobic dance class, don't do aerobic dance. If jogging makes your breasts bounce too much and your knees hurt, don't jog. If swimming makes you dread being seen in a bathing suit, don't swim, says Brumley. Instead, pick an activity that you do enjoy – or at least don't hate.

Plan for contingencies. Before making any big change, whether you're beginning an exercise programme or giving up smoking, you need a game plan, says Elizabeth Howze, Sc.D. The first step in that plan is to make a list of potential deterrents and ways to get around them. Here are some questions to ask yourself.

➤ What will I do if it rains or snows?

➤ How can I balance my exercise with my family life? What will I do with my children while I exercise?

➤ What will I do during autumn or winter when it gets dark early?

"When difficulties arise, willpower alone won't help. You need a practical strategy," says Dr. Howze. "People who make changes are more successful if they first plan for how they are going to deal with difficulties."

Start with an activity that appeals to you. If you're intimidated by exercise, try something that you already know how to do. For many, that means walking. But think about all the aerobic activities you have tried. Ask yourself, Which was comfortable?

Avoid post-traumatic gym syndrome. If you're like many women, you may have bad memories of a dreaded day in gym class when you were forced to run a mile in under 10 minutes or you were the last girl to be picked for netball. If you know from experience that a particular exercise isn't for you – if running seemed like torture or if team sports embarrassed you – cross it off your options.

Be patient. If your list of "not to do" exercises outnumbers your list of "to do" activities, don't give up hope. Experts say that in their experience, most women can find at least one activity they enjoy. Although you may need to experiment, you'll find something you like.

Turn to your chores for exercise. If you don't like the idea of formal exercise sessions, make daily activities your exercise, says Dr. Howze. Keep track of the amount of time you spend walking up the stairs, washing your car or vacuuming – anything active that you do during the day. Then make sure that you spend a total of at least 30 minutes a day on these activities, which can be just as effective as walking, swimming or other aerobic activity, says Dr. Howze.

Challenge yourself. Once you select an activity, vary it somehow to make it more interesting. If you like to walk, for instance, make it a little harder by walking up a big hill. Or walk faster for a block. And try to do a more difficult activity once a week, like stairclimbing or cross-country skiing, says Mangan.

Find the time. First, take stock of how you now spend your time. For about a week, keep a record of your time, much as you would enter expenditures in your cheque book, says Virginia Bass, a time-management consultant. Then review your time log. Chances are, you can nip and tuck parts of each day to free up bits of time. Instead of talking to a neighbour on the phone, maybe you could take a walk around the neighbourhood together. Instead of satisfying your addiction to TV news from the easy chair, you could soak up the news while you pedal a stationary bike.

Start with as much time as you can spare. Exercise doesn't have to be an all-or-nothing venture. "As little as 10 minutes a day helps," says Susan W. Butterworth, Ph.D. Once

exercise becomes a habit, chances are you'll find more time to do it.

Designate a time slot for exercise. Once exercise is on your "to do" list, decide when to do it. Otherwise, you won't always get to it.

Early birds who work out in the mornings believe that they are much more likely to stick to their programmes than people who leave it until later, when unexpected demands can knock the best intentions off-balance. Others find that working out at noon is best, so they don't have to find a baby sitter for the kids. Some people prefer a walk, followed by a bath, as a nightcap. So the "right" time to exercise is whatever time that works for you.

Block out the time. Write your exercise appointment on your calendar or in your diary. "You don't have to tell your secretary or business associates what the appointment is for. It's just an appointment," says Dr. Butterworth. Treat it the same way you would a business appointment or other obligation, she says.

Strategise with your family. Explain that exercise is important to you, and ask your family to help you find ways to fit it in. Maybe your husband or kids could cook dinner on your exercise nights, for instance.

Make exercise a family outing. You can have your five-year-old ride his bike alongside as you jog. Or you can enroll him in a gym activity, such as a karate class, while you do aerobics, says Dr. Butterworth. You might also try to schedule family fitness hours, with the entire family doing something active like cycling, walking at the zoo or tossing a Frisbee.

The Weight You'll Want
A Crash Course in Resistance Training

Here's what weight training won't do.

It won't make your leg muscles as thick as tree trunks. It won't make your biceps bulge beyond femininity. And it won't make thick, ugly veins pop out all over your body.

Sure, you've probably seen women who look over-muscled and gnarly – in muscle magazines. Those women often take drugs that enable them to build bigger muscles than they could ever develop naturally.

Without taking drugs, you might get strong enough to bench-press your husband, but you won't end up looking like him.

Why Weights Work Wonders

When combined with aerobic exercise, weight training effectively provides the one-two knockout punch in the slugfest against fat. While aerobic exercise helps you to burn off calories, weight training helps to build toned muscle and sculpt the body. A pound of muscle is smaller, firmer, and more shapely than a pound of fat. So as you replace fat with muscle, your body will take on a firmer shape.

Aesthetically, muscle looks better than fat. Fat, which has more "give," hangs from the body, while muscle, which is harder, hugs the body and provides a more shapely appearance.

"Large muscle mass helps burn calories, too," says Miriam Nelson, Ph.D. That's because muscle requires more oxygen and more calories to sustain itself than fat does. And strength training is more effective than aerobic exercise at building and maintaining muscle. So you burn more calories, all day long, all week long.

Lifting Lessons

What could be easier than lifting weights? Up, down, up, down, up, down. But there are some general guidelines to follow to get the most benefits.

Three times spells success. You can get away with lifting only twice a week, according to Catherine Brumley, certified trainer. But you'll get leaner faster if you lift three days a week.

Take every other day off. Do the routine two or three days a week, resting at least one day between workouts, says Brumley. A day or two off will give your muscles a chance to recuperate.

Warm up. The biggest difference between your weight-training regimen and the one your 20-year-old niece does is probably in what you do before and after the actual weight workout. She's probably ready to start after a 3- to 5-minute warm up. But muscles that have been on the planet for a little longer need a little more time. According to Brumley, 5 to 10 minutes of brisk walking ought to grease your joints and tendons so that movements are easier to do and you don't injure anything when you start your weight workout. Follow the warm-up with some limbering range-of-motion movements, as explained below.

Make a dry run. To ready your muscles, quickly go through the motion of the exercise five to ten times without weight before actually lifting the weight, says Brumley.

Take breaks. After each exercise, be sure to rest for up to two minutes before moving on to the next exercise. Rest breaks give your muscles a chance to recuperate and prepare for further effort. When you first begin to work out, you may need to rest for the full two minutes before you feel able to do the next exercise. As time passes, however, you will probably be able to shorten your rest time, says Molly Foley, an exercise physiologist.

Work in sets. You want to lift the weight 8 to 12 times (called repetitions). After each set of repetitions, rest for one to two minutes to let

WOMAN TO WOMAN
Lifting Weights Lowered Her Weight

For Karen Craig, a radiological engineer in Manchester, losing weight was losing its appeal. Bored by exercise, Karen was unable to stick to a workout routine, and consequently she carried around 10 last, frustrating pounds. Then she discovered that working out didn't have to feel like work. Here's how she lifted off that unwanted weight.

What I had planned to gain through my college years was a degree and a better sense of myself, not an extra 2 stone. But when I walked off campus for the last time, I carried 10 stone on my petite frame.

As I entered my post-college years, I vowed to slim down. So I joined a gym. With determination, I reached 9 stone. But before long, I tired of the treadmill and the aerobics routines. And reading magazines was the only way I could make using the StairMaster or stationary bike tolerable. I was close to my goal weight, but I would have been relieved if the gym had burned down.

your muscle recover then do a second set of the same exercise. As an alternative, to save time, you can work a different muscle or opposing muscle groups between sets instead of resting. You can alternate between arm and leg exercises, for instance: First curl a weight 10 times to work your biceps, then do 10 squats to work your legs while you allow the biceps muscles in your upper arms to rest, then work your biceps again. Or for variety, says Brumley, you can add a circuit workout to your weight-training routine. In this type of workout, you might lift a weight 10 times, jog in place for two to three minutes, lift the weight again, jog again and then move on to your next exercise.

Start light. Most people overestimate the amount of weight they can lift, says Karen Rucker, M.D. "They think 10 pounds is

Fortunately, I had a change of heart. I was leaving aerobics class one day when I saw a woman lifting weights. I was instantly inspired. That was the build I wanted.

I recruited a guy from work to be my trainer and spotter. He also became a source of encouragement, since struggling with a barbell can be intimidating when you're in a room that's packed with men. But I was hooked instantly. In no time I could feel new muscles forming, and in two months definition emerged.

The best part? I never get bored! I'm continually challenged by new weight-lifting goals, and since breaks between sets is a must, working out is very social.

I lift for an hour during my lunch breaks on Monday, Wednesday and Friday, working two muscle groups each day. Midday workouts head off the too-tired-after-work excuse. In fact, they leave me energised in the afternoons.

At 8.5 stone, I'm healthier, more confident and not weight-conscious anymore. To top it off, my metabolism has increased, so I eat whatever I want.

nothing, yet they need two hands to lift a two-litre water bottle (about 4 pounds)," says Dr. Rucker. To find out which weights to begin with, consider what you lift in a day. A shopping carrier bag with two cans of soup, two oranges, one grapefruit, a 2-litre carton of milk and a head of broccoli, for example, weighs about 10 pounds. Can you lift that 12 times in a row? If that's too much weight, see how the water bottle feels.

"We start out very slowly for the first two or three weeks, at about 50 percent of the weight people can lift. This is to prevent injury. If the training isn't enjoyable, you may not continue," says Margarita Smith Treuth, Ph.D.

Push the limit. For true strength gains, you want to work your muscles to failure – the point at which your muscle is so tuckered out that it can't lift the weight one more time – during each set. Working a muscle to exhaustion helps to make it stronger, says Brumley.

Breathe. Exhale while you lift the weight – during exertion – and inhale as you lower it, says Nancy C. Karabaic, a certified personal trainer.

Take a minute. That's how long it takes a muscle to get stronger: one minute. Here's how: Take two whole seconds to lift the weight. Exhale while you are lifting, then take four seconds to lower the weight. This doesn't mean just counting to four; it means four seconds (you know, one, one-thousand, two, one-thousand). The whole exercise just took six seconds, times 10 repetitions. You have just built your biceps (or whatever muscle you're working on).

Follow the rule of 12. "Resistance training for muscle strength and size should always be done with a weight that you can only lift 8 to 12 times before fatiguing," says Maria A. Fiatarone Singh, M.D. The key is to make your muscles tired, because after being completely fatigued, a muscle will recharge itself and bounce back even stronger. If you can lift your current amount of weight 12 times but there's no way you could go for number 13, you know that you're using the correct weight. When you can do 12 repetitions with strength to spare, it's time to increase the weight.

Stretch after your workout. In the course of lifting weights, muscles contract and shorten, making them less flexible. So you'll want to stretch after lifting, while your muscles are still warm, to restore muscle length and keep them flexible. Hold each stretch for 20 to 30 seconds, says Brumley.

TONING: ANYTIME, ANYWHERE

You don't have to have dumbbells and a weight bench to work your muscles. In fact, you can help strengthen and tone your muscles during many of your day-to-day activities. Here are some ideas from fitness experts.

Be your own squeeze. When driving, standing in a queue or sitting in a waiting room, squeeze your buttocks, thighs, and abdominals to give your muscles a workout, says Mia Finnegan, a fitness trainer.

Give yourself a raise. While washing the dishes, do toe raises to work your calves, says Teresa Flunker, an exercise physiologist.

Squat, don't bend. When getting clothing out of the washing machine, instead of bending over, do a squat to work your leg and bottom muscles. Do the same when picking things up from the floor, says Flunker.

Do television waist-whittlers. While watching TV or doing any other activity that involves sitting, you can still work the muscles along your waist, says Peggy Norwood. Place one hand on your opposite knee and lift that leg about six to eight inches off the floor. Flex your stomach muscles as you gently apply counter-pressure to the top of your knee with your hand, allowing your elbow to bend slightly.

Listen to your body. Various lifestyle factors, such as how much sleep you've had or lost, when you ate your last meal and how much stress you're under, can change how much weight you can lift in a day. So listen to you body and ease up if you don't feel up to your usual workload some days.

Measure success by weight lifted, not by weight lost. Healthy changes in the amount of fat and muscle in your body may not show up on the scale, but they'll certainly show up on the weight stacks in the gym. Write down the weights you use when you start. One pound? Two? Measure that against what you are lifting even as little as 16 weeks later. If that doesn't suit you as a way to measure success, try your waistbands. Even when the workout benefits don't show up on the scale, they'll be evident in the fit of your clothing. Skirts that clung a little too much before may look just right now.

Perfect Your Technique

When you lift, proper form is as important as frequency. Heed these tips.

Give yourself enough room. Women who begin to lift weights often don't give themselves enough "elbow room," says Karabaic. We tend to keep our arms at our sides and our legs close together in order to appear ladylike. To train properly, she says, you need to spread out and take up as much room as you need to be comfortable.

Pay particular attention when you're doing squats, says Karabaic. To do a squat correctly, you have to stick your bottom out, which at first makes women feel self-conscious, she says.

Visualise the exercise. To lift weights correctly, you need to feel your muscles move. Yet some women who are overweight or uncomfortable with their bodies for any reason tend to be out of touch with what it takes to move their bodies, says Kathy Mangan, a certified personal trainer. So at first, weight lifting may feel foreign. Visualisation can help overcome that awkwardness and help you lift correctly, says Mangan. Before you actually start the strength-training exercises described on the following pages, picture yourself doing the motions depicted in the illustrations. In particular, think about which parts of your body you will use to do the motion correctly and how that might feel.

Don't lock your joints. When doing any exercise, don't lock your elbows or knees. If you do, you'll end up putting weight on the joint instead of the muscle, possibly causing elbow or knee pain, says Karabaic.

Use good posture. Good posture will help protect your joints and spine from strain, says Tereasa Flunker, an exercise physiologist. Before each movement, check to make sure that you have good posture. Whether you are standing up or lying on your back on a bench, plant your feet on the ground or bench about shoulder-width apart. Bend your knees slightly and let your arms relax at your sides. Lift your breastbone by pulling your shoulders back and down. Roll your pelvis so that your lower back is straight instead of curved inward.

Smart Equipment Choices

You don't have to join a large gym with dozens of exercise machines to tone up. A few simple items will suffice. Here's what to look for.

Buy varying sets of weights. Because some muscles will be stronger than others, you'll need more than one pair of dumbbells. Buy sets of 3-, 5-, and 10-pound dumbbells. Later, as you become stronger, you'll probably need heavier ones, but most beginners don't need anything heavier than 10 pounds, says Flunker. You can save money on dumbbells by going to a second-hand sporting goods shop, scouting car boot sales or offering to buy lighter weights from bodybuilders who've moved on to heavier ones, says Flunker.

Go for comfort. Unlike purchasing a treadmill, stairclimber or other exercise machine, buying dumbbells doesn't require a lot of research or comparison shopping. Dumbbells haven't evolved much since the day of their invention. Your main objective is to find dumbbells that are comfortable to hold, says Mangan. They vary in length and width; you'll probably feel more comfortable with shorter ones. The longer the dumbbell, the more unwieldy it is, she says.

You also want a comfortable bench. Since some are wider than others, lie on the bench at the shop to make sure that it is wide enough to support your body, says Mangan. You don't want your shoulders or sides hanging over the edge, making you feel as if you might fall off. Also, some benches are taller than others. Make sure that your feet can comfortably touch the floor when you are lying down, she says.

Slip on the gloves. You can get through your routine without them, but you'll feel more comfortable with a pair of weight-lifting gloves. They help you grip the weight securely and prevent calluses.

Quick-and-Easy Weight Lifting

You want to train all of your major muscle groups to get the best benefits. That means your arms, legs, abdomen, back and rear end. Here's a short total-body weight-lifting routine designed by the fitness professionals at a health spa.

Dumbbell Bench Press

MUSCLES TONED: the chest (pectoralis major), front of shoulders (anterior deltoid) and back of upper arms (triceps)

WHAT TO DO: (A.) Lie on your back on a bench with your feet flat on the floor. Your buttocks, upper back and head should stay in contact with the bench during the exercise. Hold a dumbbell in each hand and lift them so that they are directly above your shoulders. Your elbows should be straight and the ends of the dumbbells should touch each other.

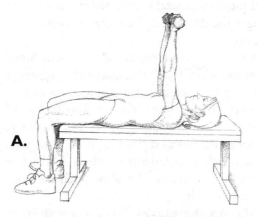

A.

(B.) Slowly lower the dumbbells by bending your elbows and bringing your arms down to the sides. Keep the dumbbells perpendicular to your torso until they are even with your chest. Your elbows should be bent at a 90-degree angle. You should feel a stretch in your chest. Then press the dumbbells upwards and together to return to the starting position and repeat.

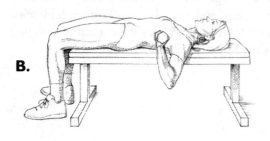

B.

Dumbbell Row

MUSCLES TONED: upper back (latissimus dorsi), back of shoulders (posterior deltoid) and front of upper and lower arms (elbow flexors)

WHAT TO DO: (A.) Stand sideways next to a bench. To support your lower back, place one hand – with your elbow extended but not locked – and the corresponding knee on the bench. Your hand should be directly under your shoulder and your standing leg slightly bent and under your hip. Keep your back straight and your shoulders parallel to the floor during the exercise. In your free hand, hold a dumbbell with your palm facing your body and your arm extended directly below your shoulder.

(B.) Lift your elbow towards the ceiling, keeping it close to your body, and raise the dumbbell until it is even with your chest, keeping your torso as stationary as possible. Your elbow will be above your back. Then slowly lower the dumbbell to the starting position and repeat. Complete all repetitions with one arm before switching to the other side.

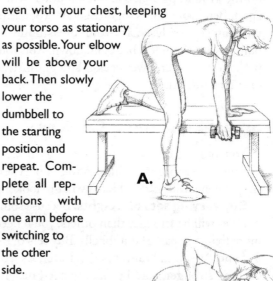

A.

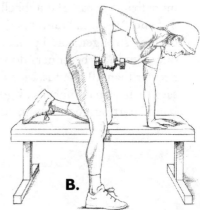

B.

Squat

A.   **B.**

MUSCLES TONED: buttocks (gluteus maximus), front of thighs (quadriceps) and back of thighs (hamstrings)

WHAT TO DO: (A.) Stand with your feet slightly more than shoulder-width apart and your toes pointed straight forward or slightly out. If you are using weights for more resistance, hold your arms straight down at your sides throughout the exercise.

(B.) With your back flat, your chest up and your eyes focused straight ahead, lower your body into a squat, as if you were sitting down in a chair, until your knees are bent at a 90-degree angle. Your knees should be directly above (never beyond) your toes. Keep your back straight and your heels on the floor. Keep your weight balanced back towards your heels to prevent yourself from leaning too far forward. Rise from the squat by forcing your hips in line. Extend your hips fully at the top and squeeze your buttocks muscles before beginning the next repetition.

Overhead Press

MUSCLES TONED: shoulders (deltoid), back of upper arms (triceps) and lower neck and upper middle back (trapezius)

WHAT TO DO: (A.) Sit sideways on a bench with your feet flat on the floor and a dumbbell in each hand. Your elbows should be bent and your palms facing forward at shoulder level, with the dumbbells slightly more than shoulder-width apart.

(B.) While keeping your back flat, press the dumbbells up and extend your arms overhead until the ends of the dumbbells meet. Lower the dumbbells and repeat.

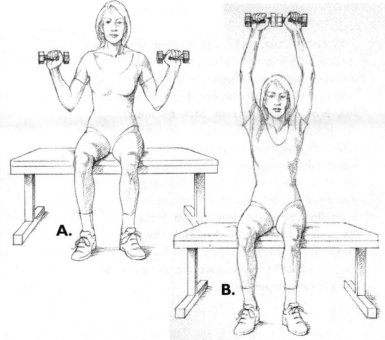

A.   **B.**

Biceps Curl

MUSCLES TONED: front of upper arms (biceps)

WHAT TO DO: (A.) Stand with your back to a wall with your feet about a foot from the wall and your knees slightly bent. Press your lower and upper back flat against the wall. With your palms facing out, hold the dumbbells with the ends touching at about midthigh.

(B.) Keeping your elbows pressed against your sides, bend your elbows as you lift the dumbbells up towards your shoulders. Do not arch your back in order to provide extra momentum for your lift. Slowly lower the dumbbells to the starting position and repeat.

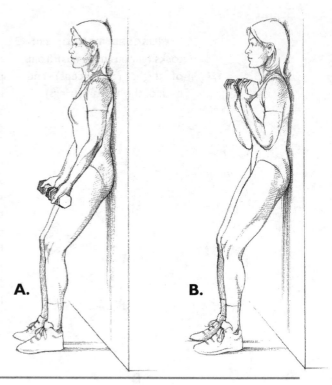

A.

B.

Back Extension

MUSCLES TONED: lower back (spinal erectors), buttocks (gluteus maximus) and back of thighs (hamstrings)

WHAT TO DO: (A.) Lie face down on the floor with your elbows bent to the sides and your hands palms down under your forehead. (A note of caution: Those with disk problems or current back spasms should consider an alternative exercise.)

(B.) Lift your head, chest, arms, feet and legs simultaneously. Lift only as far as you can without discomfort. Be sure to keep your head and neck aligned while you stare at the floor. Keep your legs straight. Hold the position for two to five seconds, then slowly lower yourself back to the floor. Touch the floor lightly but don't rest before doing the next repetition.

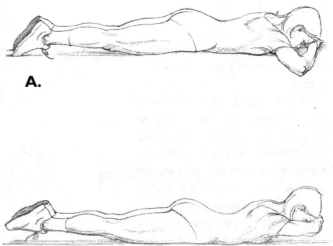

A.

B.

Abdominal Crunch

MUSCLES TONED: abdominals (rectus abdominis)

WHAT TO DO: (A.) Lie on the floor with your legs bent at an angle that allows you to keep your feet flat and your lower back pressed against the floor. Place your fingers behind your head for support, with your elbows back.

(B.) Use your abdominal muscles to lift your shoulders while keeping your lower back pressed to the floor and raising your buttocks no more than 2.5 to 5 cm. Be sure not to use your fingers to jerk your head off the floor. Hold for a count of five, then slowly lower your shoulders and buttocks to the floor. Start your next crunch immediately; don't take any time to rest. If you have difficulty raising your shoulders and buttocks at the same time, try raising your shoulders first and then raise your buttocks so that both are up at the same time.

(C.) If you have lower-back pain, do the exercise with your legs resting on a bench, being sure to keep your lower back pressed to the floor.

(D.) For a more advanced workout, hold your legs up with your knees and hip joints bent at a 90-degree angle. Then curl your upper and lower body together, trying to touch your elbows to your knees.

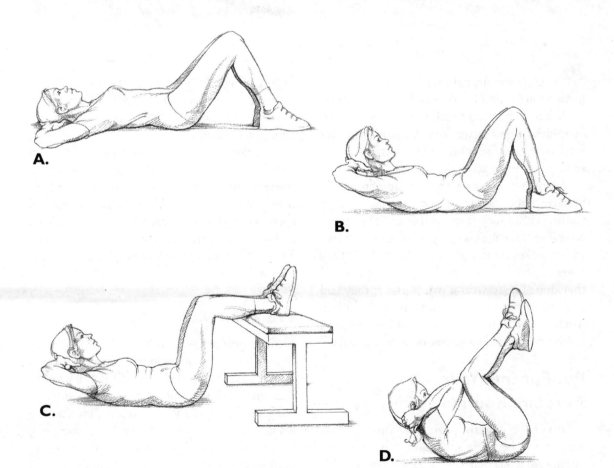

A.

B.

C.

D.

The Ultimate Fat-Burner

Getting the Aerobic Edge

Sweat. Complicated calisthenics performed to loud music. Taut bottoms and perky ponytails.

If that's what you think of when you think "aerobics," think again. You can work aerobics into your exercise programme without even setting foot in an aerobics class.

"Many women hate to exercise aerobically because they define it too narrowly," says Catherine Brumley, certified trainer. "They think aerobic exercise means going to an aerobics class, which makes them feel uncoordinated. Or they think aerobic exercise means being in a pool, and they don't like to wear a swimsuit. Or they feel uncomfortable in a gym environment. When women realise that they have other options, however, most find an aerobic exercise they enjoy."

Put Fun into Your Aerobics Routine

Forget the negatives with aerobic exercise: pain, sweat, breathlessness and boredom. Too often, erroneous beliefs – "I have to sweat a lot to lose weight"; "jogging is the best calorie-burner"; "I can never miss a day"; "if I don't hurt, I'm not working hard enough" – deter our efforts, says Brumley.

Even doing household chores and playing with your kids or grandkids could count, as long as you're moving your body with a purpose and not sitting on your rear end. The only "rule" is that you spend enough time exercising to burn at least 1,600 calories a week, according to researchers. That's the equivalent of walking for an hour at a four-mile-per-hour pace five days a week.

Walk Off the Weight

Since you've been walking since you were about 18 months old, you may think you know all the basics. But there are different ways to walk, and some give you a better aerobic workout.

Heel-to-toe walking, for instance, involves the whole body in one great gliding, heart-pumping, joint-flexing, muscle-working, calorie-burning motion. Because it protects the knees, this kind of walking is safe for women over age 40 or those who have never exercised, says Brumley.

All you need to do is coordinate your arms, hips and feet while you maintain proper posture. Here's each step broken down.

Assume the correct posture. Stand tall, with your chin up and your weight slightly forward on the balls of your feet. Lean forward just slightly from the ankles without bending at the waist. Imagine that your body is a board and it's starting to tip forwards, all in one plane. Avoid a swayback by tucking in your buttocks and your stomach, but don't strain. Keep your shoulders relaxed. This lean allows gravity to help you move forward. (You can check your posture by standing in front of a mirror and getting into position just before a walk.)

Start walking. Try to point your feet straight ahead. And make gentle corrections if you notice your feet pointing out or in. Land on your heel with your toes and forefoot raised at about a 25- to 30-degree angle off the ground. (Landing on your heel this way helps straighten your knee, which diverts impact from your knee joint.) Allow yourself to roll forward on your foot, pressing down on the outside portion of the bottom of your foot so that you feel continuous contact with the ground. Push off with your toes.

Practice walking barefoot. At first, just walk around the house barefoot to get the feel of it. You'll notice a distinct push forward when

WOMEN ASK WHY

Why is it that exercise looks so easy when other people are doing it but is so hard when I'm doing it?

If you're thinking of exercise instructors on TV who smile through hour-long aerobics routines, remember that they've been at it for quite a while. Doing crunches is a heck of a lot easier for them because they have chiselled abs. Unfortunately, they got those abs by doing a lot of crunches! Whether you're doing crunches, playing tennis, or jogging, you have to stick to it if you want to see results. But if you exercise too much, too soon, it's going to get harder before it gets easier.

So if you're a beginner, start slowly. You can't necessarily hop on the stationary bike at the gym and hammer away, working at the same resistance and speed as the last person, no matter how easy she made it look. Start with low-intensity, low-duration workouts until you build up your endurance and strength. The workouts should be challenging, but not so difficult that you end up spending the rest of your day trying to recover.

Some forms of exercise, such as playing racket sports or using a cross-country ski machine, take a certain amount of skill. And exercise is always tougher than it looks when you choose an activity that requires practice to master. Conversely, exercise comes naturally if it takes little skill. That's why walking is always a good place to start, since it's simple to do and is accessible to virtually everyone. And some exercise machines are easier than others, especially something like a stationary bike that requires very little skill. Others can be a bit awkward.

So start simply and have fun, and you'll stay motivated in the long run.

Expert consulted
Janet Walberg-Rankin, Ph.D.

you use this rolling motion, in contrast to your normal, more flat-footed stride. Go slowly, and you'll also realise just how strong your toes are and how much motion you can get out of your whole foot. You'll also notice greater use of your buttock muscles than in regular walking.

Use your hips properly. Hips that waddle side to side are a result of faulty technique. When you heel-to-toe walk with proper form, you look powerful and graceful, not anything like a duck.

To correct your technique, stand in front of a mirror and try this exercise suggested by Elaine Ward, walking coach. Walk in place by moving your knees forwards and back. Stand tall and let your arms swing naturally at your sides. Next, let your hips swing forwards and back with your legs. You'll feel a twisting motion at your waist. If it's hard to get your hips moving, pretend you're holding on to a towel and drying off your bottom. Notice that the movement of your arms helps your hips move forwards and back even further. When you are walking, this hip movement allows you to keep your back foot on the ground a bit longer, extending your stride behind you and giving power to your push-off.

Move your arms. Arm movement complements leg and hip movement and turns walking into a total-body workout. When you walk using your arms properly, you'll feel a sense of rhythm and coordination, plus extra power. Your shoulder joints stay flexible, too. Bend your arms at least to a right angle, but a little more is better, according to some coaches. Let them swing like pendulums from your relaxed shoulders. Hold your hands cupped in a

GET THAT EXTRA BURN

When it comes to burning calories, every little bit counts. Here are 50 ways to burn an extra 150.

- Iron clothes for 68 minutes.
- Shoot pool for 58 minutes.
- Canoe leisurely for 50 minutes.
- Cook for 48 minutes.
- Wash and wax a car for 45 to 60 minutes.
- Wash windows or floors for 45 to 60 minutes.
- Paper a wall for 45 minutes.
- Play volleyball for 45 minutes.
- Ballroom dance for 43 minutes.
- Stock shelves for 40 minutes.
- Play croquet for 38 minutes.
- Reel in a large, feisty fish for 36 minutes.
- Mop floors for 36 minutes.
- Food shop for 36 minutes.
- Walk moderately for 1¾ miles in 35 minutes.
- Dust for 34 minutes.
- Vacuum for 34 minutes.
- Play horseshoes for 33 minutes.
- Play table tennis for 33 minutes.
- Garden for 30 to 45 minutes.
- Wheel yourself in a wheelchair for 30 to 45 minutes.
- Do a country line dance for 30 minutes.
- Shoot basketball for 30 minutes.
- Bicycle leisurely for 5 miles in 30 minutes.

loosely clenched fist as you swing each arm forwards and back, forwards and back.

Don't hunch up. Your hands should swing no higher in front than the midline of your chest, and they should swing straight ahead, not on the diagonal. As you swing back, your hands should go back as far as an imaginary back pocket, but no farther. Your elbows should stay

- Dance fast for 30 minutes.
- Push a pushchair for 1½ miles in 30 minutes.
- Rake leaves for 30 minutes.
- Walk briskly for 2 miles in 30 minutes.
- Mow the lawn with a power push mower for 29 minutes.
- Snowmobile for 29 minutes.
- Golf without a power cart for 26 minutes.
- In-line skate leisurely for 26 minutes.
- Stack firewood for 25 minutes.
- Snorkel for 24 minutes.
- Bowl for 23 minutes.
- Play badminton for 22 minutes.
- Play Frisbee for 22 minutes.
- Scrub floors for 20 minutes.
- Saw wood by hand for 18 minutes.
- Skip rope for 18 minutes.
- Groom a horse for 17 minutes.
- Backpack with an 11-pound load for 17 minutes.
- Ride a motorcycle for 16 minutes.
- Fork hay for 16 minutes.
- Twirl a baton for 16 minutes.
- Bicycle fast for 4 miles in 15 minutes.
- Shovel snow for 15 minutes.
- Climb stairs for 15 minutes.
- Do the Twist for 13 minutes.
- Snowshoe in soft snow for 13 minutes.

close to your body. (Check your arm swing by walking in front of a mirror.)

Pointers for Beginners

If you're out of shape, don't expect to walk for an hour five times a week. If you do too much, too soon, you'll hurt. Start with what feels comfortable, maybe walking 10 minutes a day.

"Kind of underdo it each time, so you don't hurt or exhaust yourself. Don't create a reason to stop doing it," says Suki Munsell, Ph.D. First, focus on frequency: Work up to five times a week. Then work on duration: Extend the time spent walking each day. Last, increase intensity: Speed up your pace or take on steep hills. Follow these guidelines.

Begin by taking several short walks in the course of a day. If it seems like there's no good time to walk, consider the prime-time opportunities: before or after a meal, after a long meeting, at the end of the workday, or a couple of hours after dinner.

Increase by 10 percent a week. If you started by walking for 10 minutes a day for the first week, walk for 11 minutes a day the following week, says Dr. Munsell. Gradual increases should allow you to eventually work up to at least a half-hour four to six times a week.

Talk to yourself. Walk at a slow enough pace that you can talk about what happened on *ER* last night but not so slowly that you can hum the show's theme song.

Hold your head high. Keeping your head aligned with your shoulders – not tilted forwards or arched back – will help your neck support your head, says Dr. Munsell. If you lead with your chin, you'll probably end up with neck pain.

Don't lead with your hips. Some people walk with their hips thrust forward, as if someone had just yanked their upper body backward. Walking that way strains the lower back, says Dr.

Munsell, so try to keep your hips aligned with your shoulders.

Mix it up. To stay motivated and avoid overuse injuries, change terrain. Opt for areas where the ground offers a variety of surfaces, or switch routes.

Other Aerobic Options

If you don't like to walk, you can choose from a wide variety of other aerobic exercises. You want to find a couple of kinds of aerobic exercise that are easy and enjoyable and that you're likely to do today, next week, next month, next year – and the rest of your life.

First and foremost, find something you enjoy. But think about other criteria, too. Can you afford the equipment or fees? Is it convenient? Is it comfortable? Here's what top exercise and weight-loss experts have to say about a few of the more common types of aerobic exercises.

Aerobic dance. *Pros:* At home, you can do aerobics at any time of the day by popping a videotape into the VCR. If you go to a gym, spending time with other women who want to be healthy and firm can help keep you motivated. You get great calorie burn. *Cons:* You have to keep up with the instructor. High-impact classes can be hard on the joints.

Cross-country skiing. *Pros:* It's easy on the joints and works the upper and lower body for increased calorie burn. *Cons:* Indoor machines require coordination. Skiing outdoors requires skis, boots and poles, adequate amounts of snow, and access to suitable terrain.

Cycling. *Pros:* You get high calorie burn with

WATCH OUT FOR FAUX AEROBICS

If you're like a lot of people, you may think that certain activities are aerobic when they're not, says Barbara Ainsworth, Ph.D.

It's surprisingly easy to take the "aerobic" out of an activity, says Dr. Ainsworth. Here are 10 activities that may or may not be aerobic, depending on how you go about doing them.

1. Playing a round of golf. Pushing the accelerator and climbing into and out of the seat of a golf cart between swings won't do much for your cardiovascular system. Build in more aerobic activity by walking and carrying your golf bag.

2. Doing the laundry. Like many other domestic activities, modern conveniences have made washing clothes a no-breather. You can, however, work in a little exercise by hanging your clothes on the line instead of tossing them in the dryer.

3. Cutting the lawn. Whom can you fool perched comfortably on the seat of a riding lawn mower? Certainly not your body. To get better exercise, use a push mower.

4. Putting in a hard day at the office. Unless you are painting the office – or building it – your desk job probably isn't strenuous. Walking letters down to the post room, taking the stairs between floors instead of the lift and hand-delivering documents to co-workers can help improve the aerobic state of your job.

5. Playing tennis. If you play doubles, there are too many

---

little pressure on your joints. Cycling also has a high convenience level. You can ride outdoors or indoors. You can ride with your husband or kids. You can even cycle to work. *Cons:* Women with back pain should consider recumbent stationary bicycles, which allow you to lean back while you pedal.

Dancing. *Pros:* There's little or no boredom here. Any dance style – square dancing, rock and roll, disco, belly dancing or salsa, for instance – counts. There's minimal training needed. You

opportunities for people to end up standing around watching or only hitting balls at arm's length. If you don't play vigorously with four people, opt for singles matches more often, or at least volunteer to chase a lot of balls.

6. Cheering your kids' football team. Watching a game from start to finish – and attending all the practices – makes you a loyal fan, not a physically active parent. Walk around the pitch or volunteer to be a referee or a coach to improve your aerobic effort.

7. Running errands. Your errands probably don't generate more physical exertion than walking from your house to your car. When you can, leave your car in one centralised spot and use it as a storage area for your packages while you walk to, from, and between as many places as you can.

8. Watching the kids. Too many adults sit on a park bench or sofa while their kids run free. Join in the fun. Why should they get all the exercise?

9. Catching up on family news. Lounging around while everyone catches up on the day's events can make a family feel closer, but it doesn't contribute to their fitness. Go for a long walk, play catch, garden or go on a bicycle ride instead.

10. Housekeeping. Maintaining a house takes a lot of time. Unfortunately, cleaning up, dusting, cooking and washing clothes, in themselves, don't make you fit. Put more oomph into it and mop, scrub, vacuum and sweep with vigour.

buy a rowing machine, join a gym that has rowing equipment or find a boat.

Stairclimbing. *Pros:* Stairclimbing works women's primary trouble spots – the bottom, thighs and hips. It's easy on the joints. *Cons:* It's easy to cheat by leaning on the console or gripping the handrails too tightly, both of which lower your calorie burn.

Swimming. *Pros:* Swimming is kind to the joints. The water resistance can also build muscle, but not as well as during a water aerobics class. *Cons:* Unlike out-of-water exercises that increase your body's inner temperature and squelch your appetite, swimming in cold water may actually increase your craving for calories to keep your body warm. (If possible, select a pool heated to about 82°.) Of course, you need to know how to swim.

Water aerobics. *Pros:* The gentle support of the water nearly guarantees against injury and discomfort while helping to make your body more flexible. Water resistance helps build muscle strength while you burn calories. *Cons:* You need to attend a class or have a pool in your back garden. You have to wear a swimsuit in front of other people.

can't go wrong, calorie-wise, even if your dance form leaves a little to be desired. And dancing costs next to nothing: Pop in your favourite compact disc and do it in your living room. *Cons:* Almost none, unless you are rhythm-impaired.

Jogging. *Pros:* It incinerates calories. *Cons:* It's tough on the ankles, knees and hips.

Rowing. *Pros:* Rowing works the upper and lower body for increased calorie burn while not overstressing the joints. *Cons:* You need to either

Mini-Aerobics Add Up

You don't have to burn all of your calories in one long aerobic burst. Instead you can slowly but consistently add them up throughout the day by doing things like taking the stairs or walking from the car park. You want to accumulate a half-hour or more of such activities a day, says Maria A. Fiatarone Singh, M.D.

This approach works best for people who hate

to exercise. "It's sort of like putting small amounts of money in the bank. You get in 10 minutes here, 5 minutes there and 10 minutes another time. Your time adds up," says Elizabeth Howze, Sc.D.

Here are some examples of how small bursts of aerobic activity add up.

Take up climbing. Whenever you have the chance, climb the stairs instead of getting in the lift. You burn 10 times more calories climbing stairs than you do standing still. If this means that you need to allow yourself a few more minutes to get to your office or to make your way through an airport, so be it, even if you have to leave earlier for your destination.

Relay the groceries. Carry your shopping bags into the house one at a time, says Kathy Mangan, a certified fitness trainer.

Boycott the car wash. Don't take your car to a drive-through car wash. Instead, get out the hose and the soap and do it yourself, says Mangan.

Kid around. Rather than popping in a video to keep your children or grandchildren entertained, play actively with them. Play catch, skipping, climb on the monkey bars, push them on a swing or run foot races, suggests Vicki Pierson, a personal trainer.

Make dancing dates. Go once or twice a month to a dance club, says Pierson. Or take dance lessons.

Give up sunbathing. While at the beach, stay active by swimming, wave surfing, renting a rowboat or paddle boat or playing volleyball or paddle ball, says Pierson.

Get back to basics. If you have a riding mower, switch to a push mower. If you have a

REAL-LIFE SCENARIO
Ex-Jogger Can Still Maintain Her Weight

Jennifer was a slender, five-mile-a-day jogger until two children, a new job and aging parents took over her free time. Now she's lucky if she can exercise on the weekends, and walking is more her speed. Keeping her weight down is a struggle, and she's constantly hungry on what she describes as her "rabbit-food existence." Is there a better substitute for running, other than starvation?

It sounds as if Jennifer is operating under two popular misconceptions about dieting: One is that in order to lose weight, you have to be hungry all the time. The second is that you have to run five miles a day – or devote an hour or more to some other strenuous effort – to get the benefits of exercise. Both are myths.

The best way for a busy woman like Jennifer to achieve her goals is not rigidly adhering to a narrow notion of what constitutes exercise or living on a diet of celery and lettuce. Rather, she needs to focus on an exercise routine that she can live with and a healthy eating plan.

While Jennifer may no longer have the luxury of a full hour to devote to running, if she can carve out 15 minutes a couple of times a day to walk, she's still going to burn calories. Even if she doesn't have a structured exercise programme, she can make other lifestyle changes that will

power push mower, switch to a manual, says Pierson.

Be a Ms. Fix-it. Whenever possible, take on home improvement projects such as painting and wallpapering yourself. You'll not only get a workout but you'll also save money, says Pierson.

Keep moving. Take five minutes here and there throughout the day and play a game with yourself: Do anything except sit or lie down, says Peggy Norwood. Walk out to your garden and

help her burn calories, such as taking the stairs instead of the lift at work, for instance. When kids are in the picture, there are tons of things you can do around the house to exercise. You can walk up and down the stairs, dance around to the radio or pop in an aerobics videotape (preferably one that also contains some strength-training techniques to tone the muscles). Sometimes kids will even follow an aerobics routine with you; they usually think it's fun.

Once Jennifer finds an exercise programme that fits her life, she'll feel more energised and she'll also be able to maintain her weight more easily.

To keep her metabolism stoked, burn calories and further maintain her weight, Jennifer also needs to adopt a low-fat eating plan based on complex carbohydrates (found in whole grains, fruits and vegetables), with a moderate amount of protein (such as beans, low-fat dairy products, fish and lean meat). She should also try to eat small, frequent meals so she never finds herself getting too hungry. If she eats often enough, she'll be less likely to impulsively choose high-fat, high-calorie indulgences.

The surest way to succeed in weight control is to devote some time to both exercise and a well-rounded diet, even when demands on your time change.

Expert consulted
Debra Wein, R.D.

check the tomatoes, for example, or carry some clutter up to the attic. Empty the dishwasher. Pace the floor while you talk on the phone.

Hide the remote control. Without a remote control, you have to get up and walk to the television to change the channel. You also may watch less television, says Norwood.

Pull up short. When you are taking a cab, allow some extra time and have the driver drop you off a few streets away from your destination.

If you're taking a bus, get off a stop or two before you need to, then walk.

Run with the dogs. If you're the proud owner of a sprightly canine, you know your pup is eager to go out anytime. Give in to the eager pleading in those friendly eyes. The more you walk your pet, the more excess fat you lose.

Lunch away. Walk somewhere at least 5 minutes from your work area to eat your lunch. After eating, return by a roundabout route so you enjoy a 10-minute walk.

Take exercise breaks. During breaks at work, walk the stairs or walk around the building instead of reading the paper or visiting the watercooler, says Pierson.

Hike to the ladies room. Start using a toilet on a different floor than the one on which you work, or at least one that is further away from your office, says Mangan.

Put It All Together

Whatever approach you select or whatever combination you choose, keep these guidelines in mind.

Start slowly. Precede each session with at least five minutes of gentle warmup that mimics your upcoming aerobic activity or sport, moving at an easy pace. If you stretch, do it gently, without bouncing movements, after your muscles are warmed up. Otherwise you may cause injury to your joints.

Wind down. At the end of each aerobic session, keep moving until your heart rate gradually returns to normal. Dr. Fiatarone Singh says that this cooldown period, however brief, is critical from a health and safety standpoint because it allows the body to return gradually to its pre-exercise state. Never stop exercising suddenly. After some heat-generating exercise, you might be tempted to come to a standstill, sit down, or start talking to a friend. But don't let anything distract you from a sensible cooldown period of up to five minutes.

Use major muscles. To burn more calories, try to do an exercise that uses large muscle groups in both the upper and lower body such as walking, jogging, stairclimbing (without holding on to the rails), using ski machines and rowing, says Dr. Fiatarone Singh.

Write it down. We usually overestimate the amount of time we spend exercising by 50 percent, says Susan J. Bartlett, Ph.D. Tracking the amount of time you spend exercising can help ensure that you are getting in enough activity as well as help you stay motivated.

Crank It Up

Once you make aerobic exercise a habit, you can look for opportunities to burn a few extra calories. Here are some suggestions.

Go longer, faster. When you begin to exercise, starting off slow and easy is prudent. Then, when you're ready for more action and you feel you can keep it up for the rest of your life, go for it. "The more you do, the better off you are," says Adele L. Franks, M.D. "You can achieve measurable health benefits by exercising moderately for 30 minutes five days a week. But you can get an even greater benefit if you increase the time or the intensity."

Sweat in short bursts. Research shows that high-intensity training, such as sprinting, burns the most calories and also elevates your metabolism for a longer time than lower-intensity activities. If you can increase the intensity a notch or two a few times during your workout, you'll reap increased calorie-burning benefits afterward, says Dr. Fiatarone Singh. So if you're working out on an exercise bike, for instance, cycle as fast as you can for 90 seconds, then slow down, catch your breath and continue at your normal pace. Then do it again once you feel comfortable.

Stretch your time. "It's known that the only way to maintain weight loss forever is to increase the amount of physical activity you do," says Miriam Nelson, Ph.D. Indeed, a survey conducted by *Prevention* magazine of its female readers found that although women of optimal weight were no more active in their daily lives than overweight respondents, they did participate in more intentional exercise. In the optimal weight group, most women said their workout sessions lasted between a half-hour and an hour. Severely overweight women most commonly reported the shortest exercise sessions – less than 20 minutes.

PART FOUR

Think
Yourself
Thin

Feel-Better Food
Stop Eating for the Wrong Reasons

Name a feeling, and most women can name the food that goes with it.

Angry? Maybe you turn to potato crisps. Sad? Ice cream is the perfect antidote. Joyful? Nothing satisfies like pizza.

Why do you turn to food when moodiness strikes? Most likely you can blame it on your parents and your pediatrician. When you were an infant, your parents fed you whenever you cried. As a young child, you may have been offered a chocolate bar after you skinned your knee. Or perhaps you always got a lollipop after braving a booster injection. And you got to celebrate good report cards and sporting triumphs with trips to the local pizza place.

Even if you were never rewarded with food, though, you probably worked out its healing emotional nature on your own. Fat- and sugar-laden treats taste good and feel good in our mouths, providing instant pleasure that elevates a bad mood, if only for a few fleeting moments, says Dianne Lindewall, Ph.D. "On that level, it's hard for a carrot to compete with a bowl of ice cream," she says.

Also, foods like ice cream, cakes and chocolate are rich in carbohydrates that may also elevate levels of a feel-good brain chemical called serotonin, temporarily boosting a woman's sense of well-being, says Dr. Lindewall.

This carbohydrate connection may be especially strong during the second half of the menstrual cycle, after ovulation. At that time, progesterone levels rise, causing a drop in blood sugar and increased food cravings, says Elizabeth Lee Vliet, M.D.

Snipping the Food/Mood Link

It's okay to turn to chocolate chip biscuits – occasionally. But if we turn to pistachio fudge and marble pound cake to soothe our everyday disappointments, we're headed for trouble, says Linda Smolak, Ph.D. Habitually seeking solace with rich "comfort foods" can lead to overweight. Here's how to hold off the pounds no matter how bad the emotional crisis.

Don't deny yourself completely. You're more likely to turn to food for comfort if your diet leaves you feeling deprived, says Dr. Smolak. Studies show that restrained eaters – women who diet or strictly control food intake to maintain a low weight – seem especially susceptible to responding to strong feelings by reaching for something to eat. If you want to slim down, don't crash-diet.

Keep a food/mood journal. Jot your thoughts in a pocket-size notebook, in your day planner or on a three-by-five card. Answer the following questions.

❧ Am I physically hungry?

❧ What do I want to eat?

❧ What am I feeling?

❧ What am I saying to myself?

❧ Who is with me?

❧ What's been going on in the past hours or the past day?

Pause before you eat and identify your true needs – emotional or physical hunger, says Donna Ciliska, R.N., Ph.D. "Once you identify your emotions, the long-term goal is finding new ways to cope." Keep the journal for a week, review your notes, and search for your emotional eating triggers.

Find solutions that don't involve food. Once you've identified a situation that makes you turn to food for comfort, you need to come up with a different response. If your boss makes you feel unappreciated, think about strategies to deal with it that don't involve eating.

Share your feelings. Tell your children, your partner and your close friends about the positive feelings

WOMAN TO WOMAN
She No Longer Runs to the Refrigerator for Comfort

At one time, emotional ups and downs sent 34-year-old Joanne Held, of Edinburgh, to her refrigerator for solace or stimulation. But not anymore. When Joanne reached 15.5 stone, eating began to invoke distress, not comfort. So she decided to learn all she could about what she was eating, and more important, why she was eating it. Now, instead of running to the fridge, Joanne runs to her bookshelf. She credits this tactic with enabling her to lose 3.5 stone and to keep it off for the past 10 years. Here's what Joanne learned about food – and about herself.

For me, food and my emotions – good or bad – were closely intertwined. If I felt empty, I ate to fill the emotional void. If I felt anger, I ate to stuff it down. If I felt excited, I ate to contain my emotions.

Emotions are a part of life. So is food. And unlike smoking or other bad habits, you can't give up eating. So what I needed to do was learn how to control my love of food.

I learned everything I could about fat, calories and serving sizes. Now I can rattle off the number of calories or fat grammes in just about any food. I can look at a plate of food and know exactly how big the portions should be. And I discovered reduced-fat substitutes for my high-fat favourites. If I really want chocolate, for example, I'll grab a handful of Cocoa Puffs cereal instead of a chocolate bar. If I have a yen for potato crisps, I make air-popped popcorn instead.

That's not to say that I totally deprive myself. Another thing I learned is that sacrificing "forbidden foods" creates a negative mindset and sets me up for failure. But I am more aware that if I do eat something like a small chocolate bar, I'm eating four grammes of fat. I just count the fat content in my quota for the day, and it balances out. That way, any food can be incorporated into my "diet."

For me, channelling my energy into learning about food instead of eating mindlessly is positive and exciting. I take pride in what I've learned about food, and my success has replaced my urge to run to the refrigerator.

THE BEST (AND WORST) MOOD FOODS

Regardless of whether we're celebrating a job promotion, lamenting a romance on the rocks or fervently plotting the downfall of a rival, we usually reach for something that's loaded with fat and calories. Yet we could easily satisfy our moody yearnings with healthier alternatives, says Susan Olson, Ph.D. When various moods strike, here's what we eat and why – and what to grab instead.

ANGER AND STRESS

What we usually eat: Potato crisps, tortilla chips or nuts.

Why: Crunching hard foods releases aggression and tension in the jaw.

Better alternatives: Sugarless gum, pretzels, carrots or low-fat crackers.

SADNESS, A BROKEN HEART OR DEPRESSION

What we usually eat: Chocolate, ice cream or cheese.

Why: The smooth consistency soothes us. Chemically, chocolate contains a mood-elevating substance that acts like an antidepressant.

Better alternatives: Non-fat chocolate frozen yogurt, hot chocolate or vegetable soup.

HAPPINESS

What we usually eat: Pizza, crisps with dip or cake.

Why: Traditionally, we associate such foods with celebrations.

Better alternatives: Vegetarian pizza (without cheese), prawn cocktail or watermelon.

---

drives you to eat, a support group like Overeaters Anonymous can be helpful. Even if there is someone to talk to at home, it's often easier to discuss difficult circumstances with people who share them, says Dr. Smolak.

Treat yourself well. Instead of reaching for food, take time out for a walk, soak in a warm bath, play your favourite CD, call a friend, indulge in a manicure, pedicure or facial, relax with a new book or sign up for a low-fat cooking class.

Use self-talk. Words are powerful. By repeating an affirmation that focuses on the solutions you can use instead of overeating when you feel unloved, you actually make it less likely that you'll turn to the pantry for nurturing, says Nan Kathryn Fuchs, Ph.D. Try repeating the following statements for 5 to 10 minutes every day: "I handle my problems well. I eat food to nourish myself." Or come up with your own affirmation. Put it in the present tense, even if this is not what you are now doing. In time, you will.

Encourage yourself. Listen to how your self-talk is going throughout the day, suggests Barbara Dickinson, R.D. Is your inner voice critical or self-defeating or full of commands? Counter negative messages with truthful, positive responses. Turn a comment like "I can't talk with my new co-workers, they won't like me," for example, into "I'd like to get to know them better – I'll begin with some questions about our office during coffee break."

---

you have for them, says Gail Post, Ph.D. Don't rely on making them a batch of biscuits to express how you feel.

Seek out support. Sometimes the problem is that there's no one you can talk to. If loneliness

Put moods in perspective. "Tell yourself, 'This feeling will pass if I eat or not,' " says psychotherapist Mary Anne Cohen. Sometimes women cannot tolerate discomfort because they think it will last forever. You need to realise that feelings have a beginning, a middle and an end.

Solve the problem. What's prompting you to reach for food at the moment? A work deadline? A conflict with your spouse? Try to focus on solving the problem, rather than distracting yourself with food. If the issue cannot be resolved immediately, write the solution down and get on with your day.

Take a time-out. For 10 minutes, resist the urge to nosh and ask yourself what's going on. Figure out what's behind that craving, says Sandra Campbell, Psy.D. And make it a habit to tune in to your inner feelings at these times.

"Sometimes you just need a few minutes to pull yourself together," says Susan Moore, R.D.

Reach out and call someone. A brief phone call to a friend or relative may distract you and provide the emotional connection you really crave, says Connie Roberts, R.D. "You don't have to tell them you were about to eat four chocolate cupcakes," she says. "Just chat. It helps."

Delay. Come up in advance with a list of alternative activities to do when the eating mood strikes. At work, pin the list to your calendar. It could include reading your post or the newspaper. At home, sew a button on that skirt that's been out of commission for months. Polish your shoes. Re-pot your favourite fern.

Practice safe snacking. We all need an emotional pick-me-up once in a while. Try satisfying your need with tasty foods in small portions. This approach also keeps you from fearing the foods you desire. "I get patients to practice buying one chocolate truffle and enjoying it to the utmost," says Roberts. "Sometimes denying yourself the one thing you want can lead to eating more calories somewhere else."

Plan. If you must eat, tell yourself in advance what snacks you'll turn to when emotion-driven episodes occur, says Roberts. Possible examples include air-popped popcorn or a muffin.

Nurture yourself. Take care of yourself, suggests Dr. Ciliska. You may need more rest, more creative and intellectual stimulation or the opportunity to express your feelings and be heard.

You may need new sources of comfort, nurture and love, which could range from setting aside time for a relaxing bath or listening to your favourite music to developing new friendships.

Speak your mind. If you stuff down anger, learning to ask assertively for what you need can help, Dr. Ciliska says. This may require taking an assertiveness training class, she says.

"I don't know any women, myself included, who haven't benefited from some assertiveness training," notes Dr. Lindewall. "Learning to speak up for yourself, without being timid or intimidating, is a very important skill."

Make time for simply doing nothing. Are you stressed? Are mealtimes and snack times the only times you allow yourself to relax? If so, you may be eating just to get a breather from a nonstop routine, notes psychotherapist Sue Irish.

"A lot of women feel tremendous guilt if they stop working for even a minute," she says. "You work hard all day, eat lunch at your desk and then spend the evening doing laundry, taking care of the kids and cleaning the house. You may have a snack or spend a long time over dinner because for most of us, it's the only time that we give ourselves permission to stop working." Next time, try listening to music, reading, watching a film or simply not doing anything at all, she says.

Put some excitement in your life. Are you bored? Instead of perking up a dull day with chocolate-covered cherries, seek new job challenges, revive a long-lost hobby or find a new one, suggests Dr. Ciliska.

"I've known people to ask their supervisors for more diverse job responsibilities," she says. "If you feel bored at home, think about past activities you've enjoyed, such as a sport or a handicraft." Or peruse the community calendar of your local newspaper for new activities, from volunteer opportunities to quilting circles, tennis classes to wild flower-identification walks.

Eat every four hours. Skimping on breakfast and lunch can leave you hungry, irritable, and vulnerable to emotional eating, says Dickinson. The antidote? Eat the right foods, at the right times.

Most people find that a substantial breakfast that totals about 400 calories is helpful. Include a protein food (such as low-fat or non-fat milk, yogurt or cottage cheese), grains (like whole-wheat toast, oatmeal or a high-fibre cereal) and fruit, says Dickinson. "Plan on eating lunch four hours later and dinner four hours after that," she says. It's also good to have a small amount of a healthy fat, from avocado, peanut butter, nuts, canola oil or olive oil. These fats, comprised largely of monounsaturated and polyunsaturated fats, help you feel satisfied.

Do something with your hands. For some women, unwinding with food can easily be replaced by gardening, a craft or even computer games – "anything that involves fine motor movement of the fingers and hands," says Irish. Somehow, small, repeated movements help us chill out after a long day.

Work out what you want. If you've paused

> ## QUIZ: DO YOUR EMOTIONS DRIVE YOUR EATING HABITS?
>
> Getting a handle on emotional eating is the very first step towards successful weight control, says Ronette Kolotkin, Ph.D. How can you tell if you are an emotional eater? As you read the following questions, circle yes for the statements that are true for you and no for those that don't apply. Then check your score below.
>
> 1. I often eat for reasons other than hunger.
>   Yes   No
> 2. When I am overwhelmed, I often eat to find relief.
>   Yes   No
> 3. I usually eat to calm myself down.
>   Yes   No
> 4. When I am angry, I turn to food.
>   Yes   No
> 5. Whenever things feel out of control, I eat more.
>   Yes   No
> 6. If someone dislikes me or puts me down, I often turn to food to feel better.
>   Yes   No

and still want to nosh, think of ways to minimise the binge. Before you grab a chocolate bar or a big slice of cake, be clear about the food experience you're seeking, says Moore. "Find out what you really want," she says. "Will a cup of coffee do, or do you really need a chocolate bar? Are you looking for a specific taste, or do you want to fill up? If it's a special taste, then maybe a small chocolate bar is all you need. If it's volume you're after, maybe fruit or popcorn is a smart choice."

Bargain down the size. Once you've decided what you want, ask yourself how much you really need, says Moore. Half a chocolate bar or a whole one? Will half a piece of cake satisfy

er,a

,ar

7. When I'm happy, eating makes me feel happier.
   Yes   No
8. When I want to reward myself, I eat.
   Yes   No
9. Food is more than nutritional fuel. It's my best friend, my comforter, my escape, a source of unconditional love.
   Yes   No
10. If I'm lonely or bored, I'll overeat and feel better.
   Yes   No

If you answered yes to five or six of the questions, food is moderately important in your emotional life, says Dr. Kolotkin. If you have seven or more yes answers, food has a central role in your emotional life. You may eat to avoid unpleasant feelings or as a substitute for love, intimacy, achievement or even fun. Keeping a food/mood diary and using other tactics suggested in this chapter to prevent emotional eating episodes may help you meet those needs and avert feeding frenzies and weight gain.

you? "By keeping the size down, maybe to just a taste, you control overeating," she says.

Interrupt yourself before the next bite. If you find yourself on automatic pilot, mindlessly reaching into the biscuit bag, stop for a moment. "Ask yourself if this is really what you want to be doing and if there is anything else you'd rather be doing instead," suggests Dickinson. "Often, emotional eating is done quickly. You don't realise what's going on until the food is all gone. Pause, and be aware."

Balance the calories. Think about how much your indulgence will "cost" in terms of calories, then plan accordingly. You can compensate for the extra calories that come with an episode of emotional eating by eating less at another meal or two or by getting more physical activity, says Moore. Compensating for a 250-calorie chocolate bar, for example, would mean skipping bread and butter at dinner and walking an extra mile.

"If you think about balancing the calories ahead of time, you might decide that the chocolate bar just isn't worth it," Moore says.

Defuse high-risk times. Your mother's coming for a visit? Almost time for the annual family holiday gathering – and all the tense moments that come with it? "If you can predict high-risk situations and get ready for them, you can balance out the added calories in some way," Dr. Lindewall says. "You can always eat a little less before and afterward."

Challenge all-or-nothing thinking. If you do find yourself crunching instead of coping, don't despair. "That doesn't make you a bad person or mean that you've ruined everything," says Dickinson. "Even if you still experience some overeating, remember that you're making a change. It takes time. Don't lose sight of that."

The Stress Monkey
The Real Reason That Diets Fail

Stress – it's so familiar, you can taste it. Inside your body, your adrenal glands start pumping out the hormones epinephrine and norepinephrine, which tense up your muscles and speed up your heart rate, blood pressure and breathing. And you're as jumpy as a cat in a car wash.

A few thousand years ago, such tensed muscles and palpitating heart would have helped you run a few hundred yards in record time – hopefully fast enough to escape being gored to death by some really big, hairy animal with sharp fangs.

Today, such a sensation makes you reach for a dozen or so chocolate chunk biscuits or some other majorly fattening comfort food. In today's world, stress and weight gain go hand in hand.

The Stress of a Woman

Indeed, stress breeds bad eating habits. And women are particularly vulnerable.

"Women are probably under more stress than ever before," says Camille Lloyd, Ph.D. At work,

we have more responsibility but less job security. At home, we're juggling demands made by our families. Our relationships are less secure. (Consider the divorce rate.) And we're less likely to have extended family and lifelong friends to lean on, since everyone relocates so often, she says.

"We're trying to do it all," says Sylvia Gearing, Ph.D. "The bottom line is, women feel that they are in a particularly challenging time of our history. We don't have clear rules. Do we stay at home? Work? How will we raise the children?" Men are less apt to face conflicting demands.

Also, there's evidence that women turn to food more often than men when feeling stressed; we choose sugary foods and wash them down with copious amounts of coffee. Overweight women report that stress is one of the top two reasons that they overeat, says Ronette Kolotkin, Ph.D.

"If a woman is under stress constantly, she must take time to take care of her body," says Georgia Hodgkin, R.D. "The key is to set aside time and energy for good meals and good snacks, plus get plenty of sleep, exercise and relaxation."

Soothing Solutions

Here's how to get that fattening stress monkey off your back.

Take a moment to relax. Stress is most damaging if it's unrelenting. Just a few moments of relaxation can help considerably, says Susan Heitler, Ph.D. "Take mini-breaks," she says. "If you're at work and you start feeling stressed, get up and stretch or talk to a co-worker for a couple of minutes." If you're home, take a break in a quiet room.

Give yourself a longer break at least once every day, says Sharon Greenburg, a clinical psychologist.

Talk it out. If you have more to do than you can realistically handle or too little control over your schedule to get things done, speak up, says Deborah Belle, Ed.D. At work, talk to your boss. She may have no idea that you are overloaded or that your assignments are so ambiguous that you spend an extra hour each day trying to work out what's expected, she says. Or consult co-workers to find out if and how they've handled similar situations.

"If nothing else, you'll feel less powerless because you've spoken up, and that sense of control can significantly reduce the negative impact of stress," says Dr. Heitler.

At home, talk to your spouse. "In relationships, poor communication is often the source of stress," says Rosalind Barnett, Ph.D.

Go easy on yourself. "If you're in a job where expectations are unrealistic, you'll only feel more stressed if you tell yourself, 'I'm really incompetent,' " says Dr. Greenburg. "Instead, be objective. Tell yourself, 'I'm

---

ONE MORE REASON TO DE-STRESS

Even if you manage to avoid fatty, sugary foods when stress knocks on your door, you could still gain weight. Why? Stress seems to encourage your body to store fat, regardless of your eating and exercise habits.

Stress triggers a starvation response, an unconscious tendency to conserve energy from food, as if your body was preparing for famine. So when stress hormones begin coursing through your body, you start storing calories as fat. Also, during stress, blood sugar is shunted away from the chemical pathways that would burn it, so instead of being burned for fuel, it is stored as fat.

In addition to making your body store more fat, stress even changes where it is stored. An overweight woman who has a lot of stress in her life will usually store fat in her belly rather than on her thighs or buttocks, research shows.

So to avoid the fat-stress connection, you need to do more than practice good eating and exercise habits: You need to learn to cope with stress. That's why breathing techniques and other relaxation exercises are so important.

---

doing as much as anyone could – and more.' "

At home, accept the fact that you can't give the people you love everything, says Dr. Barnett. "So do the best job you can and be okay with that."

Off-load some chores. Women who work full-time outside the home still do more than half of the housework, especially tasks such as grocery shopping, meal preparation and cleanup and child-oriented duties such as bathing and helping with homework, studies show. Strive for a more even split. Your husband actually may enjoy some of his new responsibilities. "Our research finds that, for many husbands, being with the kids actually feels like a reward after a hard day at the office," says Dr. Barnett. "When husbands and wives share more equally, everyone feels less stress."

Think before you cut. Many women assume that all of their obligations add more stress, says Dr. Belle. "But research actually suggests that people with many roles – worker, parent, spouse, community volunteer – fare better," she says. Evidently, the satisfaction you get from one role can buffer the stress that you feel in another. So before you give up your post as a den mother, ask yourself what you're getting out of it, says Dr. Belle. It may be providing leadership opportunities that are lacking at work, for example. By the same token, the sense of satisfaction and mastery that you get at work could be the ideal antidote to the stress you feel while raising a teenager. More roles may also mean a wider stress-relieving social support network.

Exercise. The feeling of well-being that you get from physical activity can counter pressure at both home and the office, says Dr. Lloyd. Activities that get you moving, such as tennis, volleyball, running, swimming or walking, are ideal because they burn off stress-related chemicals. They also strengthen your heart so that it can withstand the future ravages of stress.

Pop bubbles. One study found that students were able to reduce their feelings of tension by popping two sheets of bubble wrap used in packaging. "Now we know why people hoard those things," says Kathy M. Dillon, Ph.D.

Carry a humour first-aid kit. Laughter is a tremendous release, says Linda Welsh, Ed.D. "You're changing your brain chemistry and putting yourself in an altered state," she says. "It works physically as well as emotionally in that it lets go of the tension and improves your outlook."

TAKE A DEEP BREATH AND CLOSE YOUR MOUTH

Proper breathing is one of the most effective ways to lower stress levels and head off stress-induced feeding frenzies.

"People who are stressed don't breathe properly," says Martha Davis, Ph.D. "To demonstrate this, I'll often ask my students to follow my finger as I wave it back and forth in front of their eyes. Then I'll ask how many of them stopped breathing. If they're honest and paying attention, most will realise that they stopped breathing for a few seconds. If they stopped breathing with something as mundane as my waving my finger, then how often do all of us stop breathing during the more stressful moments in our lives?"

That's where breathing exercises come in. If you practice breathing on a regular basis, you'll train yourself to breathe deeply and calmly when you encounter any stressful situation. Here are a few exercises to try.

➤ Lie on your back on the floor. Place your left hand over your chest and your right hand over your belly button. Now,

Stop and smell the apples. Keeping a green apple on your desk may calm your nerves. Research shows that the scent of the apple can significantly reduce stress and anxiety levels in women.

Think twice about caffeine. Some studies show that a little caffeine can increase alertness. But drinking coffee, tea or other caffeinated beverages is apt to leave you feeling jittery and irritable in the long run, says Dr. Hodgkin. In fact, researchers have found that caffeine can actually stimulate the body's fight-or-flight response to stress.

Keep your hands out of the sugar bowl. Too much sugar robs your body of vital nutrients, causing nervous tension and anxiety. It also fuels the fight-or-flight response, which overworks your adrenal glands and triggers

without consciously altering your breathing, notice which hand moves. If your right hand rises first and falls last with each breath, that's great. You're breathing with your diaphragm, which is how it should be. An ideal breath should fill the bottom third of your lungs first, then the middle third, and finally the top third; the order should be reversed when you exhale. If when you do the exercise, your left hand rises first or it rises more than your right hand, you're a chest breather.

❥ Lie on the floor with a book on your stomach. Concentrate on making the book rise and fall with each breath. Alternately, lie on your stomach and concentrate on pushing your belly into the floor with each inhalation. This exercise will train you to belly-breathe.

❥ Breathe deeply for a count of four, pause, then breathe out for a count of five. Do this for a couple of minutes, and it will have a tranquilising effect on your body and mind. Counting keeps your breath regulated and gives your mind something to concentrate on.

vasoconstriction, or narrowing of the blood vessels, further contributing to stress. High-sugar foods also make blood sugar levels rise, promoting an infusion of insulin that ushers the sugar into your cells, which in turn drops blood sugar levels, says Dr. Hodgkin. "When blood sugar levels drop, you can feel irritable, tired and unhappy, which is the last thing you need under stress," she says.

Plan for snack attacks. If you snack, avoid high-fat, high-calorie snack-machine fare by bringing your own treats, says Dr. Hodgkin. Stock a desk drawer with apples and oranges, low-fat microwave popcorn, or single-serving boxes of crunchy, low-sugar cereal.

Delay. Do you crave a packet of chocolate-covered raisins when a deadline looms? Wait 10 minutes and the urge may pass, says Carla Wolper, R.D. "Or have a nice cup of caffeine-free tea. Or take a short break. Distracting yourself for 10 minutes could be all you need," she says.

Decide what you can deal with and forget the rest. List the most stressful situations in your life. Then list the ones you can change (like leaving too late for work in the morning) and the ones you can't (like getting caught in the daily traffic jam). Prioritise the ones you can control, then outline a de-stressing action plan.

Defuse. Even when you're pressed for time, you can take three minutes to defuse a stressful situation and derail the need to eat, says Dr. Kolotkin. How? Step outside for some fresh air. Close your office door and stamp your feet, punch a pillow, or turn on a relaxation tape for a few minutes.

Balance thinking and feeling. Under stress, our conscious selves may recognise that we're not at fault or not in trouble, but our emotional selves may not, says Dr. Gearing. "There may be some feelings stirring around in there that you can't calm," she says. "Remind yourself that this will pass, that it will be over soon. Continuing to obsess will not help – it only takes energy away from doing what you have to do."

Get your daily requirement of play. Unwind, suggests Connie Roberts, R.D. Set aside playtime. "Go to an art museum, see a film or take a walk with a friend," she says.

Know your trigger points. The ultimate stress-control strategy is to know yourself, says Dr. Kolotkin. "Look for patterns," she says. "If you start crying every Sunday night and find you're eating all night long, it could very well be that you're having some feelings about your job and things aren't right," she says. "Sometimes you have to either accept that this is a stressful job and find less stressful work, or take steps to make the job more tolerable. The same is true of relationships. Ultimately, you have two choices – change the situation or accept it."

Take a hike. Walking is one way to attack all of your symptoms at once: It can help you lose weight, give you the perfect chance to sort out goals and priorities and reduce stress in a big way.

Put time on your side. Stressed-out women often seem overwhelmed because they're disorganised. They're the ones who don't start making the kids' Halloween costumes until the night before. They also tend to apply equal vigour to every task, even though some tasks are more important than others, and so they feel out of control – a leading cause of work-place anxiety.

If you recognise the symptoms of disorganisation in your habits at home and on the job, come up with a system to keep track of your tasks. You might use a notebook, for example. Make a list of everything you need to do and check off each item as you go along. The most pressing tasks go at the top and the least time-sensitive go towards the bottom.

List your de-stressors. Plan your bad-mood strategy by making a mental or written list of pleasurable activities. The next time you feel stressed out, for instance, try calling a friend, reading a book, having a bath, going to the gym, writing your feelings in a journal, playing with your kids or your dog, getting a massage, going to a film, taking a walk, buying flowers, listening to music, taking a nap, doing volunteer work, visiting a neighbour,

REAL-LIFE SCENARIO
Mindless Nibbling Can Add Up

Lynn's newspaper design job is a pressure cooker of deadlines. There never seems to be time for a real meal, so she's always nibbling at her desk. Even though she brings healthy foods from home, she's constantly dipping into the biscuits, sweets and other goodies that always seem to be around. At times she doesn't even know she's doing it. No wonder she's overweight! What can she do to get her eating under control?

Although Lynn probably won't like it much, the best thing she can do is keep an actual record of what's she's munching on all day. That way, she'll be more aware of when she's eating, what she's eating, and the amount she's eating. If she's willing to do that, she'll be taking a big step towards regaining control over her eating habits.

What Lynn *will* like is that there's no need to completely cut out her favourite snacks, even if she's trying to lose weight. In fact, she will probably be more successful at keeping the weight off if she doesn't feel that she's totally

taking a yoga class, meditating or praying.

Listen to music. Music can produce the most profound states of mental and physical relaxation. "In fact, the right music in the hands of a trained music therapist can yield reductions in blood pressure, heart rate and even the levels of stress hormones, such as cortisol, that the body produces," says Cheryl Dileo, Ph.D.

Listen to your heart. In a study, 22 middle-aged women who were highly anxious spent 10 minutes a day simply paying attention to their heart rates using wireless monitors. At the end of 12 weeks, their anxiety levels had dropped to normal. You don't need a monitor to get the same effect. You can listen to your breathing

depriving herself while she's dieting. What is important is that when she's nibbling on those favourite goodies, she knows she's doing it. Keeping a food notebook of everything she eats can really help her keep tabs on when she digs into the sweets and just how many pieces she actually grabs.

One thing Lynn can feel good about is the fact that everything she's eating at work isn't junk; after all, she does bring some nutritious foods from home. But as she knows all too well, that packed lunch of healthy stuff probably isn't the first thing she grabs when she's facing a killer deadline. If she becomes more aware that it's stress, not hunger, that makes her so ravenous, however, she can work out other ways to reduce that stress. She may just need to "take five" to walk around a bit or call a friend. And if Lynn becomes in tune with herself enough to know the difference between actual hunger and an oversize appetite due to stress, she can still eat a couple of goodies once in a while without the worry of losing control.

Expert consulted
Annette Pederson, R.D.

midmorning and mid-afternoon can prevent the low energy that leads to anxiety and stress, says Barbara Dickinson, R.D.

Drink lots of water. Fit in eight glasses (250 ml each) of water a day – and drink before you get thirsty, Dickinson suggests. Dehydration can cause headaches and fatigue, so you may think you need a snack when all you really need is cool, clear water, she says.

instead. Sit in a quite place and close your eyes. Observe yourself inhaling and exhaling. Don't try to slow your breath or make it deeper; just let it be natural. Focus on the sensation of breath as it passes through your nostrils or the back of your throat. Practice anywhere from 2 to 20 minutes a day.

Eat in the morning. Stress levels rise when your body is low on fuel, says Susan Moore, R.D. "Experiment with a combination of foods until you find out what gives you long-lasting energy," she says. "Some women need more than a bagel and juice; a little protein and fat, like a dab of peanut butter, gives them staying power."

Add a snack. Small pick-me-ups at

Stop the Saboteurs

Sidestep the Four Most Common Weight-Loss Pitfalls

Do you ever swear off chocolate only to eventually find yourself eating a jumbo bag of Smarties?

Does your mouth say yes while your brain says no every time a co-worker brings baked goods to the office?

Do you avoid eating "forbidden foods" in public but then binge on those same foods in private?

Have you quit your weight-loss programme because your goal seemed too far away, too hard, and too impossible?

If you answered yes to any or all of these questions, you have fallen into one or several of the most common weight-loss traps, according to Joyce D. Nash, Ph.D. Many times, say psychologists, weight loss fails not only because we are eating too much food or exercising too little but also because we are mentally sabotaging ourselves. The good news is that you can sidestep the sabotage. All you need to do is arm your brain for psychological warfare.

Diversify Your Thinking

Too often, women think in terms of all or nothing. The thought process goes something like this: You tell yourself that you are not allowed to eat chocolate chip biscuits. You swear them off. You get through a week, maybe even two, before you see a dozen chocolate chip biscuits sitting in the company break room with a large "free for the taking" sign taped to the box. You take one. Then two. Then you tell yourself, "I already messed up. I might as well eat all of them." Then you feel horrible. Guilty. And you pledge to never do it again. A week later, you find yourself in the same situation.

Why did you end up eating not one but a dozen biscuits? Because your weight-loss plan didn't give you any latitude. Rather than make space for one, two or even three biscuits, you allow yourself none. And when you slip up and have one, you quickly eat all of them while you still can. Such thinking is probably the number one psychological pitfall of any fat-fighting plan, says Carolyn Costin.

In reality, sometimes you'll stick to your plan, but sometimes you'll overeat. Likewise, sometimes you'll exercise regularly and sometimes you won't. Here are some strategies to pick yourself up, forgive yourself and keep going.

Avoid making rules. Do any of the following phrases sound familiar?

➤ "I have to lose 1 stone before the class reunion."

➤ "I can't ever snack."

➤ "I'm giving up chocolate."

If you've made similar resolutions, you're not alone. Women tend to set all kinds of rules for themselves and make promises like that all the time. The trouble is, rigid rules create sabotage traps, says Costin. "The more you deprive yourself of a food, the more you want it," she explains. That's why dieting often fails.

"There's such a big emphasis on resisting food," says Susan Olson, Ph.D. Once you stop following such rules, however, you easily lose weight, says Dr. Olson.

So if you have trouble quitting cold turkey, make sure you have a backup plan. "If you have to set up a rule for yourself, know that you need to be flexible," says Costin. Ask yourself, "If I break this rule, what do I do?" The answer? "I get back on track." The *Fight Fat* plan advises you to keep your fat intake below 25 percent of your daily calories, for instance. What happens if one day you eat 30 or 40 percent? You go back to eating 25 percent the next day.

Imagine a teeter-totter. When you find that you're tottering – maybe you had a lot of fatty foods at dinner – don't make up for it by teetering to the other extreme. Hold your teeter-totter steady – that is, head for balance, says Costin. If you eat a few biscuits, for instance, don't resort to eating the whole bag. Also, don't

try to make up for it the next day by skipping breakfast. Just start the next day with a clean slate with your teeter-totter in the centre, balanced position, says Costin.

Set realistic expectations. Instead of trying to eat perfectly 100 percent of the time, try instead to make healthy food choices 80 percent of the time. Then chalk the rest up to human nature, says Dr. Nash.

Give yourself credit. Instead of obsessing about the one day out of an entire week that you overate, focus on the six that went just fine.

Say No to the Food Pushers

She makes brownies just for you. She stands in your office doorway. You can tell that she won't leave until you try one. So when you eat the brownies, you mentally blame it on her – after all, she talked you into it. But shifting responsibility to others is flawed thinking. The food pusher isn't the one who's trying to lose weight or the one who's eating the extra calories. You are.

In the end, you have to deal with the damage. "Nobody really has the power to make you eat more; only you can open your mouth and put food in it," says Ronna Kabatznick, Ph.D.

Although you and you alone decide what you will eat and when, saying no to food pushers can be tricky. "You have to be vigilant, know what your emotional vulnerabilities are and understand that eating is often connected to times when you're feeling less strong or powerful," says Dr. Kabatznick. But, she adds, this is a terrific opportunity to practice standing up for yourself. Here's how to say no, graciously and firmly.

Practice assertiveness. We have a tough time standing up for ourselves because we have been socialised to take care of others' needs before our own, says Dr. Nash. To make things easier, use this four-step assertiveness process to get people to understand your point of view.

1. Describe the problem. How is the person hindering your fat-fighting efforts?

2. Express how you feel about the problem, without blaming the person.

3. Specify what you would like that person to do instead.

4. Explain the consequences of making that change.

You can say, for instance, "Sweetie, I've been trying to slim down. But every night before bed you get a big bowl of ice cream and ask me if I want some. I have a hard time saying no to such temptation. It would really help my efforts if you wouldn't offer me the ice cream."

Persuade others to buy into your plan. Some people will have a personal stake in your weight-loss plan. Your husband and family may not want to eat low-fat, for instance, while you do. So think about all the people who may be affected by your weight-loss efforts. Then explain to them why this fat-fighting plan is so important to you, how you think it may affect them, and what you need them to do to help you out. Ask how you can make the process easier on them. And ask them to let you know when your efforts are really cramping their style, says Dr. Nash.

Compromise. Sometimes you need to do more than express your feelings. You need to find a middle ground. If your husband has absolutely no intention of eating "diet" food, for instance, strike a compromise. He could agree to buy his own fat-laden snacks and keep them somewhere in the house that you never enter. Or he could go

WOMAN TO WOMAN

She Hung Her Large-Size Jeans Next to the Fridge

Kathy Cyphers, a 37-year-old accounts receivable supervisor from Milton Keynes, used a lot of willpower – and a dash of creativity – to lose 4.25 stone in six months. Here's her story.

I was very unhappy with myself and my life. I've never been thin. In fact, as a chubby child, my weight gained special privileges for me – shopping trips alone with my mum and no second hand clothes from my skinny sisters. But as an adult, my size wasn't so beneficial. At 4.25 stone over my ideal weight, I developed a negative attitude about myself and my job. Since no one said anything about my weight or my disposition, I kept trudging down my gloomy path. I wanted to do something about my weight but lacked the courage to do it.

I didn't own a scale, so it was easy to ignore how much weight I had gained. And I chose not to notice my expanding dress size. Then I was a bridesmaid in my sister's wedding. I saw the family pictures on Christmas day, and I couldn't believe what I looked like.

Suddenly I realised I had to do something.

That day I vowed to eat no more sweets, knowing that if I could get through Christmas without them, I could do it any other time as well. I thought taking weight loss one bite at a

out for fast food as long as he doesn't expect you to go along.

Outrun the Food Police

They watch the way you eat. They read the menu for you. They make faces and click their tongues when they see what you put in your shopping trolley. They are the food police, imagined or self-appointed arbiters of your eating habits. They exist among the ranks of

time – cutting out sweets first, then fat, then adding exercise – would break it down into manageable pieces.

As simple as my plan was, it almost derailed. I quickly learned that many saboteurs conspire to keep people from meeting their weight-loss goals – kind office-mates bearing chocolate chip biscuits, commercials taunting "you can't eat just one," or comforting family members reassuring you that "you look just fine." On top of that, my husband worked late and wanted dinner at 8:00 P.M., leaving me vulnerable to snacking until he got home.

The saboteurs' voices formed a chorus. I needed to hush them up.

When I started down the weight-loss road, I wore size 18 jeans, and they were tight. After I lost a bit of weight, I needed some motivation to continue, plus I didn't know what to do with my old jeans (which I hoped never to wear again). So I tacked them up on the wall. Right next to the fridge – a big denim badge of courage.

And it worked. When I wanted to quit – or have just one chocolate bar – I'd look at the jeans and remember that I never wanted to wear them again. I lost 10 pounds the first month, and the voices of the saboteurs subsided.

Once I started losing weight, my whole attitude changed. Now I'm more positive about myself and my job. My outlook on life is 100 percent different now. I know where I'm going in life, and I have the courage to get there. You can do it, too.

your friends, co-workers and family – and some are even strangers. Your husband or mother may be chief of the food police. And they make you feel guilty every time you eat.

So you eat on the sly, devouring hundreds or thousands of calories in a short period of time, says Connie Roberts, R.D. Recognising the food police is easy. If you get a tense feeling in the pit of your stomach, a tightness every time you and someone else are around food together, trust it. That person is a food cop. And he or she is someone you want to either avoid or confront, says Dr. Olson. Here are some strategies.

Define what you need. Figure out exactly how you want others to treat you and then tell them. Do you want them to champion your successes and ignore your failures? Or do you wish they would never bring up the topic of food, exercise or weight loss in your presence? For many women, the latter holds true. Explain that seemingly complimentary comments can pack a sting. You could start by describing how benign comments such as "Wow, I can see you've lost some weight" make you feel pressured to lose more, says Dr. Nash.

Rehearse those encounters you dread. Think about, act out or even write out how confronting a food cop will turn out. Imagine what you are going to say. List the possible responses of the saboteur. Then decide how you will respond to each scenario, recommends Dr. Nash.

Tell them once, tell them twice tell them again. "Sometimes it takes more than one time of saying 'Here's what I need from you. Please don't watch over me. Please don't watch everything I eat. And please don't give me those looks,'" says Dr. Nash.

Keep a safe distance. "Sometimes no matter how good you are at communicating your needs, particularly with mothers, they don't seem to get the message," says Dr. Nash. One woman who consulted the doctor, for instance, was able to get her mother to stop commenting on her weight. But then her mother began making comments about her cousin's weight problem. Her mother just didn't get it. And even though she loved her mother and her mother loved her, the woman decided to limit the time they spent together until she felt stronger about her efforts.

Take the Emphasis Off Your Weight

The simple phrase "I'm trying to lose (blank) pounds" can be a huge pitfall. Even though you may do everything right – you eat low-fat, you exercise and you practice portion control – the weight may not slide off as quickly as you'd like. You may occasionally hit plateaus. And so you say to yourself, "This isn't working" – and you quit.

When that happens, you tend to revert to eating high-fat foods and watching television, so you gain even more weight.

Instead of obsessing about every pound you lose – or don't lose – experts say that you would do better to focus on the beneficial changes you are making that may eventually help you lose. In other words, focus on the process rather than the outcome. "Focusing on a weight number is a way to sabotage yourself. It really is better to focus on changing your habits," says Dr. Nash. Slowly cut back on the amount of fat in your diet and slowly increase how much time you spend exercising. Then "let your weight fall where it may," says Dr. Nash.

Many women, however, have an intimate relationship with the bathroom scale. And breaking off that relationship can be tougher than getting out of a dysfunctional love affair. Here are some strategies.

NO MORE NASTY THOUGHTS

Depending on what you tell yourself, the ongoing dialogue about weight loss that takes place in the space between your ears can help or hinder your fat-fighting efforts, says Susan Olson, Ph.D.

When You Catch Yourself Thinking...
I'm not losing weight fast enough.

I've starved myself and haven't lost weight.

I've been more consistent than Joan, but she's losing weight faster. It's not fair.

I don't have the willpower.

I'd be able to lose weight if it weren't for my (husband/kids/job).

I get so nervous I have to eat.

I'm doomed to be fat just like Aunt Sally.

There goes my diet. That coffee cake just cost me two pounds.

Go in small increments. If you still catch yourself taking a peek at your weight and continuing to set a weight-loss goal, try to break up your goal into small, manageable increments of 10 pounds or less. If you feel that you have 7 stone to lose, for instance, focus on the first 10. Then, once you lose 10, focus on the next 10, says Dr. Nash. That way you won't feel overwhelmed.

Talk to the scale. Your scale is your assistant, not your boss, your mother or your guru. If the number you sneak a peek at today happens to be higher than the number you noticed the last

Here are some common sabotaging thoughts, along with alternatives to put you in the right mindset. According to Dr. Olson, these were originally identified by Michael J. and Kathryn Mahoney, authors of *Permanent Weight Control*.

Tell Yourself Instead...

If I continue my healthy eating habits, I'll lose the weight eventually.

Those pounds took a long time to get there. I'll settle for any progress.

Who says life has to be fair?

There's no such thing as willpower, just poor planning. Let's take one day at a time.

My schedule isn't any worse than other people's. I just need to be a bit more creative.

Eating doesn't solve my psychological problems, it creates them.

If fat is an inheritance, I want it to be cut out of the will.

What is this, the food Olympics? I don't need perfect habits, just improved ones. I'll cut back someplace else.

menstrual period is here (or fast approaching). And while it's not fair, sometimes your weight goes up for no discernible reason at all.

The real questions to ask yourself as you hop on and off the scale are "How am I eating?" "How often am I exercising?" "How do I look?" "How do I feel?" The more you come up with answers you like, the more you'll realise that the number on the scale is just a number.

Tally your score. One way to focus on the process rather than the weight-loss goal is to track your food and activity habits. Tallying makes you aware of your habits and keeps your goals and your successes right there in front of you. Use a plain sheet of paper to track every activity you do (including things like taking the stairs instead of the lift) and all the food that you eat (including the amounts). If you face a special challenge, put that on the paper, too.

If one of your goals is to eat regular meals rather than "picking" at food all day, for instance, write down the time of each meal and snack (or try writing it beforehand). Once you are at your ideal weight, you can try to keep track of food and activities mentally for a while. Just return to paper record-keeping if you notice that your healthy habits are beginning to go astray.

time, regardless of the fact that you've been eating sensibly and exercising in the interim, it may be because you drank more water than usual, because you consumed more water-retaining salt or monosodium glutamate, or because your

Motivation Made Easy

Find the Spark That Keeps You Going and Going

The first few weeks on any weight-loss plan are the easiest, "but the honeymoon ends a few weeks into the attempt," says Susan J. Bartlett, Ph.D. So you make excuses. ("I can't walk again today – I'm too tired. And I need to make time to clean the oven.") Or you cheat. ("If no one sees me eat it, the calories don't count.") Or you find yourself complaining. ("My body's not co-operating, so why bother?")

And you fall off the weight-loss wagon.

The thing is, you can make that early motivation-packed honeymoon last for the rest of your life. How? With careful planning.

Set Inspiring Goals

Quite possibly, motivation wanes because you have tied your goal to a number on the scale and get discouraged when you don't like what the scale tells you. First of all, scales can lie: Fluid shifts can hold the scale steady even though you have actually slimmed down. Second, like setting out for a distant destination without a map, setting a goal in itself offers no clues about how to get where you're going.

For more motivation, set a series of short-term goals that break your weight-loss task into achievable sections, giving you a strategy that leads to your long-term objective. Here's a breakdown of the characteristics that experts say your goals should have for best results.

They are achievable. Saying "I'll never eat sugar again" usually lands you in the pantry a week later with a handful of biscuits and a big load of guilt, says Susan K. Rhodes, Ph.D. A more realistic goal: For the next few weeks, put a reasonable number of biscuits into your food plan.

They are specific. Effective goals define not only what you plan to do but how, where and when you'll do it, such as, "At least four times this week I'm going to try to write down my meals before I eat them."

They are focused on behaviour. Beware of the "I'm going to lose a pound this week" trap. You can't guarantee yourself a weight change. What you can say is, "I'm going to walk every day this week" or "I'm going to nibble on carrots rather than chocolate this week."

They are just a little beyond reach. A weight-loss goal that's too difficult will make you want to give up. A goal that's too easy may not get you anywhere. At first, set modest goals that you can achieve quickly, such as switching from whole milk to low-fat milk. Then begin to set more ambitious goals, such as switching to non-fat milk.

Here's some other advice on how to set inspiring goals.

Reward yourself. You can choose anything for a reward as long as it is enjoyable, immediate and available only when the goal is met. Some people do better if they reward themselves each time they accomplish a difficult task. They'll put a pound in a jar after each exercise session, for instance, or allow themselves to soak in a hot bath for 30 minutes.

Think of at least 20 small, non-food rewards for yourself. They should be simple, short-term things you would like to have or do that don't take a lot of time or money, such as having a mineral bath, gathering a bouquet of fresh flowers, calling a friend for a long chat or reading a chapter of a novel you never seem to have time to finish. Then write each one on a separate slip of paper and put the paper in an empty biscuit tin. Each day, as you accomplish a mini-goal, draw from the reward tin.

Time your rewards. Instead of always rewarding yourself after the fact, find ways to reward yourself during an activity. If you like to watch Oprah, for instance, but you can't usually find the time, only allow yourself to take part while pedalling a stationary bike. Or reward yourself by watching a sappy film that your husband doesn't want to see – as long as you do it while you're on the treadmill or stationary bike.

Write it down. Seeing your goals on paper, where you can update them, will make them seem more real and boost your motivation to achieve

them, says Virginia Bass, who teaches executives to do this for all kinds of goals. So put your mini-goals on paper, then give yourself a star once you accomplish them. Or make a formal contract with a friend. Include your goal and the reward for reaching it.

See it happen. Close your eyes and visualise yourself accomplishing your week's goals. If your mini-goal is to get up 15 minutes earlier to walk the dog, for instance, in your mind see the alarm clock set at 6:15 A.M. instead of 6:30. See Spot at your bedside with his tail wagging. Your track suit and walking shoes are next to the bed, where you placed them the night before. Picture yourself getting into them and getting out there. Now you're set to really do it.

Maintaining Momentum

You can capitalise on the motivation you feel at the beginning of a weight-loss adventure by making some careful plans for later in your fat-fighting journey. Details to remember:

Do a cost-benefit analysis. Divide a sheet of paper into two vertical columns. In the left-hand column, list all the benefits of sticking to your weight-loss plan. Some examples: "I've already dropped six pounds," "I have more energy," "I deal with stress better." Under those items, jot down the costs of not sticking to the programme, like "I'll be out of shape" or "My belly will come back."

In the right-hand column, write the costs of following your programme, such as "I have to cut back on favourite foods that are loaded with fat" or "I have to make time for exercise." Then include the benefits of abandoning the programme, such as, "I'll have more time to myself because I won't be walking every day" or "I'll be able to eat and drink whatever I want."

"The things in the left column are the thoughts

that will motivate you. When your thoughts start drifting to the right column, to the costs of making the changes and the benefits of not bothering, that undermines your motivation," says Joyce D. Nash, Ph.D. Post the list where you can see it every day, as both a visual and mental reminder. Being honest and open about your negative thoughts can help you work out why you're starting to feel burned out, says Dr. Nash.

Check your records. At the beginning of your fat-fighting journey, write down your weight, body measurements, cholesterol levels, blood pressure and any other vital statistics. Also write down the amount of time you spend exercising. Then later, if your motivation wanes, check out your progress. Avoid thinking about how far you have to go to reach your long-term weight-loss goals. Instead, pat yourself on the back for the progress that you have made.

Start for the right reasons. Perhaps you decide to lose weight because someone wants you to. Maybe your husband wants you to slim down, or the family doctor keeps pushing the issue, or your mum's been nagging you. Well, ignore them.

"Trying to lose weight because others want you to creates a commitment that may cause feelings of resentment," says Dr. Bartlett, and resentment can weaken your resolve. Telling yourself that you "have to" or "should" lose weight, exercise, or stay away from particular foods brings up a rebellious twin that says, "I don't want to have to."

Write down all of the reasons that you decided to eat lower-fat foods and exercise. Each sentence must start with the words "Because I

REAL-LIFE SCENARIO
Marriage-Induced Pounds Can Come Off – With Patience

Debbie's husband is unhappy with the 10 pounds she has gained since they were married two years ago, and he wants her to lose the weight. The problem is, he doesn't have a weight problem , even though he's a meat-and-potatoes man who loves to go out to dinner with Debbie two or even three nights a week. He just bought her a treadmill for her birthday and expects to see results. What can she expect?

Debbie's husband has the typical male attitude: "Here's a problem. Let's fix it." But he clearly has a different perception and understanding of weight management than Debbie does. And since he's never had a weight problem, that's understandable.

For women, eating often has an emotional component, so it's tougher for us to control our food intake than it is for men. Also, just by the nature of our bodies, it's tougher for us to lose weight. Plus, women have hormones that create food cravings as well as hamper our ability to lose weight. And we have harried schedules, which may make it tough for us to fit in exercise. All together, this explains why it can – and should

choose to..." When things occasionally get tough, refer to the list.

List your high-risk situations and your defense strategy. Maybe you tend to overeat at restaurants or you have an aversion to working out in cold weather or you have trouble stopping at just two non-fat oatmeal-raisin biscuits. Write each of your most tempting situations on the fronts of index cards. Then think of as many counterstrikes as you can and note them on the backs of the cards. Some suggestions: Drink a glass of water and have a carrot or celery stalk to take the edge off your hunger before you leave

– take Debbie 10 weeks or more to lose 10 pounds.

A man who has never had a weight problem needs help in understanding the struggle that a woman faces. Debbie can educate her husband in various ways. She can give him materials, such as brochures or magazines, explaining why it takes time to lose weight. She can point out that eating out may cause her to eat too much food or tempt her to eat foods that she's trying to cut back on. She may suggest a compromise: They can still go out to eat, but only once a week and only to a restaurant where she knows she can order low-fat, healthy dishes.

Also, if Debbie's husband continues to breathe down her neck, "expecting to see results," she can assure him that she understands he is only trying to help, but such policing is making her nervous, which can lead to eating more. It can also lead to resentment, which could make her sabotage her own efforts. If all else fails, Debbie may even consider inviting her husband to accompany her to consult a professional psychologist who specialises in weight management so that they can work on communicating better.

Expert consulted
Joyce D. Nash, Ph.D.

for the restaurant; try shopping mall walking or gym workouts in the winter; buy individually wrapped snacks, such as non-fat oat and fruit bars, to keep you from going on a binge. With your defense at the ready, you'll be equipped to handle anything and stay motivated right to the weight-loss finish line.

Keep Going through the Tough Times

Once you are well into your fat-fighting plan, you may still experience some motivational peaks and valleys. Often you can link dips to boredom. Here are ways to liven up your routine.

Go on a food safari. Instead of making yourself as miserable as possible by forcing yourself to eat the blandest low-fat foods you can find, think of eating low-fat as a food adventure. Try different recipes. Try different low-fat foods. One low-fat brand of cheese might not taste as dry as another. One vegetarian chilli recipe may taste meatier than another. The key is to try.

Spice up your diet. Give your tastebuds a treat: Try a new, exotic fruit or vegetable, a different type of fish, or a new low-fat or non-fat product each week. Start a herb garden and add fresh sprigs of basil, oregano, coriander or parsley to your recipes. Every time you go to the supermarket, hunt down one new, low-fat food that you've never tried before. It could be a frozen meal or an exotic fruit.

Change your workout routine. Take your act on the road. Instead of stationary cycling, traverse wooded trails on a mountain bike. Walk in a new area or with a new partner. Try a workout in the morning instead of waiting until the afternoon. Take up a new sport or switch from weight-lifting machines to a free-weight workout. Or experiment with interval training: After a 10- or 15-minute warm-up, step up your pace for about 2 minutes. Slow down to catch your breath, recovering for about 1 minute, then speed up again for another 2. Vary your workouts as much as you like in order to keep them fresh and exciting.

Get a partner. Two exercisers are better

WEIGHT-LOSS CHEERLEADERS YOU DON'T NEED

Just as some girls get dropped from the school cheer-leading team, some family members and friends ought to be dropped from your weight-loss cheerleading section. Here's why. Although they may mean well, some would-be-weight-loss supporters can actually become weight-loss hindrances, says Susan Olson, Ph.D.

Your mum or best friend, for example, may be very good at explaining what to eat and what not to eat, but they're so good that you end up eating tons of food as soon as you're safely out of their sight. Or best friend number two may be fighting a weight-loss battle of her own. Your fat losses might make her jealous, so she keeps baking you treats to even out the playing field.

To pick a true weight-loss motivator, look for someone who treats you like an adult and encourages you to act like one, says Dr. Olson. You want the type of person who generally makes you feel good about yourself, who's willing to hear about your struggles, and who encourages you to reach your goal. She won't tell you everything you've been doing wrong. Rather, she'll remind you of all the things you are doing right. "Such a person will give you the message that you can do anything you set your mind to," says Dr. Olson. "And that person will help you in any way that *you* want, not anyway that she wants."

than one. On those days when you feel like copping out, your partner can talk you into working out.

Break up your exercise session. Some people find exercise less boring if they break it up into numerous short sessions instead of one long, arduous workout. Try walking for 10 minutes before work, 15 minutes at lunch and 10 minutes after dinner, for instance. Doesn't

seem like a 35-minute workout, does it?

Distract yourself. Studies show that fast, upbeat music can help motivate you to exercise and keep you going longer. Other effective tactics include watching television or reading while working out on stationary equipment.

Holding Firm

Once you've lost all the weight you've planned to lose, you take on a new motivational challenge. "During maintenance, there isn't that psychological reward of getting on the scale and seeing a smaller number," points out Judy E. Marshel, R.D. "Now your goal is to see the same number all the time, and for some people it's not nearly as satisfying."

You can keep your motivation going strong, however, just by switching mental tracks. Now you no longer have a weight-loss goal, but rather a lifestyle goal. Weight maintenance is a lifetime endeavour.

In order to stay motivated and value your efforts, look for new ways to pat yourself on the back. Each morning as you get dressed, for instance, remind yourself how well your clothes fit. Or each time you get on the scale and the number has not budged, consider the event a cause for celebration. You may have completed the weight-loss race, but now you are embarking on a new, more challenging adventure.

Your Time, Your Weight

A Sensible Programme Takes Time and Patience

At a weight-loss centre, coordinator Beth Bussey, R.D., won't let women lose more than 10 percent of their weight within three months. If the women start to lose weight too quickly, Bussey tells them to eat more.

As you can imagine, the women complain. They want those pounds off fast. They want them off now. After all, for a 12.75-stone woman, 10 percent is just 18 pounds dragged out over three months' time.

At that pace, fat-fighting doesn't even seem worth the time spent exercising, reading labels or shopping for non-stick cookware. In reality, however, weight that comes off as slow as molasses is weight that will stay off.

In This Race, the Last Will Be First

If Bussey could, she'd actually make women lose weight even more slowly, over the course of a year. But she speeds it up for two reasons. First, many of the people she counsels are what doctors describe as morbidly obese – in order to avoid heart attack and other life-threatening conditions, they need to lose weight as quickly as possible within the limits of medical safety. Second, most people simply won't wait an entire year for a 10 percent loss.

So Bussey puts them on the 12-week plan. She tells them to be patient. To help ease their urgency, she explains over and over again why slow weight loss is worth the effort.

The odds are that you're probably in the same kind of fat-fighting rush as the women Bussey counsels. So here are all the reasons that you want to lose fat slowly.

❧ While you could initially lose weight faster by severely restricting your food intake, you'll have a harder time reaching your goal weight. Eating too few calories slows your metabolism – the rate at which your body burns calories – causing a weight-loss plateau. So regardless of how few calories you eat, your weight essentially remains stagnant well before you hit your goal. To keep your body from conserving calories, you need to eat at least 1,200 calories a day.

❧ Rapid weight loss usually brings on

WOMAN TO WOMAN

No-Excuse Time Management

Lisa McMillen of Newcastle, had tried 10 times to lose weight. She tried fad diets and joined health spas and support groups, but each time she failed – until she learned to make time for weight loss. Now, for the first time, she weighs less than her husband. Here's how she found time.

I don't have the time" is probably the most common excuse for putting off weight loss. I know I've used it a few times. Whenever I tried to slim down, the demands of work, family and friends seemed to interfere. Life's just not set up for putting ourselves first.

But I got tired of buying larger and larger clothing. As a dental office manager, it was getting to the point where, if I didn't buy new uniforms, I would burst out of them.

It took me eight months, but I lost the 2.5 stone that I needed to feel better about myself. I decided to exercise at 5:15 A.M. I dusted off my treadmill and began walking five or six days a week for a half-hour. Surprisingly, I actually enjoy this time. I watch the morning news or just zone out.

I also started taking time to cook things that are better for me. I use the microwave a lot. It took a while, but I learned to make recipes that included more vegetables.

I used to resent the extra time it took to become healthier. After a while, it became more natural. I just kept telling myself that I was worth the time and the effort it was taking to lose the weight. Now, I take the time, no matter what else is going on in my life. No more excuses.

plumper returns. Once you start eating more food after ending a low-calorie diet, you gain weight faster than before you began dieting because your metabolism isn't burning calories as well. Then, every time you crash-diet to get rid of this new fat, your metabolism slows down even more quickly, which makes weight loss even harder.

⟡ If you restrict calories long enough, your metabolism can drop to as low as 500 calories a day. When your body burns so few calories, you may feel cold, even in the summer. You may also feel tired and notice other side effects, such as dry skin, constipation and depression. A diet of fewer than 800 calories a day can also pose significant health risks such as heartbeat irregularities and mineral imbalances, which can be life-threatening.

⟡ Another potential by-product of rapid weight loss is also a painful one: gallstones. Usually the gall-bladder contracts to empty itself of bile and cholesterol. When food intake is low, however, the gall-bladder loses its ability to contract, so cholesterol is more likely to build up and thicken into painful gallstones.

To get over the urge to crash-diet and shed those pounds fast, try to focus instead on the tons of lifestyle changes that you are making. Reward yourself for making the switch from whole milk to skimmed, for instance. Pat yourself on the back for eating breakfast. Give yourself a cheer for walking this morning. The more you focus on the small external changes you make to lose weight, the less you'll obsess about how much weight you are losing and how fast.

Fitting in Weight Loss

You might think that cooking healthy food

and exercising take too much time. Not true.

For one thing, exercise actually creates time. After the first week or so of a regular exercise programme, many people report that their levels of energy and stamina surge to the point where they feel as if they've actually gained extra productive hours in each day. Exercise also helps you gain time in the most literal sense: By reducing your risk of heart disease, osteoporosis and other life-threatening diseases, you can add days and even years to your life.

Still, you'll be more likely to stick with your fat-fighting habits if you learn to fit them into your schedule. Here's how.

Plan your attack. Smart cooking begins with a plan, says Judy Gilliard, author of *The Guiltless Gourmet* and other cookbooks, who started to cook healthier meals when she was diagnosed with diabetes.

"We don't always have time to prepare food, so we make unhealthy choices, like grabbing a doughnut for breakfast. The key is to take a little time each week to pre-plan what we'll cook," says Suzanne Havala, R.D.

Devote part of a weekend (or other convenient time) to planning your meals and making a shopping list, Gilliard suggests. Select healthier recipes that you'd like to try.

Reorganise your larder. If your foods aren't where you can easily find them, you'll waste time hunting

WOMEN ASK WHY

Why is it so hard to lose weight and so easy to gain it back?

There's really no clear-cut answer. But there are a few possibilities.

For one, women usually lose a lot of water and sodium during their first couple of weeks of weight loss, especially if they are on a low-carbohydrate diet. This water loss amounts to a significant drop in weight on the scale. But it's deceiving. The water comes mostly from muscle and other parts of the body, not from fat. Fat contains no water, and the tissue surrounding fat has very little. If a woman resumes a normal diet after only a couple of weeks, the water she lost will come back almost instantly. While it took a week or two to lose a few pounds, those pounds can return within a day, so it seems as if you've regained your weight instantly. But the truth is that you never lost fat; you just lost a lot of water.

On a longer diet, you typically lose weight for about three months and then plateau. It's not exactly clear why the body responds this way. But the result is that your lower body weight requires fewer calories to maintain. To continue losing weight, you may need to modify your calorie intake further, increase your level of exercise, or both. If you don't, you may find the pounds creeping back on.

Also, when you crash-diet, you may lose some muscle tissue, which slows your metabolism. But when you gain the weight back, unless you are exercising, you may gain back fat, not muscle. So the next time you try to lose weight, you start off with a slower metabolism than you had initially because you have less muscle to start with.

Not every woman loses muscle when she diets. You can reduce the chances of muscle loss by exercising and holding your weight loss to a pound or less a week.

Expert consulted
Judith S. Stern, R.D., Sc.D.

when you could be cooking, says Gilliard. "Group your canned tomato products – tomato sauce, tomato purée, stewed tomatoes and the like – in one logical, convenient place, for instance. Do the same with canned beans, grains, oils, condiments and so forth."

Out with the old. Go through your refrigerator, cabinets and larder and clean them out, says Gilliard. "Get rid of high-fat items and old items," she says.

Presoak rice. To reduce the cooking time of regular brown rice, soak it overnight, says Marion Burros. Then, when you want to prepare it the next day, it will cook as quickly as white rice.

Leave the chopping to someone else. Take advantage of time-saving precut fresh produce at the supermarket, such as broccoli florets, carrot coins, watermelon cubes and pineapple spears, as well as bags of frozen veggies.

Save the work for a rainy day. What else do you have to do? On a blustery, rainy, or generally dreary day, prepare several low-fat, freeze-ahead meals and save yourself cooking time later in the week.

Walk and talk. Time that you usually spend chatting – on the telephone, over lunch or across a desk – may provide an opportunity for fitness. Whether it's an intimate tête-à-tête with a good friend or a brainstorming session for an annual fund-raiser, consider carrying on the conversation while you walk for fitness.

Improve your mind. Get fit while you get the news: Ride a stationary bike while reading the paper or watching TV news.

Shop for fitness. If you leave the car at home, you can turn hauling home the shopping

---

MAKE TIME, WITHOUT GUILT

Here are six ways that you can make time for exercise and other fat-fighting habits without feeling the tiniest pang of guilt, according to Virginia Bass.

Give the TV a rest. If you are watching for a few hours a day, your television time could be the easiest spot to cut back. You don't have to give up television for good. Just stick to your favourite shows and click off the tube when you realise that you are merely vegetating.

Get out of bed. You can create more time by getting up a few minutes earlier in the morning. Set your alarm a half-hour to an hour earlier, then get up and go for a walk.

Let your timesaving devices do the job. Do you wash your dishes before sticking them in the dishwasher? Look for ways to use such appliances so that you can shave a minute here and a minute there off your preparation and cleanup time in the kitchen. "It's very important to look for where minutes can be shaved."

---

into an effective workout. Make sure your shopping is fairly evenly divided between two handled bags when you leave the shop. Grab one in each hand and, as you walk, raise and lower the bags by bending your elbows one at a time or, better yet, at the same time. When your arms get tired, simply carry the bags normally for a block or two. Repeat until you get home.

Exercise on the go. Is travelling a big part of your job? Make those pockets of time work for you and your fitness regimen. Plan on getting to your destination 30 to 60 minutes early so you can use the hotel gym or jogging path. Stuck at the airport between planes? Check your carry-on luggage in a locker, tie on your trainers and do a couple of brisk laps around the terminal.

Play to your preferences. Combine fun with a physical challenge. Do you love to shop? Forget the TV shopping channels. Instead,

Take a shorter shower. Sure it feels great to stand under that stream of hot water while you daydream about who knows what for 5 or 10 minutes. But do you have to? If you normally have a 15-minute shower, try reducing it to 10. Over the course of one week, that small change will give you a half-hour to spend exercising or planning healthy meals.

Say no to time-sappers. You might refuse altogether: "No, I can't do that for you." You might reschedule: "No, I can't do that right now because I'm on my way to the gym. How about next week?" And you might compromise: "No, I can't host the Christmas dinner. But I could bake a couple of pies."

Ask for help. Stop trying to be a domestic martyr. Free up some time for yourself by sharing the chores with your husband and kids. Even time spent on simple tasks like making the beds in the morning, clearing the table after dinner or unloading the dishwasher can add up.

fitness-walk along your favourite shopping street before the shops open and preview the window displays. Got the travel bug? Sign up for a fitness-orientated vacation. Are you crafty by nature? Then take a nature walk and collect pine cones, twigs and other found objects for your next project. Try all kinds of activities – bird-watching, gardening, table tennis, horse riding or social dancing. The best workouts aren't necessarily the ones that deliver the greatest calorie burn; rather, they're the activities that you're more likely to do because you honestly enjoy them.

Buy a pedometer. To keep track of the distance you're covering in your daily walks, buy a pedometer (just a few pounds at many sporting goods shops), suggests Judith S. Stern, R.D. Overweight women should aim for at least four miles a day, she says. If you go on holiday pack your pedometer along with your walking shoes. Holidays often mean added indulgence, so try to increase your walking to offset the extra food, says Dr. Stern. If you're at the beach or in the country, you'll have lots of opportunities for outdoor walking. But even if it's a city vacation, you can cover plenty of ground visiting museums and other sites of interest.

Be creative. "Did you know that, during a typical hour TV show, there are between 8 and 10 minutes of commercials? Use that time," says Dr. Stern. "When a commercial comes on, get up off the couch and walk around the house. Every time you do that, you get in an extra few minutes of exercise. You notice that I'm not telling women to stop watching TV, just to make the most of it. The idea is to build good habits. The hope is that when exercise opportunities, such as taking stairs, present themselves, you'll automatically take advantage of them."

Have your stuff handy. Nothing can derail your intentions faster than trainers that are still soggy from the weekend hike or personal stereo batteries that are so run-down that they make Frank Sinatra sound like Lurch from the Addams family. Flatten those paper-tiger obstacles by keeping your gear ready to roll and, above all, handy. If you have to trip over your walking shoes on your way out the door, you're one step closer to leaving with them on.

Hitch exercise to an essential. Attaching exercise to something you absolutely have to do every day will boost your chances of doing it. Some exercisers leave the house without showering so that they have to go to the gym on their way to work. Think about the things you can't live without and learn to use them to your fitness advantage.

Spare Time You Didn't Know You Had

Every day we waste time – lots of it. If you take advantage of all of that time, cooking healthy foods and exercising won't seem so time-consuming. Here's how to round up some extra time.

Keep a time log. For about a week, write down how you've spent your time. This gives you a way to tell at a glance what occupies your day. Then look for tasks that are expendable or that you can at least cut back.

Do first things first. People often mistake activity for productivity. But simply by spending too much time on frivolous tasks, a person can be very busy and still not get anything important done. Every Sunday, make a list for the week of things that either need to be done or that you'd simply like to do. Choose the five most important items on the list and schedule time for them. Then arrange the less important tasks around those five. Finally, add the things you'd like to do if any time remains. Even if you don't follow through on everything, the five most important items will likely be taken care of. (And if being healthy and feeling good are important to you, don't forget to include exercise among your top priorities.)

Never do one thing when you can do two. Don't you find it really frustrating to dash out to the hardware shop for paint only to get home and realise that you need to go back out to get a birthday cake at the bakery – which just happens to be next to the hardware shop? Keep a magnetic note board on your refrigerator and maintain an ongoing list of errands. Before leaving the house, check your list to see if there isn't some way to combine two or more of them.

Buy several generic greeting cards. If someone has a baby, you need to go out and buy a baby card. Someone has a birthday – another visit to the card shop. Forget it. Make one trip and buy 10 attractive cards that have no pre-printed message inside. Keep the cards with some stamped envelopes and simply reach for one when you need it, penning in inscriptions appropriate to the occasion.

Make haircuts a breeze. Some chains offer a walk-in service that requires no appointment. But if you don't want to waste time reading outdated magazines while waiting for a chair, the best time to go is Monday to Wednesday between 1:00 and 4:00 in the afternoon. Avoid weekends before the three busiest haircutting times of the year: Mother's Day, Easter and before the kids go back to school in the autumn.

Box it. Somewhere between no filing system at all and one that's so meticulous that it takes an hour a day to maintain, there's a simpler way to never lose another piece of paper: the three-box system. Keep one box to toss bills into, another for recipes and coupons and a third for miscellaneous stuff that you don't need right now but probably will soon. Once a month, go through the boxes. Pay the bills, use the coupons and throw out what you don't need.

Hire help. While a live-in maid, a full-time gardener and a cook might be a bit more pricey than most of us can afford, there's no reason that you can't hire some occasional help when it's less expensive than doing it yourself. The rule of thumb is this: Work out what your time is worth by calculating your hourly rate at the office. If you make £10 an hour and little Timmy down the street will rake your leaves for £2.50, that's a bargain.

Make your next appointment during your current one. You know you'll need another haircut in eight weeks, so why not make the appointment while you're at the salon for a trim today? The same thing applies to dental appointments, medicals and even car services.

Put things back where you found them. Sure, it's one of the oldest tricks in the book – so old that nobody seems to pay it any mind. To see just how much simpler life could be when it's orderly, compare the amount of time it takes to consistently hang your car keys on a nail beside the front door with the amount of time, anger and cursing it takes to try to find them under a couch cushion or by the phone.

Get a cordless phone. Around the house, having a cordless phone means uninterrupted conversations while walking on the treadmill, chopping vegetables or even dusting or cleaning the fridge.

Let your grass grow. You can waste a lot of time and sweat cutting your grass more than necessary. The optimal grass length is 2½ to 3 inches in the summer. That allows the grass to grow more slowly. Whenever you cut grass shorter, it shoots up at the fastest rate possible. Also, at the recommended length, your lawn will become dense enough to crowd out weeds, reducing the need for you to crawl on your hands and knees to pull dandelions.

Shop at the right time. In general, you'll find the smallest number of shopping lines on Tuesday and Wednesday. But even those days have their rush periods. Peak daily times include the lunch hour and the hours between 4:30 and 7:30 P.M., when the office crowd does its shopping.

Use automatic deposit. It's the 1990s. There's no need for you to drag a paycheck over to the bank, write slips and stand in a queue. Your company's payroll department will probably be happy to set up a direct deposit system for you.

Mind over Platter
Mental Techniques to Achieve Your Goal

Practiced regularly, mind-body techniques such as imagery and visualisation can be powerful tools to aid you in your weight-loss journey. Regularly picturing how you'll look newly thin and wearing a sleek black cocktail dress, for instance, can actually go a long way towards making that dream come true.

The Pizza Principle

To get an idea of how strong the mind-body connection is, try this exercise: Picture a big gooey pizza. The smell of garlic, tomato and basil tickles your nostrils. The cheese is all bubbly and the crust is golden brown. Imagine picking up a slice and taking a bite. You taste the tangy sauce, and the chewy cheese is stretching like a mozzarella rubber band from the slice to your mouth.

If your mouth waters just at the thought of that pizza, you have an idea of how your thoughts trigger physical reactions in your body.

The mind-body connection centres in the hypothalamus, the section of your brain that regulates the autonomic nervous system, which controls automatic processes such as breathing. The hypothalamus regulates two branches of the autonomic nervous system, the sympathetic, which responds to stress and gets the heart pumping, and the parasympathetic, which calms the body's responses, says Judith Green, Ph.D. "These parts of the brain are set up so they'll respond to our thinking and feelings," says Dr. Green. So if your brain regulates your body and your thoughts regulate your brain, it only makes sense that you can affect many of your physical responses.

Think Yourself Thin

Two effective mental tricks in your fat-fighting arsenal are visualisation and imagery. To relax, for instance, you might visualise a restful beach scene. Then you could incorporate the surrounding images through your senses: Hear the waves. Feel the breeze. Smell the salt air.

"Imagery is the primary language of the body," says Dr. Green. "The body understands

English and you can talk to it directly, but it truly loves images."

Here are some other techniques for seeing your way to weight-loss success.

Sit quietly and comfortably. Once you are in position, start breathing deeply. Your eyes should be closed and your belly soft. Let that softness spread from your belly into your legs and upper body. Doing so will relax you, helping you to concentrate on the images that you visualise.

Imagine a bright white light. Picture a bright light going through your body, surrounding and protecting you and keeping out negative energy. Practice this visualisation for 15 minutes twice a day, once in the morning and once at night, says Archana Lal-Tabak, M.D.

See yourself rejecting food. Once you've learned how to use visualisation to relax, you can turn it against the fat in your body by envisioning yourself avoiding the pitfalls of overeating. Visualise a situation that makes you feel vulnerable to cravings. Maybe you know that you're going to find yourself home alone with half a cheesecake left over from a dinner party. Imagine smelling it, looking at it, letting the craving develop and not fighting it. The next step is to see yourself destroying the food or putting it away in the refrigerator, out of sight. Then, when the situation arises, your mental rehearsal will keep you from devouring the food. Practice your craving-control visualisations two or three times a day for about five minutes.

Picture a slender you. Seeing yourself losing weight programmes the subconscious mind to do what you want. Imagine how your body will feel and what it will look like. See yourself wearing the kind of body-hugging outfits and doing the kinds of things – such as proudly walking across a crowded beach – that might not feel comfortable for you quite yet. Keep forming these pleasant mental pictures, and you'll find yourself motivated to make them a reality.

"Keep that mental picture of yourself at your desired weight in the forefront of your mind and keep retrieving it. That will help you make the decision about whether to eat just a small piece of that food you crave – or maybe not eat it at all," says Judy E. Marshel, R.D.

Daydream while you exercise. Dissociation is a form of controlled daydreaming in which you consciously direct your mind away from the task at hand and onto more pleasant thoughts. The result is a more enjoyable workout – one that you'll look forward to instead of one that you dread.

Researchers studied the effects of dissociation on women exercisers. Students cycled for 15 minutes while their heart rates were monitored. Some were asked to concentrate strictly on their exertion levels during the exercise, while others were asked to try to remember the names of every teacher they'd had since nursery school. While the actual exertion was similar for both groups, those who were busy conjuring up schoolmarms of yore rated their level of exertion as significantly less than did their self-focusing peers.

Give yourself an imaginary helping hand. Any psychological ploy to make your task seem easier than it is can help you finish a workout. This kind of positive thinking can help anyone perform better, says Diana McNab.

To squeeze out a few more crunches when you do abdominal exercises, for instance, envision a string connecting your navel to your spine. As you curl up, imagine that string pulling down on your navel and tugging it towards your backbone, she says. Or picture a string around your waist that pulls you as you walk, run or cycle uphill. Or pretend those last few laps around the track are part of the end of a race-walking event.

FOCUS ON ONE GOAL AT A TIME

Did you ever have a friend who could snub her nose at the most tempting cheesecake, hold herself to just a couple of bites of the greasiest fried onion and somehow make herself show up for every single aerobics class, rain, snow, sleet or shine? Does it seem that she got an extra helping of willpower?

It's possible that she may not have had any more willpower than you do. Rather, she focused her willpower on her priorities. It seems, according to one study, that we all possess a limited amount of willpower, so when we need self-control for one task, such as resisting food, we lose self-control for another task, such as resisting the urge for a cigarette or making ourselves study for an exam.

In a study, researchers split students into three groups. Two groups of students sat in a room stocked with two kinds of food — a dream supply of freshly baked chocolate chip biscuits and radishes. One group was allowed to eat only biscuits, and the other group could eat only radishes. The third group sat in a different room with no food at all.

All three groups were given the tedious task of tracing various geometric figures, but they were allowed to give up their tracing task whenever they felt tired. The second group of students, who had to resist the urge to stuff their faces with chocolate chip biscuits, gave up tracing first.

What's the weight-loss moral here? When you are in the midst of making various food and lifestyle changes, don't further tap your self-control by simultaneously taking on another resolution such as quitting smoking, going back to college or cutting back on impulse shopping, says Ellen Bratslavsky. Otherwise you'll risk overwhelming yourself, in the end accomplishing none of your goals.

Beat Cravings with Contemplation

If you've ever tried to drown your sorrows with a bag of biscuits or a plate of ravioli, you know that as soon as the food's gone, the pain and pounds return.

Enter meditation, a form of contemplation that's thousands of years old and rooted in the traditions of the world's great religions. Meditation is really the art of paying attention to or becoming mindful of your actions, including eating. When you pay attention to how your body reacts to having a steak or a cheeseburger, you'll find that you feel sleepy and sluggish and that your thinking is fuzzy. Suddenly, wise choices become obvious.

When you meditate, you concentrate on your breathing while you dismiss any distracting thoughts. Although it sounds simple, it takes practice, and the longer you practice, the easier the process becomes, says Deeja Napier. After about 10 minutes a day of practice, you'll soon be able to get your mind off food in any stressful situation. Here's the four-step meditation process.

1. *Go to your special spot.* "Set aside a special place you go to each day, a place in which you're comfortable and where you are less likely to be interrupted as you meditate," says Napier. "Mark it with something simple like a cushion and a flower. A corner of your bedroom is often a good place to meditate."

2. *Get into position.* Sit in your most comfortable place, either on the floor with your back supported or in a chair. If you like, you can lean against a wall, using a cushion for added support.

3. *Just breathe.* During your first few meditation sessions, simply concentrate on the physical act of breathing, without trying to

control or change your normal breathing pattern.

4. *Dismiss distractions.* If you get distracted by passing thoughts (and you will, especially in the beginning), avoid delving into them. Tell yourself that you'll deal with them later. Then return to concentrating on your breathing.

Once you get the hang of it, you can add some twists. Here are some ideas to try as you use meditation.

Write off distractions. If you find that your thoughts keep racing, keep a pad and pencil nearby. Write down the worries, concerns, or problems that you're afraid will distract you from meditation and promise yourself that you'll deal with them when you're finished.

Take a mental holiday. Close your eyes and concentrate on a soothing, tranquil place where you feel safe and calm. As distractions flutter through your mind, remind yourself that you'll deal with them when you're finished meditating. A quiet beach is an ideal mental destination for many women, says Eileen F. Oster. Picture yourself resting on the sand. Feel the sun on your skin, hear the water lapping the shore, listen for the sounds of seagulls, or see the ships gliding out to sea. You can use this routine for any beautiful, serene place that calms you.

Choose a meditative word. A word like *serenity*, which alternates vowels and consonants and feels good when you say it, works best. Repeat the word of your choice. Chant it. Focus

GOOD DISTRACTIONS

You're bored: You eat. You're depressed: You eat. You're stressed: You eat. You're mad: You eat.

Often, though, you can derail such behaviour by doing something else to take your mind off your craving. Here are 20 things you can do to keep your mind off the high-fat food you crave.

1. Drink two glasses of water.
2. Brush your teeth and gargle.
3. Have a walk.
4. Have a nap.
5. Have a bath.
6. Call or write to the person who upset you.
7. Go to a film.
8. Buy yourself a non-food gift.
9. Have sex.
10. Snack on safe food such as an apple, rice cake or carrot.
11. Call a friend.
12. Meditate.
13. Eat some fruit.
14. Leave the building for 10 minutes.
15. Play on the computer.
16. Catch up on office news with a co-worker.
17. Walk to the watercooler, get a drink and walk back.
18. Go to the toilet and splash cool water on your face.
19. Review your appointments for the upcoming week.
20. Walk up a few flights of stairs.

on nothing else but the word. "Let the sound of the word vibrate through your body. Let the word resonate up from your abdomen and let it go to your hands and your feet. Let your muscles move as you chant the word," says Oster.

QUOTES TO INSPIRE YOU

When fighting fat gets tough, remember: Even famous women struggle with weight. Here's what some of the more well-known women of the world have to say about their personal weight-loss journeys.

[Weight loss] takes time, effort, desire and arming yourself with tactics and education. It's about learning to use those elements that we know work, like fat reduction and portion control, and applying those to everyday cooking. It's about identifying your vulnerable points, your habits, what it is you're doing wrong, and then breaking those habits and replacing them with things you can do right — things that you enjoy!

— Joan Lunden in her book *Healthy Cooking*

I am easier with myself these days, more forgiving, more content. I have learned, for example, that there is Life After Cellulite. When I'm in the company of a model, I don't wish to have her figure. I've got my own, and it's perfectly nice — it's me, after all.

— Sarah Ferguson, Duchess of York, in her book *My Story*

This new way of eating very low fat, low sugar, low salt (I like to call it clean eating) has made such a difference in my life. I feel better. But do not be misled: Changing the way you think about food is only the first step towards achieving and maintaining a desirable weight. It was only through a comprehensive plan of healthy eating, daily exercise and changing my self-defeating behaviour that I was able to release weight as an issue from my life.

— Oprah Winfrey in her book *In the Kitchen with Rosie*

Food is one of the greatest pleasures in life. It is not your enemy! Yet most people approach the meal table with tension. I look forward to each and every meal. I know I'm going to eat wonderful food and enjoy the company of my friends and loved ones.

— Suzanne Somers in her book *Eat Great, Lose Weight*

Send Your Body the Right Message

We think 450 to 1,200 words a minute. The messages you send yourself throughout the day can have a tremendous impact on your self-image — and the success of your weight-loss programme. Whether you know it or not, you talk to yourself all the time, although not necessarily consciously or out loud. If you see a chocolate cake on the counter, for instance, your body isn't automatically drawn to it. In deciding whether or not you will have a piece, you might say to yourself, "I've had a tough day. I deserve this" or "I've been dieting all week and haven't lost a pound, so I might as well eat it."

What's your next likely course of action? You'll probably eat the cake. But what might happen if you said to yourself, "I've had a bad day, but it won't solve anything if I eat cake. It won't make me feel any better." This kind of self-talk may well prevent you from eating.

The point is that self-talk plays an important role in determining how you'll act and how you feel about yourself. If your self-talk is negative and defeating, you may end up engaging in self-destructive behaviours such as binge eating and nibbling when you're not even hungry, says Joyce D. Nash, Ph.D. On the other hand, if your self-talk is positive, you can often prevent inappropriate eating and the bad feelings that trigger or accompany it.

Use the following three-step process to turn self-defeating self-talk into empowering talk.

1. *Reflect.* Each time you feel that you've strayed from your goals, reflect on your thoughts before, during and after you ate.

2. *Analyse.* Ask yourself if your thoughts are rational, true or helpful. For example, suppose you've already eaten three biscuits while waiting in a traffic jam and you find yourself reaching into the bag for more. Ask if it's really true that you can't wait until dinner. After all, will eating the biscuits make the traffic jam break up? Will you really feel better after eating a whole bag of biscuits? In the long run, will three biscuits make any difference in your weight?

3. *Change.* Come up with more positive, helpful self-statements, such as "I can wait until dinner; if I wait, the hunger may pass" or "Eating will not solve the problem." As for the classic "I may as well eat the whole bag," challenge it with "Three biscuits won't make me gain weight, but eating the whole bag might." Instead of thinking "There's no way I can cut back with Christmas coming" or "I deserve to eat it since I've been so good," say to yourself, "It's hard to watch what I eat when I go out, but I can plan ahead" or "I do deserve to celebrate, but I'll buy myself something other than food."

Here are some more ways to talk your way to a lower weight.

Firm up with affirmations. Affirmations are simple words or phrases that you can repeat to yourself whenever you feel a funk coming on. Thinking about skipping today's workout? The minute the thought comes to mind, say to yourself, "Stop." Take a deep breath. Now refocus your thoughts in a positive light: "I'm on the road to fitness. I want to stay there."

The more positive messages you send to yourself, the more you'll want to do what's needed to slim down. Each day, write or say aloud these kinds of affirmations, suggests Laura Stein, author of *The Bloomingdale's Eat Healthy Diet.*

- I'm losing weight now.
- I'm enjoying how I'm feeling now.
- I love the food that makes me thin.
- I love the feeling of making progress.
- Losing weight is effortless.
- I'm making things easy for myself now.
- My body is getting stronger, slimmer and healthier every day.

It's important, she adds, that all of your affirmations be in the present tense to give them a greater sense of power and immediacy. If you talk about the ways you hope to be and feel in the future, you'll be less apt to take action today.

Find power. Get into the habit of switching "pain words" to "power words," says Susan Jeffers, Ph.D., author of *End the Struggle and Dance with Life.* "It's important that you monitor your words, using phrases that empower rather than weaken you," she insists. "So eliminate the can'ts, shoulds, problems and struggles from your vocabulary and replace them with power words." Here are some word swaps that she recommends.

- I can't = I won't
- I should = I could
- It's a problem = It's an opportunity
- Life's a struggle = Life's an adventure
- I hope = I know
- If only = Next time
- What will I do? = I know I can handle it.

Snap out of it. Every time you give yourself a negative message, snap your fingers. Not a loud, finger-popping snap, just a gentle one. "These messages tend to happen very quickly," says Julia Boyd. "And since no one can hear them except you, you have to make sure you're not letting them just fly by unnoticed." For each snap, make a mark on a piece of paper. At the end of the day, count the marks. If you can remember what you told yourself, write it down, then see if you can come up with a more realistic message. Instead of telling yourself "I'll never be pretty because I'm too fat," for instance, say "I don't like being this heavy, but I'm still attractive."

Love yourself. When the static of self-doubt creeps in, the most important messages we can give ourselves are "I'm lovable" and "I am worthwhile." These two simple messages won't make us media stars, nor will they make others accept us. They will, however, affirm our right to be ourselves and cut through unhealthy messages that feel burdensome. Try writing two affirming sentences on index cards, placing them on your bathroom mirror, and reading them first thing every morning and last thing at night as a reward to yourself.

A Grab Bag of Mental Strategies

In addition to visualisation, meditation and affirmation, there are numerous other ways to think yourself thin. Here's a potpourri of tips to try.

Visualise your future. A technique known as neurolinguistic programming enables you to focus mental energy away from feeling-orientated, in-the-moment gratification to making very specific plans and schedules that track you from the present into the future. Make holiday plans, career plans, education plans or exercise plans. Think about them. Visualise them. In fact, see the future unfolding in your mind's eye. This may help for more than one reason. One, it helps get your mind off the immediate attraction of food. Also, seeking the future actually engages a different brain system – the visual system, in contrast to the feeling system. Eating things that you know aren't good for you is a feeling-orientated, in-the-moment activity. You eat the piece of cake because it will feel good to eat it now. Weight change, on the other hand, is a visual, future-orientated activity.

Get more sleep. Many people work too hard and get too little sleep. We may even eat to compensate for our lack of sleep. It may give us a quick boost, but we end up storing the extra calories as fat. When you need to work long hours, try walks or showers rather than chocolate bars to boost your energy.

Laugh yourself thin. Are you too tired to hit the gym? Then pop a Marx Brothers tape into the VCR and yuck your way to fitness. Laughing 100 times is the physiological equivalent of working out on a rowing machine for 10 minutes.

Index

Underlined references indicate boxed text. *Italic* references indicate illustrations.